Contraception Across Cultures

Cross-Cultural Perspectives on Women

General Editors: Shirley Ardener and Jackie Waldren, for The Centre for Cross-Cultural Research on Women, University of Oxford

ISSN: 1068-8536

Vol. 1:   *Persons and Powers of Women in Diverse Cultures*
     Edited by Shirley Ardener

Vol. 2:   *Dress and Gender: Making and Meaning*
     Edited by Ruth Barnes and Joanne B. Eicher

Vol. 3:   *The Anthropology of Breast-Feeding: Natural Law or Social Construct*
     Edited by Vanessa Maher

Vol. 4:   *Defining Females: The Nature of Women in Society*
     Edited by Shirley Ardener

Vol. 5:   *Women and Space: Ground Rules and Social Maps*
     Edited by Shirley Ardener

Vol. 6:   *Servants and Gentlewomen to the Golden Land: The Emigration of Single Women to South Africa, 1820–1939*
     By Cecillie Swaisland

Vol. 7:   *Migrant Women: Crossing Boundaries and Changing Identities*
     Edited by Gina Buijs

Vol. 8:   *Carved Flesh/Cast Selves: Gendered Symbols and Social Practices*
     Edited by Vigdis Broch-Due, Ingrid Rudie and Tone Bleie

Vol. 9:   *Bilingual Women: Anthropological Approaches to Second Language Use*
     Edited by Pauline Burton, Ketaki Dyson and Shirley Ardener

Vol. 10:   *Gender, Drink and Drugs*
     Edited by Maryon MacDonald

Vol. 11:   *Women and Mission: Past and Present*
     Edited by Fiona Bowie, Deborah Kirkwood and Shirley Ardener

Vol. 12:   *Muslim Women's Choices*
     Edited by Camillia Fawzi El-Solh and Judy Mabro

Vol. 13:   *Women and Property, Women as Property*
     Edited by Renée Hirschon

Vol. 14:   *Money-Go-Rounds: Women's Use of Rotating Savings and Credit Associations*
     Edited by Shirley Ardener and Sandra Burman

Vol. 15:   *'Male' and 'Female' in Developing Southeast Asia*
     Edited by Wazir Jahan Karim

Vol. 16:   *Women Wielding the Hoe: Lessons from Rural Africa for Feminist Theory and Development Practice*
     Edited by Deborah Fahy Bryceson

Vol. 17:   *Organizing Women: Formal and Informal Women's Groups in the Middle East*
     Edited by Dawn Chatty and Annika Rabo

Vol. 18:   *Women Plantation Workers: International Experiences*
     Edited by Shobhita and Rhoda Reddock

Vol. 19:   *Beads and Beadmakers: Gender, Material Culture and Meaning*
     Edited by Lidia D. Sciama and Joanne B. Eicher

Vol. 20:   *Cross-Cultural Marriage: Identity and Choice*
     Edited by Rosemary Breger and Rosanna Hill

Vol. 21:   *Extending the Boundaries of Care: Medical Ethics and Caring Practices*
     Edited by Tamara Kohn and Rosemary McKechnie

Contraception Across Cultures

Technologies, Choices, Constraints

Edited by
*Andrew Russell, Elisa J. Sobo
and Mary S. Thompson*

Oxford • New York

First published in 2000 by
Berg
Editorial offices:
150 Cowley Road, Oxford, OX4 1JJ, UK
838 Broadway, Third Floor, New York, NY 10003-4812, USA

Berg is the imprint of Oxford International Publishers Ltd.

Library of Congress Cataloging-in-Publication Data

A catalogue record for this book is available from the Library of Congress.

British Library Cataloguing-in-Publication Data

A catalogue record for this book is available from the British Library.

ISBN 1 85973 381 6 (Cloth)
     1 85973 386 7 (Paper)

Coventry University

Typeset by JS Typesetting, Wellingborough, Northants.
Printed in the United Kingdom by WBC Book Manufacturers, Bridgend,
Mid Glamorgan.

Contents

Acknowledgements   vii

List of Figures and Tables   ix

Notes on Contributors   xi

Part 1 Approaches and Methods

1   Introduction: Contraception across Cultures
Andrew Russell and *Mary S. Thompson*   3

2   Psychosocial Data and Cross-Cultural Analyses:
Challenges to Anthropology and Contraceptive Research
Mary S. Willis and *Marion Pratt*   27

3   Responding to Reality: The Efficacy of Anthropological
and Participatory Methods for the Implementation of
Sustainable Contraceptive Programmes
Joshua Levene   51

Part 2 Contraception in its Political and Economic Contexts

4   Fertility Running Wild: Elite Perceptions of the Need for
Birth Control in White-Ruled Rhodesia
Amy Kaler   81

5   A Clinic in Conflict: A Political Economy
Case Study of Family Planning in Haiti
M. Catherine Maternowksa   103

Part 3 Contraceptive Policy and Practice: User Perspectives

6   'Weak Blood' and 'Crowded Bellies': Cultural Influences
on Contraceptive Use Among Ethiopian Jewish Immigrants
in Israel
Jennifer Phillips Davids   129

7 New Reproductive Rights and Wrongs in the Galilee
Rhoda Kanaaneh   161

8 My Body, My Problem: Contraceptive Decision-Making
among Rural Bangladeshi Women
Nancy Stark   179

**Part 4 Contraceptive Policy and Practice:
Provider Perspectives**

9 Uzbekistan in Transition – Changing Concepts in Family
Planning and Reproductive Health
Monika Krengel and *Katarina Greifeld*   199

10 Family Planning or Reproductive Health? Interpreting
Policy and Providing Family Planning Services in
Highland Chiapas, Mexico
Mary S. Thompson   221

Index   245

Acknowledgements

The majority of chapters in this volume have been developed from papers originally presented at a two-day international conference 'Changing Contraceptives: Technologies, Choices and Constraints' held at University College Stockton (since renamed 'University of Durham, Stockton Campus') from 12–14 September 1996. Our thanks are due to the Mellon Foundation in New York, and the Overseas Development Administration (now the Department for International Development) and the Simon Population Trust in London, for their generous financial support for the conference, participants at the conference for their camaraderie and insightful comments, and to the staff at University College Stockton for their hospitality. We are particularly grateful to Shirley Ardener, founder and previous director of the Centre for Cross-Cultural Research on Women at Queen Elizabeth House, Oxford, and editor of the series of which this book is a part, for her enthusiasm and support both for the conference and this book. As reviewer for the series, Anne Coles gave very helpful comments on individual chapters, and contributors worked with diligence and commitment to complete their work within a tight timeframe. We would also like to express our thanks to Kathryn Earle and the staff at Berg Publishers for their advice and alacrity, and to members of the Centre for the Study of Contraceptive Issues and the Department of Anthropology at the University of Durham whose intellectual interest in this project has helped keep it on track. A number of employers are represented amongst the contributors to this book. However, the views expressed within it are those of the individuals concerned and do not necessarily reflect the opinions of their employers.

Royalties from the sale of this book will be shared between the Centre for Cross-Cultural Research on Women and the Centre for the Study of Contraceptive Issues.

Andrew Russell
Elisa J. Sobo
Mary S. Thompson

List of Figures and Tables

Figures

1.1 Countries represented in *Contraception across Cultures*   4
3.1 Diagrammatic representation of modernity   54
3.2 For sustainable development to be a reality, the diagram must present a notion of holism, where all the dimensions inter-link and interact   55

Tables

3.1 Contrasts between verbal and visual modes   60
3.2 Table of exercises and applications   69
6.1 Number of women who participated in semi-structured interviews, by age and immigration cohort   137
6.2 Number of women who participated in semi-structured interviews, by residence and marital status   137
6.3 Percentages of current contraceptive users, by method type (n=33)   139
6.4 Results of a multiple regression analysis of the factors that affect the interbirth interval in Ethiopia (n=275 births)   141
6.5 Results of a multiple regression analysis of the factors that affect the interbirth interval in Israel (n=111 births)   143
6.6 Number of responses to the question 'Do you want any more children?' by number of live births (n=72)   146
6.7 Number of responses to the question 'Do you want any more children?' by ever-use of contraception   147
6.8 Number of responses to the question, 'Do you want any more children?' by current use of contraception   147
8.1 Reported side-effects of contraceptive methods (n=50)   187
8.2 Individuals consulted for contraceptive side-effects (n=47)   188
8.3 Treatment for contraceptive side-effects (n=48)   189
8.4 Further treatment for contraceptive side-effects (n=9)   189
8.5 How husband learned of contraceptive use (n=70)   191

Notes on Contributors

Jennifer Phillips Davids has a Ph.D. in anthropology and an MPH in international health from Emory University. Since 1993, she has conducted research among the Ethiopian immigrant community in Israel on reproductive decisions, fertility transition, and life course change. In addition, she has conducted research on teen pregnancy and perinatal outcome among African Americans in Atlanta, piloted methods for the field determination of reproductive status (among the Hadza in Tanzania), and examined the social context of interpersonal relationships among patients with Alzheimer's disease. She is currently a visiting lecturer at Hebrew University, Jerusalem.

Katarina Greifeld has a Ph.D. in social anthropology (1984) and is an international health consultant and a medical social anthropologist. She works for different cooperation agencies all over the world, mainly in relation to target group issues in health and environment. She lectures at the University of Heidelberg and was recently assigned by the European Commission to expert panels in health, ethics and environment.

Amy Kaler has a Ph.D. in sociology and a minor in Feminist Studies from the University of Minnesota, awarded in 1998. She is presently a postdoctoral fellow at the Population Studies Center at the University of Pennsylvania, where she is working on several research projects concerning culture, gender and reproductive technologies in southern and eastern Africa.

Rhoda Kanaaneh received her Ph.D. in anthropology from Columbia University in 1998. She is Assistant Prof. of Women's Studies at New York University. Her forthcoming book on nationalism, globalization, medicalization, gender and reproduction among Palestinians is entitled *The Reproductive Measure: Negotiating Babies and Boundaries in the Galilee,* to be published by University of California Press.

Monika Krengel has a diploma in sociology and received her Ph.D. in social anthropology from Heidelberg University in 1988. She currently holds the position of a research fellow at the South Asia Institute in Heidelberg, conducting research in the Central Himalayas (India) on a project entitled Customs, Law and Moralities. She also works as an international health consultant. She has been teaching at Heidelberg and Frankfurt (Main) Universities and conducts research in environment, gender and health-related projects.

Joshua Levene was a student on the Human Sciences degree course at University College Stockton (now renamed University of Durham, Stockton Campus) when he first went to Tonga under the auspices of the Overseas Training Programme run by Voluntary Service Overseas. He has subsequently returned to the South Pacific as a consultant for the World Bank, and has conducted other participatory action research projects amongst intravenous drug-users in the UK.

M. Catherine Maternowska has a Ph.D. in medical anthropology from Columbia University (1996). Her involvement with Haiti dates from 1984. She has also worked as an international health consultant in Tunisia, Jordan and, most recently, Mali, incorporating gender-based strategies into reproductive health programmes. In 1993 she helped found, and is now Executive Director to, the Lambi Fund of Haiti. This non-profit alternative development organization works to sustain Haiti's popular democratic movement. She also holds a faculty position in the School of Public Health and Tropical Medicine at Tulane University/Arkansas Campus.

Marion Pratt, who earned a doctorate in sociocultural anthropology from Binghamton University in 1995, currently holds the position of Social Science Advisor for the U.S. Office of Foreign Disaster Assistance (OFDA). At OFDA she focuses on the cultural, environmental and gender contexts of disasters in Africa and Asia.

Andrew Russell is a lecturer in the Department of Anthropology at the University of Durham, and is involved in teaching on the Human Sciences and Health and Human Sciences degrees at its Stockton campus (UDSC). His doctoral research was conducted in East Nepal, and he has subsequently conducted further fieldwork in Nepal and north-east India. He is currently involved in a number of health-related projects in the north-east of England, and is convenor of the Centre for the Study of Contraceptive Issues at Durham and UDSC, which seeks to bring together a cross-disciplinary section of people, including practitioners outside academia, to facilitate contact and collaboration in research issues. He is editor (with Iain Edgar) of *The Anthropology of Welfare* (1998).

Elisa J. Sobo (Center for Child Health Outcomes; Children's Hospital, San Diego) has published numerous journal articles and several books, including *One Blood: The Jamaican Body* (1993), *Choosing Unsafe Sex: AIDS-Risk Denial among Disadvantaged Women* (1995), *The Cultural Context of Health, Illness, and Medicine* (with M. Loustaunau; 1997), and *The Endangered Self: Managing the Social Risks of HIV* (with G. Green; 2000). Other co-edited books are *Using Methods in the Field* (with V. de Munck; 1998) and *Celibacy, Culture and Society: The Anthropology of Sexual Abstinence* (with S. Bell; forthcoming). Dr Sobo is on the editorial boards of *Anthropology and Medicine* and *Reviews in Anthropology*.

Nancy Stark is a Research Associate and Cancer Control Fellow in the Department of Public Health Sciences at Wake Forest University School of Medicine, Winston-Salem, NC. She is currently working on breast cancer survivorship issues and health-related quality of life research.

Mary S. Thompson works for the UK Department for International Development attached to Unicef-Guyana as a consultant on Unicef's Amazon Programme. She has a doctorate from the University of Durham on 'The Social Context of Family Planning Policy in Highland Chiapas, Mexico' and remains involved in the work of the Centre for the Study of Contraceptive Issues at the University. Her current action research on the Amazon Programme involves implementing a rights-based strategy in development projects amongst Guyana's indigenous peoples.

Mary S. Willis was awarded a doctorate in biological anthropology in 1995 from Washington University in St Louis. She then completed the Science and Diplomacy Postdoctoral Fellowship, sponsored by the American Association for the Advancement of Science, in the Center for Population, Health and Nutrition at USAID. Dr. Willis is currently an Assistant Professor at the University of Nebraska Lincoln. Her research and consulting projects are focussed on health-related issues, culturally relevant instruments, and service delivery programmes.

PART 1

Approaches and Methods

1

Introduction: Contraception Across Cultures

Andrew Russell and *Mary S. Thompson*

Conceptions and Contraceptions

The development of new contraceptive technologies over the last fifty years has profound implications for social relationships between men and women. Conversely, gender and other power relationships at local and global levels have implications for the way the new contraceptive technologies are developed, disseminated and used. The aim of this volume is to investigate the impact of contraception on society, and of society on contraception, from a cross-cultural, anthropological perspective using case studies and overviews from around the world (see Figure 1.1).

Compared to recent interest in the new reproductive technologies within anthropology (e.g. Strathern 1992; Edwards *et al.* 1993), attention paid to contraception has been relatively scant.[1] While no-one can deny the awesome social and cultural implications of many of the reproductive technologies that anthropologists have addressed, such as in vitro fertilization, the fact remains that few people worldwide are ever likely to have the chance to use these innovations. Contraception, on the other hand, impinges on the lives of the majority of heterosexual couples in their childbearing years, irrespective of income or social status.

In light of this, Andrew Russell and Elisa Sobo convened an international conference, 'Changing Contraceptives: Choices, Technologies and Constraints', in September 1996.[2] The conference examined contraception cross-culturally, and the methodological approaches anthropologists and others use to shed light on contraception-related patterns of thought and action. The majority of chapters in this volume were first presented as papers at the conference.

This chapter outlines the themes and theories that underlie the study of contraception across cultures, drawing together the work of the other

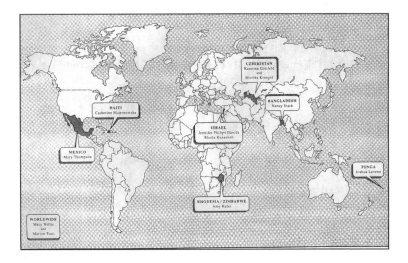

Figure 1.1 Countries represented in *Contraception Across Cultures*

contributors to this volume and those from outside. Contraceptives are important new technological 'facts' on the global stage. However, as importantly, they are mental 'conceptions'. It is in exploring these conceptions cross-culturally that the analyses of anthropology have so much to offer the study of contraception. We must be concerned with the definitions accorded different types of contraception, what they contain and what is left out. We need to examine the methods with which anthropologists and other cross-cultural researchers can explore what is missing from such definitions (such as the human agents, and the beliefs, relationships, institutions and power structures within which they operate). What and how is contraception 'conceived', both in terms of institutions and social relationships 'on the ground' and as ideas in people's heads? These are the questions and issues that form the subject matter of the rest of this chapter.

Defining Contraceptives

Contraception entails the use of drugs, chemicals, devices, surgery or behaviour that control fertility amongst sexually active heterosexual people.[3] The various methods of contraception can be categorized by mode of operation, whether they are traditional or modern, and whether they are provider- or user-dependent.

'Mode of operation' covers the differences between hormonal, mechanical, and surgical methods. Of these, hormonal forms of contraception are the new contraceptive technology of the second half of the twentieth century par excellence (Watkins 1998). In addition to the range of oral contraceptive pills now available, the so-called 'morning after pill' (which can actually be used up to 72 hours after intercourse with contraceptive effect), injectables, implantables and the contraceptive 'patch' fall into the 'hormonal' category. Many of these hormonal preparations were developed, at least ostensibly, for non-contraceptive purposes (see Oudshoorn 1994).

Mechanical devices include 'barrier' methods such as the cap, diaphragm and condom, vaginal rings and sponges. Condoms (which are now produced in both 'male' and 'female' forms) have come to particular prominence over the past two decades with the realization that they are the only effective way of protecting against HIV/AIDS and some other STDs. Chemical contraceptives such as spermicidal creams and jellies, and pessaries, are often used in conjunction with barrier methods to increase their efficacy. Intra-uterine devices (IUDs) are also mechanical forms of contraception but differ from barrier methods in that they require medical intervention rather than user control. Surgical methods include vasectomy for men and tubal ligation or occlusion for women.

Some writers add 'behavioural' to a list of 'modes of operation', in order to include abstinence, coitus interruptus (where the man withdraws his penis before ejaculation), the 'rhythm' or calendar method (which involves refraining from intercourse during the supposed fertile period based on counting the days of the menstrual cycle) and 'natural fertility regulating methods'. The latter rely on the observation of menstrual patterns in conjunction with observation of body temperature and/or the consistency of vaginal mucus to assess fertile periods during which abstinence may be practised, or condoms used, to avoid conception. However, the term 'natural' is problematic when applied to contraception, as it implies that all other forms of contraception are inherently 'unnatural' and that 'natural' and 'unnatural' methods are mutually exclusive (plainly not the case if, say, condoms are used as contraceptives during perceived 'fertile' periods).[4] The definition 'behavioural' is similarly problematic, since all forms of contraception, whether coitus interruptus, or taking a pill every morning, involves some kind of behavioural strategy.

Perhaps the term 'traditional' better describes practices such as abstinence, coitus interruptus, non-penetrative sex (often referred to as 'petting'

– or, in one innovative health promotion amongst teenagers in the UK, 'outercourse' as opposed to 'intercourse'), sustained breast-feeding (lactational amenorrhoea), post-partum sexual taboos and the rhythm method. Herbal concoctions and many other, 'older' forms of contraception should also be included in the 'traditional' category. Some writers (e.g. Newman 1995) call these methods 'indigenous', which are opposed to the 'prescriptive', modern methods available through clinics, family planning services, and other sources. As Newman points out, indigenous methods tend to be subsumed in the residual 'other methods' category in much contemporary demographic research, a category that tends to be ignored, misrepresented, discounted or regarded (often wrongly) as intrinsically 'ineffective'.

Another distinction often made is between 'user-dependent' methods (the 'behavioural' and 'traditional' methods outlined above, although barrier methods and oral contraceptive pills are 'user dependent' too) and 'provider dependent' methods such as injectables (e.g. Depo-Provera) implantables (e.g. Norplant), IUDs, and sterilization. Apart from the oral contraceptive pill, most new technologies have tended to be 'provider-dependent'.[5] More recent research has focussed on the possibility of a long-acting injectable, immunological contraceptive (or anti-fertility vaccine) for women. There is much interest, but as yet relatively little activity, surrounding the idea of a male hormonal contraceptive.

Such definitions present contraception as a 'fact' or 'thing', categorized only by epistemological judgements about how it works, its origins and history of use, and who controls how it is used. It is obviously important to understand the technologies involved at such a factual level – yet contraceptives are social constructs (see below) or social conceptions, as well as physical facts (cf. Latour 1993). At the very least, they are products that require human agency for their use. Contraceptives do not just 'work', they work in bodies in a wide variety of perceived ways and with a wide variety of additional effects, amongst them the so-called 'side effects' (see Etkin 1992). The ways that they work, and are perceived as working, are mediated by a variety of relationships, institutions, knowledge and beliefs (the social and cultural in anthropology). It may be argued that to put labels such as 'traditional' or 'indigenous' on particular forms of contraception does little to further our understanding of the dynamics of contraceptive processes. The 'modern' innovations outlined above are rapidly becoming absorbed into 'traditional' or 'indigenous' cultural settings around the world, thus dissolving these dualistic categories into one and providing a fascinating case study of the diffusion of technological innovations as they do so.

The mainstay of anthropological understanding of contraceptives at work is the concept of 'culture', which pervades the forms and expressions of human agency, facilitating some and constraining others. Thus contraceptives can only be understood with reference to the political and economic structures, and social and cultural forms, of the people amongst whom they are found and (perhaps) used, and the local realities that mediate and ultimately define a global phenomenon such as contraception. Cross-cutting all this is the role of 'power' in human relationships and organizational structures. Methodological issues are vital in order to deal effectively with this complex interplay of culture, power and technology cross-culturally, and will be considered next.

Methods Compared

Anthropology is perhaps the most philosophical of the social sciences, its philosophy founded on a holistic approach to the study of human affairs. It is inherently comparative and 'cross-cultural', taking its examples from societies around the world. The *raison d'être* of anthropology today is in seeking to observe and understand the many processes underlying social transformation. At the same time, anthropological research is marked by methodological pluralism. It is also, increasingly, an applied discipline with advocacy-related potential.

There has been much debate in anthropology over the validity of quantitative versus qualitative methods of data collection. Quantitative research, relying heavily on 'number-crunching', has traditionally been aligned with a positivistic, scientific label whereas qualitative research belongs to the field of interpretation. This distinction seems increasingly anachronistic in much contemporary multidisciplinary and development-focussed research compared to more balanced and holistic research practices that seek to breach this divide (Bernard 1995; Sobo and de Munck 1997). Quantitative research methods include surveys, questionnaires and polls in formats that allow for statistical analyses. Qualitative research uses an equally broad range of research tools, including participant-observation (see below), semi-structured interviews, and the use of archival and contemporary texts. Whilst quantitative and qualitative research should be mutually reinforcing each can also illuminate problems in the other which may often be attributed to poor research frameworks (Sobo 1996). Several contributions in this book bring out this point, such as Greifeld and Krengel's questioning of official statistics on abortions in Uzbekistan, and Levene's insight into the reason for the unfeasibly high usage of condoms in Tonga. Similarly, quantitative data can be used to challenge the generalization of information collected from limited data sets – the 'anecdotal', the 'case study' or the 'context-specific' – to a wider population. Both modes of research are rigorous and scientific, depending upon the quality of the research carried out. In any good anthropological research, whether quantitative and qualitative data are conjoined or not, one will observe sensitivity to issues of definition, context and meaning, as well as to numerical accuracy, by the researchers undertaking it. A careful assessment of ethics is another grounding factor.

In seeking to achieve an in-depth, holistic understanding of the situation of a particular people or community, participant-observation is the qualitative research method that has become a hallmark of much anthropological research. Participant-observation (often glossed as 'ethnography', although strictly speaking the latter should be used only to describe the written results of participant-observation) involves long-term, in-depth participatory social and cultural research amongst a particular group. Where the researcher is a member of the group in question by birth, the boundaries between participant-observation and everyday life can become very blurred (cf. Kanaaneh, this volume). Participant-observation is a vital research tool for obtaining meaningful, contextualized information in a sensitive way, about sexual and other forms of behaviour that are vital to understanding how any form of contraception 'works'. It is not a tool, however, that lends itself to rapid data collection for the kind of large-scale data sets often required by national and international reproductive health analysts. Thus, we often find that contraceptive behaviour coalesced with contraceptive methods as 'things' that are used to prevent conception within a rationalized scientific framework, rather than as a cultural process to be assessed within a socio-cultural framework (cf. Bibeau 1997).

Participant-observation can form the root of activism in anthropological research. As an essentially interpretive tool this raises questions of ethical boundaries but given the propensity for anthropologists to become participants in socio-economic and cultural milieux different from their own it is unsurprising if some decide to take up a more than observational role, such as mediator or advocate – to 're-present' as well as to 'present' the people with whom they live, as Simpson (1997) pithily summarizes it. Such activism sharpens existing issues of objectivity, politics and emotion, three core paradoxes that drive anthropology forwards in creative ways. The passion with which Maternowska (this volume) interprets the plight of the urban poor in *Cité Soleil*, for example, shines through in her account of family planning services in that community. Her activist stance often brings out the ambiguities of meaning that dominant discourses may hide – for example, the question of whose 'need' for contraceptives in *Cité Soleil* we are talking about, the need of the superpowers to 'control' population growth in developing countries, the need of population planners to meet targets, or the need of the local people (particularly poor women) for empowerment and control over their lives. The political-economic framework she adopts enables Maternowska to highlight the absurdity of a situation where the annual cost per client for the services offered by the family planning clinic in *Cité Soleil* is half the average annual income of persons living in that community.

Participant-observation, as Levene (this volume) observes, can provide anthropologists with valuable information of relevance to contraceptive delivery services that intend to meet the needs of the people they are designed to serve. However, he feels strongly that anthropological research should not be an extractive exercise, rather researchers should act as mediators, facilitating communication between the different participants in a programme or a potential programme to make sure that everyone's reality 'counts'. Levene used the techniques of participatory rural appraisal (PRA) research, derived from development studies, in his research into the feasibility of a contraceptive social marketing (CSM) programme in Tonga. He sees PRA research as most effective when conducted in tandem with more traditional anthropological methods that serve to make PRA more creative and responsive to local perceptions and conditions. [6] Levene's work demonstrates the value of such methodological pluralism. Moreover, participation has value in its own right, as a process of empowerment for the community regardless of the results of its findings (cf. Cornwall and Jewkes 1995).

Willis and Pratt are concerned that what they call 'psychosocial' research methods have been developed primarily for use amongst Western populations, not the 70 per cent of the world's population that lives in 'developing' countries. For anthropologists in international development, funding and time constraints and the frequent need for regional or national, rather than local, coverage make doing long-term ethnographic research difficult, even though this is acknowledged as the best means of data collection. Anthropologists have tended to be hesitant about involvement in development activities, even where development agencies are crying out for the input of the anthropologically trained 'culture broker' (albeit often on the agencies' own terms and conditions). This is largely due to ethical concerns about the 'neo-colonialism' of much development activity, and the possibility of inadvertently imposing Western values and assumptions in a situation where they are unwarranted and could be harmful. How to deal with the latter risk in the conduct of contraceptive research is the subject of Willis and Pratt's thorough appraisal. One point they make, like Levene, is that not only do anthropologists have to work in unconventional ways to accommodate the time frames and other constraints of development work, but they also have to be unconventional in their ways of relating to others. Gone is the image of the Malinowskian anthropologist 'set down' alone on a Trobriand beach, expected to 'fit in' with whatever is going on in an essentially non-interventionist way. In its place we see anthropologists working in research teams, sometimes in a managerial capacity, often with a highly proactive research agenda.

There are many parallels that can be drawn between the conduct of good quality anthropological research and the operation of high-quality contraceptive programmes. 'Informed consent', for example, is a hallmark of both. Riding roughshod over the principle of 'informed consent' leads to unwillingness of people to participate in future research programmes or contraceptive delivery initiatives. Issues of social distance also have to be addressed in both the 'researcher/subject' relationship in anthropo-logical research and the 'provider/client' relationship in contraceptive delivery. Researchers, like providers, do best when they can speak the same language as their informants, are socially skilful and culturally aware. However, it is not necessarily the case that providers or researchers should be 'peers' of the group with which they work, or be involved in personal relationships with them that go beyond the merely professional, even though this can sometimes be advantageous. In some cases, social distance is inevitable because it is embedded in language, with forms of address and 'modes of reference' varying with age, sex and status, which are themselves culturally ascribed markers of difference. The context in which anthropological research, like contraceptive service delivery, takes place is also important in determining how likely people are to participate in the research or take up the service respectively. In Levene's research in Tonga, for example, conducting group sessions in a church was deemed culturally inappropriate. However, overarching this issue are attitudes to the discussion of sexual matters, which also vary significantly cross-culturally. Finally, the question of confidentiality has to be addressed in both contraceptive delivery and anthropology (cf. Seeley *et al.* 1992).

What all this implies is the importance of understanding any social situation, whether it is a piece of anthropological research in a rural locale, or a family planning service in an inner city, from the inside, or the grass-roots level. This is what anthropologists call the 'emic' perspective. Concepts such as 'extramarital sex', 'ideal family size', 'libido', 'abstin-ence', 'marital satisfaction' and 'abortion' (Sobo 1996) may have totally different meanings cross-culturally, or else have no meaning at all. For example, the Xhosa, as Willis and Pratt (this volume) point out, appear to have no non-gendered equivalent for the English word Understanding language and behaviour 'emically', can lead to c appropriate recommendations, such as Willis and Pratt's suggest mint-flavoured condoms are appropriate in Zimbabwe, or Materno..ska's for non-lubricated ones in Haiti. It can also indicate appropriate or alternative ways of conducting research effectively, taking into account factors such as 'individualist' vs. 'collectivist' value structures (Triandis 1995), illiteracy, or the ways different topics may be communicated verbally and non-verbally. Such suggestions may seem almost trite when read about in isolation, but it is surprising how often they are ignored by policy makers and planners, with often disastrous consequences for the success of a development programme.

These then are some of the methods, methodological innovations and concerns in the field of cross-cultural research on contraception. The rest of this chapter examines some of the key themes brought out by these methods as they have been applied by the contributors to this volume. They coalesce around one of the major conceptual divides in anthropology, that between the social and the cultural. The two are interlinked. For example, the social can be seen both as the social institutions and relationships that form out of and impinge upon contraceptive practice, but also the ways in which these same social processes create and perpetuate concepts and values 'in people's heads' – the 'social construction' of contraception (next section). The 'cultural construction' of contraception (following section) has more to do with broader beliefs and value structures that underlie the ways in which contraceptives are regarded and used. To ask which is more important, the 'cultural' or the 'social', is to impose an impossible 'chicken and egg' question. Some anthropologists, such as Maternowska (this volume) would argue that the political and economic background of the community, region, nation or world, is the ultimate arbiter of both.

Contraception as a Social Construct

Contraception works at both biological and social levels, and the holistic perspective of anthropology acknowledges that contraceptive acts take place in the context of an entire gamut of reproductive health concerns and practices. These can be studied at a variety of different levels, from the pharmaceutical companies that develop and manufacture the new contraceptive technologies, policy makers and planners who incorporate them into their projects, the 'providers' who offer services at the local level to 'recipients', to the millions of people around the world who practice contraception. The anthropologist has much to contribute to understanding the different 'layers' through which policy and practice operate, a point made by Nader (1974) in her exhortation to anthropologists to 'study up' the hierarchy, but one that has been less frequently taken up than might be expected in subsequent research.[7]

These levels do not co-exist harmoniously. Different levels in the system have different interests and values, ranging from the capitalist desire for profit that is a major driving force (and sometimes limiting factor) in the development and marketing of new contraceptive technologies amongst the pharmaceutical giants, to the needs of people around the world for safe and effective contraceptives that enable them to control their fertility. The interests and values of the different levels are rarely discrete, however, and there are often conflicts of interest within a particular level. An example of this is the competing interests of population control and birth control in the international health development agenda.

Population control has its roots in Malthusian concerns over a perceived 'population crisis', although, as Mamdani (1974) points out, these fears are as much to do with racist and conservative fears for the stability of the world economic and political order as they are to do with the ecological and resource problems an expanding world population may cause.[8] Birth control, by contrast, derives from the struggles of the suffragette and socialist movements in the late nineteenth century (Russell 1999: 70). A shift from 'population control' to 'birth control' (via the ambivalently ...intervening term 'family planning') took place around the time of the United Nations' World Population Conference in Bucharest in 1974 (UN World Population Year). This shift, Whelan (1992) argues, may in fact have been more rhetorical than real and the two philosophies can co-exist under one programmatic umbrella, as with Planned Parenthood in the USA in the 1960s (Watkins 1998) and the reproductive health programme in Mexico today (Thompson, this volume). In Chiapas, numerical target setting (population control) runs in the face of an informed choice agenda (birth control/reproductive health) and Thompson warns about population control masquerading behind an empty rhetoric of 'participation'.

Other trends are discernible in the international policy-making agenda of the past four decades. Ulin *et al.* see a shift in focus from concern over high infant mortality rates (in the 1960s) and a need for reduction in fertility rates (1970s) to maternal morbidity and mortality (1980s) and 'total reproductive health' in the 1990s (around which a consensus of sorts emerged from the UN International Conference on Population and Development in Cairo in 1994). Contraceptive information and delivery services occupy a niche of varying centrality in these shifting agendas. Development as a 'social fact' is essentially a product of Western liberal philosophy and values and, in the arena of 'modern' contraceptive delivery services, comes with other such values as 'freedom of choice' and 'informed consent' (Thompson, this volume). While their value in theory is irrefutable, in practice all these concepts prove problematic, and Thompson queries whether the new reproductive health policy in Mexico has led to any more than rhetorical changes amongst providers in Mexico at the grass roots level. 'Freedom of choice' and 'informed consent' imply or necessitate individuals being free, socially, economically and politically, to make such choices, fully informed (in ways that are both accessible and understandable to them) about the risks and benefits involved with each form of contraception, in a situation where the risks are themselves often uncertain or, as in the case of Depo-Provera (Russell 1999), contested. There are unfortunately many examples from around the world, or provider-dependent methods being imposed without any kind of 'informed consent' whatsoever (see, for example, van Hollen 1998; Hardon *et al.* 1993).

Justice's observation of the 'momentum of international health policy, which inundates local realities as it sweeps downward from policy making circles to planners' (1986: 147) is an important corrective to those anthropologists who have tended to ignore transnational processes and concerns. However, international health policy does not wash local realities away in a uniform manner. The global picture is nothing without its local contexts. Contraception is practised, and the new technologies are developed, disseminated and used, within local systems of economic values, ethical concerns, political and religious ideologies, kinship structures and dyadic relationships: in short, the social and cultural systems of people in particular places at particular times. Different groups will ascribe different meanings to contraception depending on their beliefs, social situation, and political and economic circumstances, and history. Thus in Uzbekistan, until recently, IUDs were the only form of contraception available apart from condoms, 'natural' contraception and abortion. Greifeld and Krengel suspect that until other forms of contraception came available, health professionals felt no need to discuss the advantages and disadvantages of IUDs with their clients. Now alternatives are available, and the disadvantages of IUDs, which are perceived as causing anaemia, can be addressed. The political and economic situation in Uzbekistan has also changed, with the effect (as Greifeld and Krengel see it) that women are more likely to experience health problems such as anaemia anyway, due to their lowered economic and social status.

any different 'levels' in the social organization of contracep-
ere are multinational pharmaceutical companies that commit
us development costs, but also, potentially, enormous profits,
a new contraceptive. They often work hand in hand with
international governmental and non-governmental organizations, which
may heavily subsidize research into new contraceptive technologies (see
Hartmann 1995: 174–9). Next, there is the role of governments and
government policies that have direct effects on the development and
dissemination of contraceptives and contraceptive advice in specific
countries: policy agendas that have their own dynamics (Lee *et al.* 1998).
Such policies may be over-archingly pro-natalist, neutral or anti-natalist:
Greifeld and Krengel (this volume) remind us of the former Soviet
Union's pro-natalist practice of awarding medals to women who gave
birth to large numbers of children. Often the stance adopted may be
pro-natalist for certain sections of the society and anti-natalist for others,
such as white and black populations respectively in the former Rhodesia
(Kaler, this volume) or Jewish and Palestinian populations in the state
of Israel (Kanaaneh, this volume). It is hardly surprising, given the
history of relations between dominant and subordinate groups in societies such as Chiapas, Mexico, that family planning promotion has so
often been suspected of harbouring genocidal intentions (see Sobo 1996
on Jamaican fears of genocidal intent in family planning programmes).
Experience has shown that such fears are not always groundless where
there is a 'population control' agenda (as in the case, for example, of
Cambodian refugees in Thailand (Russell 1995/6)).

Next there are the people involved in implementing government plans
and policies at the grass-roots level, and the systems of health and social
care in which they operate. In many societies (such as Uzbekistan, Haiti,
Chiapas and the Galilee in this volume), family planning services are
offered in some kind of health arena, an example of 'medicalisation' (Zola
1975), the movement of medical interest and expertise into areas of life
that were previously outside the medical domain. One disadvantage of
the medicalization of family planning, pointed out by Thompson (this
volume) is that, where other medical services offered to women under
the umbrella of primary health care are of poor quality, it makes people
less likely to seek contraceptive advice from the same source. Health
care systems are social systems (Kleinman 1978) and there is much to be
said for anthropologists researching the social, cultural, economic and
political contexts within which secondary and primary health care workers
work, and the roles and relationships they develop in doing so. This turns
upon its head the conventional wisdom that if only people (i.e. the

recipients, or intended recipients of family planning services rather than the providers themselves) were more 'rational', then most of the problems of contraceptive delivery would be solved (cf. Sobo 1995).

Very often health development takes place without reference to or understanding of these all-important structures and personnel at all. As Porter puts it 'when sociologists began studying human reproduction they . . . took the existence and functioning of services relating to reproductive health largely for granted' (1990: 183). This 'led to a concentration on 'failures' in women's behaviour, such as the failure to use the antenatal services provided, to the exclusion of organizational and other failures in the services themselves' (ibid: 183-4). Because of this blinkered vision Thompson (this volume) sees an inherent assumption amongst most policy makers that everyone is 'rational' and, once they understand family planning they will choose to use it, those that don't being dismissed as 'ignorant' or 'superstitious'. In Rhodesia, Kaler (this volume) demonstrates how much of the discourse surrounding family planning involved the erroneous motif of the irrational, happy-go-lucky African procreating without a care for tomorrow. Stereotypic views of people can mask perceptions of variation within a group or people, and accentuate perceptions of difference between that group and others (often the observer). Such views affect not only how they are likely to be treated but also, what contraceptives they are likely to receive. Stacey (1988) cites a study in which health professionals offering contraceptive services in the UK 'stereotyped' women as to what kind of contraception the health professionals saw as being suitable for them. In Chiapas, pressure was put on women to accept provider-preferred methods (Thompson, this volume);[1] indeed, health personnel saw contraceptive delivery as being a matter of 'convincing' people rather than enabling or informing them.[9] Such factors, not to mention the lack of variety in what is provided in many clinics due to cost, do little to promote principles of 'freedom of choice' or 'informed consent' (cf. Sobo 1993).

Power relationships, manifest and latent, exist between 'providers' and 'users' (the latter often termed 'recipients') of family planning services. These are often unequal (as the 'provider'/'recipient' terminology may imply). Where this is so, the dominant perspective will often be that of the provider. It is predominantly their reality that 'counts' (Chambers 1997) in determining what happens, how, when and why, in the clinic at least. Maternowksa's chapter looks at the 'provider-recipient' (in this case 'doctor-client') relationship at the grass-roots level through a fine-grained description of a family planning clinic in *Cité Soleil*, Haiti. She provides an analysis of the structures of power underlying the relationship, arguing persuasively that these reflect and perpetuate the ideologies and political and economic realities of wider society. In the telling case-studies of individual consultations she provides, power is manifested in the routinely short, perfunctory examinations that take place and in episodes such as the doctor flinging a chart at a client, or confiding to the researcher that his clients are 'nothing'. 'Freedom of choice' and 'informed consent' are hollow concepts in such a setting, with trust (of providers for their clients, or clients for providers) often sorely lacking and negotiation of method use rare. The doctors do not appear to acknowledge the economic or cultural realities of their clients, as the examples of advice given by doctors to their clients makes plain. For their clients, acquiescence or latent resistance proves the only alternative to maintenance of the status quo, and Maternowksa's chapter finishes by indicating how such acts of resistance have started to take place collectively. In the case of Chiapas, Mexico (Thompson, this volume), 'resistance' to family planning is latent rather than expressed, but operates in the context of a low-level guerilla war, fought over the status of Mexico's indigenous population within the State of Mexico.

Not all societies appear to share the general distrust of family planning programmes, however. For example, in Uzbekistan people often express a desire to give up responsibility for family planning to the medical profession 'who know best'. Even where people want to seek professional help and advice, they may feel constrained by social pressures such as the desire for anonymity (an issue in Tonga). As Perea (1994: 17) puts it:

> There is an urgent need to document what happens in service provider-user relationships, in order to understand how conflict and inequality are manifested, and then to make this knowledge public and include everyone concerned in discussions of how to resolve these conflicts ... Mechanisms are needed so that people can be made aware of their rights and at the same time, the health services can be monitored. This is not only a question of modifying clinical practice here and there, but rather of finding ways to ensure the provider-user relations are equitable and that decisions about reproduction take place in democratised spaces.

Contraceptive decision-making also occurs, or is significantly influenced, outwith the formal institutions set up to promote it. Thus in Tonga, participants at the sessions overseen by Levene (this volume) came up with the suggestion that town officers be trained to dispense contraceptive advice and products. Greifeld and Krengel (this volume) highlight the role of the mother and the tea shops as sources of mediation and discussion on contraceptive issues for married Uzbeki men. Such arenas often go

unrecognized by planners and policy-makers, yet thei
vital to acknowledge in understanding the dynamics of con
    Finally contraceptive decision-making and use takes pla
heterosexual relationships. Issues of power, gender and trust
Woodsong and Koo 1999) infiltrate these relationships just
relationships between 'users' and 'providers' (above). In m...y of the
chapters in this volume we see women expected to defer to their husbands
in matters of contraceptive decision-making, or working behind their
backs if they wish to contracept without their husbands' (or other family
members') knowledge or consent. Women in Bangladesh and Mexico
are alike in that to deceive their husbands in this way runs the considerable
risk of male violence, and in such circumstances contraceptives that can
be administered clandestinely and infrequently (such as the IUD or an
injectable) are the contraceptives of 'choice'. In Bangladesh, however,
Stark (this volume) suggests that the decision to use contraception
'secretly' is part of a more subtle 'take and tell' communicative strategy
amongst married couples that can actually be seen as increasing female
autonomy.
    Contraceptives, then, have profound ramifications for human social
organization and relationships, and the study of contraception and the
issues surrounding it puts into high relief those aspects of human social
life, politics and economics, that both forge the compact between 'people'
and 'contraceptives' and are influenced by it. However, looking at the
social construction of contraception in this way does not exhaust the range
of meanings that contraception has in the hearts and minds of people
around the world. Contraception is as much a cultural as a social
phenomenon. We shall go on to look more deeply at the cultural significance of contraception next.

The Cultural Construction of Contraception (Or: When is a Contraceptive More Than Just a Contraceptive?)

We have examined some of the 'social facts' of contraception. However,
social reality is in people's heads as much as in their actions and
relationships. The stuff in people's heads, 'the socially transmitted
behaviour patterns, beliefs, institutions and processes' (Maternowksa, this
volume) is part of what anthropologists call 'culture'. As we have
emphasized above, 'culture' abides everywhere: it is not something
negative that adheres to certain groups of people (contraceptive users) in
contrast to the 'rationality', 'good sense' and 'professionalism' of policy
makers, planners and providers (Carter 1995). In such circumstances,

'culture' becomes politicized (Wright 1998), invoked as a 'problem' involving backwardness or hardened traditions, that explains failure of contraceptive delivery programmes when all rational explanations of the powerful have been exhausted. Thus non-attendance, for example, if not a problem of access, must be a problem of culture. The Ethiopian Jewish immigrants discussed by Phillips Davids (this volume) are suddenly in a situation of easy access to contraceptive delivery services yet often choose not to use them. In this case, 'cultural' perceptions of contraception go some way to explaining the relatively low uptake of family planning services amongst the group in question. The Ethiopian immigrants studied are not irrational (in the 'political' use of the term 'cultural'): they are simply dancing to a different tune to planners. Similarly, when they use contraceptive services they do so with an agenda not of limiting their total fertility but of spacing it in culturally acceptable ways. Even when, as in Rhodesia, the economic rationality of having many children in a society with high infant mortality rates and a need for security in old age and before may be apparent, failure to have smaller families may still be treated as cultural pathology. To reiterate, 'culture' is something that is as much embedded in the actions of 'providers' as it is in those of contraceptive 'users'.

Culture must be studied along with society: it adheres to the family planning institutions discussed above as well as to broader social formations such as class, ethnicity and gender. It pervades the anthropological analysis of all forms of contraceptive activity. It is what imbues the behaviours and technologies associated with contraception and contraceptive practice with meaning, that demonstrates how contraception is as much about concepts in people's heads as it is about products and behaviours that prevent pregnancy within heterosexual relationships.

Thus there are different ideas about what actually constitutes 'contraception', and what forms of contraception are good and bad (Sobo 1993; 1995). Several chapters indicate the fluidity of the boundary between 'contraception' as we have defined it above and what might be termed 'reproductive control' that, in the former Soviet Union (Greifeld and Krengel) as well as many other parts of the world, includes abortion. Health care planners tend to concentrate on 'modern' contraceptives and ignore more 'traditional' forms of contraception such as coitus interruptus, regarding these as 'backward' and 'unreliable' (Newman 1995). Yet perceptions of different types of 'modern' contraceptives such as the IUD (Renne 1997) also vary in clients' eyes, and will thus impinge on what contraceptives will be offered to individual users or be acceptable to (or used by) them according to people's 'emic' conceptions of such things as how their bodies work (Sobo 1993). Contraceptive providers and their clients may differ markedly in their perceptions on such matters (Erickson 1996), although there is often considerable overlap between the two.

Thus in Uzbekistan, for example, midwives expressed the view that the forty days of *jhilla* following the birth of a child was unsuitable for the insertion of an object such as an IUD, but felt it was unnecessary anyway as sexual intercourse is not supposed to happen during this time. Amongst the Ethiopian Jewish immigrants studied by Phillips Davids (this volume), a belief in the fertility-depressing, long-term effect of hormonal contraceptives and a cultural concern about their role in restricting blood flow during menstruation makes long-term use of oral contraceptives unlikely. It is noteworthy how in Japan, oral contraceptives are similarly seen as contravening 'nature' and hence are rarely used (Jitsukawa 1997).

A common theme in many of the chapters is fear of the side-effects associated with the contraceptive 'pill' and/or other devices (Etkin 1992). Such fears, that again owe much to different conceptions of the body (although this is not to deny their reality to those who suffer from them, as the medical model of care might do) are often ignored or derided by planners and implementers of contraceptive delivery services. This is particularly likely when targets are set (Thompson, this volume) or the recipients of contraceptive programmes are regarded as ignorant or wild (Maternowksa, this volume; cf. Hardon 1992). Sometimes ideas about side-effects reflect contraception operating in what Thompson (this volume) calls 'a gendered realm'. In Mexico, as in many societies cross-culturally, fertility and menstrual regulation are regarded as part of the 'female sphere of influence and knowledge'. Women fear female sterilization in case they will not be able to do the same amount of work after the operation as before, while men fear male sterilization, seeing it as almost culturally unthinkable to dispense with their virility in this way. Again, a perception that women will be put off using contraception if they are told of possible side-effects bodes ill for the principle of informed consent in the choice of method.

Contraceptives thus not only function as fertility regulators but as symbols and metaphors of other culturally salient issues. This gives them a power and potency that can have a direct impact on demographic trends. A common theme amongst contributors to this volume is the symbolic (and often very seductive) association of the new contraceptive technologies, not necessarily positively, with progress, development and modernity (cf. Ali 1996). Critchlow (1999) argues that the efforts of US policy makers to control the growth of human populations and disseminate new contraceptive technologies widely around the world have been largely successful, despite the resistance of influential institutions such as the Roman Catholic Church. In Uzbekistan, contraceptives are seen as the means whereby individuals, through regulating their own fertility, can contribute to the establishment of their country in the ranks of world nations (Greifeld and Krengel, this volume). In Kanaaneh's description of Palestinians in Galilee (this volume), reproduction (or rather the lack or control of reproduction) has become more than just a means of measuring progress and modernity, but is a source of self-identity and a means of evaluating others. The availability of contraceptive technologies in Galilee means that people can now 'make mistakes' that are seen as inexcusable, even pathological, in the eyes of those Palestinians who see themselves as upholding modernist values. 'Choice' is thus a double-edged sword insofar as it puts responsibility for controlling fertility back in the hands of individual women and men, with moral approbation and social penalties accruing to those who do not appear to take these responsibilities sufficiently seriously.

Contraceptives, then, are more than just technologies and behaviours: they operate in and represent a universe of culture, morality and emotion. As a symbol of modernity, for example, contraceptives are to be embraced, resisted or kept at arm's length – but never treated in a neutral manner. For some, contraceptive use is a marker of modernity, for others of promiscuity. In short, contraception is part of who people are, their identities and relationships. In addition, we have also seen how contraceptives are also more than just contraceptives because they come in packages that sometimes have their own meanings, they are dispensed by health and other personnel in particular cultural venues, and may be used by couples (and individuals) for a multitude of purposes beyond straightforward contraception, from condom use against STDs to (in Tonga) a form of fishing lure!

Conclusion

Contraception is a global phenomenon with local ramifications, permutations and conceptions. Anthropology as a discipline has much to offer the study of contraception cross-culturally, and this chapter has endeavoured to draw together the themes and approaches that link the chapters that follow, ordered around methodological issues and the social and cultural constructions of contraception. The holistic, cross-cultural perspective of anthropology, tempered by its focus on specific peoples and places, highlights some issues and critiques others. Good practice, in anthropology as in contraceptive delivery services, requires the 'user perspective' to be taken, with a focus on quality of care issues and empowerment (Hardon *et al.* 1997). Power relationships are all important, and providers themselves operate with serious economic and political constraints. As advocates as well as interpreters, anthropologists need to be as concerned with enabling 'choices' as with understanding 'constraints' in the dissemination and use of contraceptives, and to see such services within the wider remit of total reproductive health and the empowerment of women.

The development of new contraceptive technologies over the past sixty years has been remarkable, and they can be looked at, either individually or together, as a case study of technological innovation and its social and cultural consequences. However, the study of contraception tells us as much about social and cultural life as the study of social and cultural life tells us about contraception. This is what makes it such an exciting, never boring, topic for anthropological research.

Notes

1. Notable exceptions include Coleman (1983), some of the chapters in Ginsburg and Rapp (1995), Hardon *et al.* (1993), Mintzes (1992), Newman (1972; 1995), Nichter and Nichter (1987), Polgar and Marshall (1978), Simonelli (1986), Sobo (1993) and Stycos (1971). Other influential works in contraceptive theory and practice include Hartmann (1995) and Mirsky *et al.* (1994).

2. The conference was held at University College Stockton, which has since been renamed 'University of Durham, Stockton Campus'. Four other papers presented at the conference were published in a special issue of *Anthropology and Medicine* (Sobo and Russell 1997). Our thanks are due to the Mellon Foundation, the UK Overseas Development Administration (now the Department for International Development), and the Simon Population Trust for their generous financial support for the conference, and to the staff at University College Stockton for their hospitality.

3. Readers requiring more information on individual forms of contraception are referred to the well-maintained web pages of organizations such as the Family Planning Council (http://www.familyplanning.org/).

4. Similar problems exist with the concept of 'natural fertility' in general, which is seen, unjustifiably, as opposed to 'controlled' fertility, whereas ethnographic studies indicate that control of some sort is ubiquitous (Sainz de la Maza Kaufman 1997; Wood 1991).

5. The recently marketed 'Persona' contraception kit, is an interesting exception. It uses self-analysis of urine samples to determine a woman's fertile periods. It is very much a 'natural' method (if outside the price range of all but those in the affluent West where, in the UK, it retails for about £50 sterling).
6. For more discussion on the value of participatory research in contraception and reproductive health, see Hardon (1998).
7. A notable example of this approach in action is Justice (1986).
8. Gordon (1976) suggests that the ideology of population control is 'the successor to eugenics in every respect – ideologically, organizationally and in personnel'.
9. 'Convincing', like 'acceptability' (Reproductive Health Matters 1997), is very much part of the 'provider' mindset.

References

Ali, K.A. (1996), 'The Politics of Family Planning in Egypt', *Anthropology Today*, 12(5): 14–19.

Bernard, H.R. (1995), *Research Methods in Anthropology: Qualitative and Quantitative Approaches (2nd ed.)*, Walnut Creek: AltaMira Press.

Bibeau, G. (1997), 'At Work in the Fields of Public Health: the Abuse of Rationality', *Medical Anthropology Quarterly*, 11(2): 246–52.

Carter, A. (1995), 'Agency and Fertility: for an Ethnography of Practice', in S. Greenhalgh (ed.), *Situating Fertility: Anthropology and Demographic Inquiry*, Cambridge: Cambridge University Press.

Chambers, R. (1997), *Whose Reality Counts? Putting the First Last*, London: Intermediate Technology.

Coleman, S. (1983), *Family Planning in Japanese Society: Traditional Birth Control in a Modern Urban Culture*, Princeton: Princeton University Press.

Cornwall, A. and R. Jewkes (1995), 'What is Participatory Research?', *Social Science and Medicine,* 41(12): 1667–76.

Critchlow, D. (1999), *Intended Consequences: Birth Control, Abortion and the Federal Government in Modern America*, New York: Oxford University Press.

Edwards, J., S. Franklin, E. Hirsch, F. Price and M. Strathern (eds) (1993), *Technologies of Procreation: Kinship in the Age of Assisted Conception*, Manchester: Manchester University Press.

Erickson, P.L. (1996), 'Contraceptive Methods: Do Hispanic Adolescents and their Family Planning Care Providers Think about Contraceptive Methods the Same Way?', *Medical Anthropology*, 17(1): 65–82.

Etkin, N.L. (1992), '"Side Effects": Cultural Constructions and Reinterpretations of Western Pharmaceuticals', *Medical Anthropology Quarterly (n.s.)*, 6(2): 99–113.

Ginsburg, F.D. and R. Rapp (eds) (1995), *Conceiving the New World Order: the Global Politics of Reproduction*, Berkeley: University of California Press.

Gordon, L. (1976), *Woman's Body, Woman's Right: a Social History of Birth Control in America,* New York: Grossman.

Hardon, A. (1992), 'The Needs of Women versus the Interests of Family Planning Personnel, Policy Makers and Researchers: Conflicting Views on Safety and Acceptability of Contraceptives, *Social Science and Medicine* 35(65): 753–66.

—— (ed.) (1998), *Beyond Rhetoric: Participatory Research on Reproductive Health,* Amsterdam: Het Spinhuis.

——, B. Mintzes and J. Hanhart (eds) (1993), *Norplant: Under her Skin,* Delft: Eburon.

——, E. Engelkes, S. Kabir and A. Mutua (1997), *Reproductive Rights in Practice: a Feminist Report on the Quality of Care,* London: Zed Press.

Hartmann, B. (1995), *Reproductive Rights and Wrongs: the Global Politics of Population Control,* Boston: South End Press (first published 1987).

Hollen, C. van (1998), 'Moving Targets: Routine IUD Insertion in Maternity wards in Tamil Nadu, India', *Reproductive Health Matters,* 6(11): 98–106.

Jitsukawa, M. (1997), 'In accordance with nature: what Japanese women mean by being in control', *Anthropology and Medicine,* 4(2): 177–201.

Justice, J. (1986), *Policies, Plans and People: Culture and Health Development in Nepal,* Berkeley: University of California Press.

Kleinman, A. (1978), 'Concepts and a Model for the Comparison of Medical Systems as Social Systems', *Social Science and Medicine,* 12: 85-93. (Reprinted in C. Currer and M. Stacey (eds) (1986), *Concepts of Health, Illness and Disease: a Comparative Perspective,* Leamington Spa: Berg.)

Latour, B. (1993), *We Have Never Been Modern,* Cambridge, MA: Harvard University Press.

Lee, K., L. Lush, G. Walt and J. Cleland (1998), 'Family Planning Policies and Programmes in Eight Low-Income Countries: a Comparative Policy Analysis', *Social Science and Medicine,* 47(7): 949–59.

Mamdani, M. (1974), The Myth of Population Control, *Development Digest,* 12: 13–28.

Mintzes, B. (ed.) (1992), *A Question of Control: Women's Perspectives on the Development and Use of Contraceptive Methods,* Amsterdam: WEMOS/HAI.

Mirsky, J. and M. Radlett, W. Davies and O. Bennett (eds) (1994), *Private Decisions, Public Debate: Women, Reproduction and Population,* London: Panos.

Nader, L. (1974), 'Up the Anthropologist: Perspectives Gained from Studying Up', in D. Hymes (ed.), *Reinventing Anthropology,* New York: Vintage.

Newman, L.F. (ed.) (1972), *Birth Control: an Anthropological View,* Module No. 27, Reading: Addison-Wesley.

—— (ed.) (1995), *Women's Medicine: a Cross-Cultural Study of Indigenous Fertility Regulation,* New Brunswick: Rutgers University Press (first published 1986).

Nichter, M. and M. Nichter (1987), 'Cultural Notions of Fertility in South Asia and their Impact on Sri Lankan Family Planning Practices', *Human Organization,* 46(1): 18–28.

Oudshoorn, N. (1994), *Beyond the Natural Body: an Archeology of Sex Hormones,* London: Routledge.

Perea, J.G.F. (1994), 'The Introduction of New Methods of Contraception: Ethical Perspectives', *Reproductive Health Matters*, No. 3 (May): 13–18.

Polgar, S. and J.F. Marshall (1978), 'The Search for Culturally Acceptable Fertility Regulating Methods', in M.H. Logan and E.E. Hunt (eds), *Health and the Human Condition: Perspectives in Medical Anthropology,* California: Wadsworth.

Porter, M. (1990), 'Professional-Client Relationships and Women's Reproductive Health Care', in S. Cunningham-Burley and N.P. McKeganey (eds), *Readings in Medical Sociology*, London: Tavistock/Routledge.

Renne, E.P. (1997), 'Local and Institutional Interpretations of IUDs in South-western Nigeria', *Social Science and Medicine,* 44(8): 1141–8.

Reproductive Health Matters (ed.) (1997), *Beyond Acceptability: Users' Perspectives on Contraception*, London: Reproductive Health Matters.

Russell, A.J. (1995/6), 'Depo-Provera: Cultural Controversies in Contraceptive Decision Making', *British Medical Anthropology Review*, 3(1): 4–15.

—— (1999), 'Taking Care? The Depo-Provera Debate', in T. Kohn and R. McKechnie (eds), *Extending the Boundaries of Care: Medical Ethics and Caring Practices*, Oxford: Berg.

Sainz de la Maza Kaufmann, M. (1997), 'Contraception in Three Chibcha Communities and the Concept of Natural Fertility', *Current Anthropology*, 38(4): 681–7.

Seeley, J.A., J.F. Kengeya-Kayondo and D.W. Mulder (1992), 'Community-Based HIV/AIDS Research – Whither Community Participation? Unsolved Problems in a Research Programme in Rural Uganda', *Social Science and Medicine*, 34: 1089.

Simonelli, J.M. (1986), *Two Boys, a Girl, and Enough: Reproductive and Economic Decision-Making on the Mexican Periphery*, Boulder: Westview.

Simpson, R. (1997), 'Representations and the Re-presentation of Family: an Analysis of Divorce Narratives', in A. James, J. Hockey and A. Dawson (eds), *After Writing Culture: Epistemology and Praxis in Contemporary Anthropology*, London: Routledge.

Sobo, E.J. (1993), Bodies, Kin and Flow: Family Planning in Rural Jamaica, *Medical Anthropology Quarterly* 7(1): 50–73.

—— (1995), *Choosing Unsafe Sex: AIDS-Risk Denial Among Disadvantaged Women*, Philadelphia: University of Pennsylvania Press.

—— (1996), Abortion Traditions in Rural Jamaica, *Social Science and Medicine* 42(4): 495-508.

—— and V.C. de Munck (1997), 'The Forest of Methods', in V. de Munck and E.J. Sobo (eds), *Using Methods in the Field: A Practical Introduction and Casebook,* London: AltaMira (Sage).

—— and A.J. Russell (eds) (1997), Special Issue on 'Anthropology and Contraception, *Anthropology and Medicine, 4*(2).

Stacey, M. (1988), *The Sociology of Health and Healing: a Textbook.* London: Routledge.

Strathern, M. (1992), *Reproducing the Future: Essays on Anthropology, Kinship and the New Reproductive Technologies*, Manchester: Manchester University Press.

Stycos, J.M. (1971), *Ideology, Faith and Family Planning in Latin America,* New York: McGraw-Hill.

Triandis, H.C. (1995), *Individualism and Collectivism*, Boulder: Westview Press.

Ulin, P.R., K. Hardee, P. Bailey and N. Williamson (1994), 'The Impact of Family Planning on Women's Lives: Expanding the Research Agenda', *World Health Statistics Quarterly*, 47(1): 6–8.

Watkins, E.S. (1998) *On the Pill: a Social History of Contraceptives, 1950–1970.* Baltimore: Johns Hopkins University Press.

Whelan, R. (1992), *Choices in Childbearing: When does Family Planning Become Population Control?* Committee on Population and the Economy: London.

Wood, J.W. (1991), 'Fecundity and natural fertility in humans', in S.R. Milligan (ed.), *Oxford Reviews of Reproductive Biology, Vol. 2*, Oxford: Oxford University Press.

Woodsong, C. and H.P. Koo (1999), 'Two Good Reasons: Women's and Men's Perspectives on Dual Contraceptive Use', *Social Science and Medicine,* 49: 567–80.

Wright, S. (1998), 'Politicisation of Culture', *Anthropology in Action*, 5(1/2): 3–10.

Zola, I.K. (1975), 'Medicine as an Institution of Social Control', in A. Cox and A. Mead (eds), *A Sociology of Medical Practice*, London: Collier-Macmillan.

2

Psychosocial Data and Cross-Cultural Analyses: Challenges to Anthropology and Contraceptive Research

Mary S. Willis and *Marion Pratt*

Introduction

Developing effective, safe and practical contraceptive methods requires an understanding of subjective feelings and sexual behaviours amongst different cultural or ethnic groups around the world. Such information is derived from psychosocial research findings, i.e. information gathered on the ways in which an individual's thoughts, feelings, and behaviours compare to and affect others (Brehm *et al.* 1999). Although a minimal method mix is now available in most developing countries (e.g. oral contraceptives, condoms, intrauterine devices, injectables, sub-dermal applications or foaming tablets), there are risks associated with each method. Certain methods can compromise the health and wellbeing of the individual and/or incur significant financial or personal costs to the user or the user's family. Thus, improvements in contraceptive technology are still needed. Moreover, the HIV/AIDS epidemic has created a need for the development of new contraceptive methods that provide an effective barrier to the contraction of sexually transmitted diseases (STDs).

In order to improve currently available contraceptive options or to design new multipurpose barrier methods, an in-depth understanding of people's past history and current sexual practices is critical. Such information can provide invaluable insights, enabling researchers and users to address multiple concerns. Identifying the influence of a particular contraceptive method on the frequencies and types of sexual behaviours practised enables researchers to make changes in the overall design of a method and to improve both comfort and effectiveness. For example, the recognition that sexual activity alters the condition of genital or anal tissue might encourage the development of methods that better protect the affected areas. Determining the ages at which individuals begin sexual activity could inform efforts to revise educational materials necessary for a particular segment of the population. At a minimum, such information can help to identify features of currently available contraceptives that could be modified to increase efficacy and uptake. More importantly, this information can be used to stimulate the development of completely new contraceptive methods that further reduce the possibility of unwanted pregnancies, further limit deleterious side-effects, minimize the financial and personal sacrifices necessary to procure and use contraceptives, *and* decrease the transmission of STDs.

Contraceptives were developed originally to provide men and women with greater control over fertility options (providing or lengthening interbirth intervals and limiting overall family size) thereby improving people's health and wellbeing; new contraceptive technologies will be expected to prevent the transmission of debilitating and sometimes fatal STDs. Also, in addition to providing essential data to enhance the quality of contraceptive technology research, psychosocial studies can contribute to the development of assistance programmes administered through governmental and non-governmental organizations (NGOs). Such studies can be used to help determine overall levels of development funding for individual countries, to draft governmental policy for a specific world region or country, to influence government policy in host countries, and to design development assistance programmes for the countries that rank highest with respect to reproductive health indicators (e.g. total fertility rate, maternal mortality and morbidity rates, age at first birth). In other words, results of psychosocial research can have important implications in multiple arenas, affecting the lives of many people. Given that the pool of financial resources available for scientific research worldwide is shrinking, it is especially important that research funding be applied to projects that incorporate a rigorous methodology developed according to – or carefully adapted for – the cultural context within which data will be collected. Recent reductions in foreign assistance funding have contributed to the fact that the US Agency for International Development (USAID), for example, currently spends less money per woman on reproductive health-related development assistance than at any time since 1968 (Anon. 1999). These reductions are likely to affect negatively the progress that might otherwise have been made in the areas of contraceptive research and technology.

The goal of well-designed psychosocial research programmes is to generate high-quality results that identify *real* differences among the sample populations and thus rule out alternative or rival hypotheses (Triandis 1994). The use of reliable, valid data facilitates a comparative approach to the study of cultural groups, enabling similarities and differences related to reproductive health to emerge. The most meaningful data is acquired through long-term ethnographic studies of cultural groups throughout each region or country in question. However, funding constraints, pressure to produce results within a short time-frame (three to five years), and the need to sample multiple cultures for a single study, can force the researcher to adopt less expensive, ready-made alternatives to context-specific, ethnographic research. Usually, these take the form of psychosocial surveys, questionnaires or scales developed for Western populations – typically those in the United States and Western Europe – and applied in an uncritical manner to non-Western populations. 'Dependence on research instruments designed in the West, often in combination with an uncritical belief in their universal applicability' note Brummelhuis and Herdt, 'results in a "pick-up sticks" approach that is not only insensitive toward the local culture but even imposes Western assumptions' (1995: xxii).

If contraceptive methods are to provide choice and safety for those who wish to use them, and if uptake figures are to be increased, then data must be collected from non-Western cultures using rigorously tested research strategies. As Triandis (1994; 1995) suggests, theoretical frameworks should be constructed with the participation and collaboration of (at a minimum) representative samples of the world's population, approximately 70 per cent of whom live in developing countries. In fact, most contraceptive methods have been developed by (and usually for) individuals in Western countries and may not be as practical, efficacious or safe for use in non-Western contexts. Follow-up treatments and monitoring of side-effects may not be feasible due to the distance from the user's home to the service site, the lack of time to visit the service site, and the shortage of financial resources available for medical care. Yet modern contraceptive methods developed to accommodate the majority of the world's users could bring improved health, greater reproductive choice, and an overall increase in use for thousands of men and women around the world.

Researchers asked to conduct psychosocial studies in developing countries are usually specialists in health-related fields, most of whom have had little if any anthropological training. Anthropological training prepares its practitioners through the use of cross-cultural methods that emphasize local context, cultural immersion, and language skills. Yet anthropologists continue to miss opportunities to contribute to contraceptive research and hence to validate and enhance the value that other disciplines place on anthropological training. Anthropologists should be called upon more often to review cross-cultural research programmes, journal submissions, and grant proposals. They should assist in crafting public policy and in training members of all disciplines in ethnographic methods. Lastly, they should reclaim the anthropological methods and strategies that define the discipline and promote the observation and participation of cultures around the world. The goal of this chapter is to examine some of the aspects of psychosocial research that can impact on the quality of data gathered to improve contraceptive research and technology. The emphasis here is on the anthropological methods and insights that the cross-cultural researcher should consider, especially when funding and time constraints obligate the researcher to apply Western-designed psychosocial instruments to a wide range of cultural contexts.

Potential Barriers to Contraceptive Technology Research

In an effort to identify common methodological problems related to contraceptive research, this chapter reviews publications from several disciplines (anthropology, psychology, sociology, epidemiology and public health), in particular those that employ Western-designed scales, surveys, and questionnaires. Each citation was included for illustrative purposes only. None of the studies cited represents a large-scale contraceptive technology research programme, and hence none of the examples exemplify 'good' or 'bad' research practice. As Terborgh *et al.* (1995) have suggested, it is important to remember that not all barriers to the use of contraceptives (and, we would add, barriers to the undertaking of contraceptive-related research) are connected to issues related to the study of indigenous populations. Some are linked with the way particular programmes or health care delivery systems are implemented. The goal of this chapter is to focus on those aspects of the research protocol that are under the control of those implementing psychosocial research projects. Examples from cross-cultural research that have incorporated surveys, instruments and questionnaires illustrate some of the more problematic aspects of applying Western-designed instruments to cross-cultural settings, highlighting those that most heavily affect contraceptive research. To frame the discussion, we have selected three important components of the research process – the research team, the respondent, and the instrument – focussing on characteristics in each that can affect the quality of contraceptive-related psychosocial research. (For a general overview of cross-cultural research methods, see Bernard 1998; Browner *et al.* 1988; and Triandis 1994). We discuss issues concerning the design phase of the research process, emphasizing the development of more rigorous data collection strategies.

Issues Related to the Research Team

Who Will Benefit from the Research?
In a review of issues relating to AIDS research in Africa, Schoepf (1991; 1995) identifies this question as the most crucial. Is the topic strictly an academic exercise for the benefit of the researcher, i.e. to satisfy the requirements for a grant, dissertation, or publication? If the main beneficiary of the study is the researcher, might the results be used in policy formation or programme development? If we are going to ask members of a population to share detailed information about themselves and their sexual activity, often in direct conflict with cultural prescriptions, we should be able to provide some benefit to the individual or community involved. It should also be possible to design the research programme to target issues that are meaningful to the specific community being observed or studied. In addition, it is desirable to work in collaboration with national university students or faculty, national and regional medical officials, local community groups and NGOs, and volunteer nationals. Local community members should be involved in all phases of the research programme (design, data collection, analysis, and write-up). Through this process local people can assist in creating the actual benefits that the research endeavour will bring to the community.

Does the Community Understand the Purpose of the Research and the Goals of the Researcher? Should Informed Consent be Obtained?
Huygens *et al.* (1996) found that a study was easier to conduct when 'mobilization' exercises were undertaken prior to the onset of a study. Community discussions, visual and textual announcements, local dramas, and door-to-door visits are all methods that can provide information to the community about an impending research effort. Inviting local residents to participate in the research process can build local capacity, provide employment, establish trust, and provide insight crucial to the collection of reliable data. In 1983, the US-based Society for Applied Anthropology revised its *Professional and Ethical Responsibilities*

statement, stipulating that 'To the people we study we owe disclosure of our research goals, methods and sponsorship' and that participation should be both voluntary and informed (Fluehr-Lobban 1991: 263). Because psychosocial research, and specifically contraceptive-related research, involves the study of sexuality, informed consent may be warranted.

Although many funding agencies require a human subjects review prior to the onset of a research project, many researchers fail to comply when projects are based in developing countries. In areas of high rates of illiteracy, human rights are easily violated (Ankrah 1989). Subjects could suffer unnecessarily simply because they do not understand what they are agreeing to and for what the data will be used (ibid.). Furthermore, a research programme that is poorly designed and implemented may affect the willingness of citizens to participate in future studies (in both contraceptive technology and other development sectors), even if such programmes are designed to assist the communities being studied. Participants should be made aware that results will be published in donor reports, books, and journals, and that a description of the country and region studied, as well as data regarding sexual activity, will be presented. Finally, the participants must be told who has funded the research and for what purpose the donor has agreed to do so. If each component of the research endeavour, described above, is shared with the community and some method is employed that allows a participant to acknowledge his or her understanding, then 'informed consent' has been achieved. (See Van Willigen (1993) for a comprehensive discussion of ethics.)

How Might the Respondent be Affected by Characteristics of the Interviewer?

An interviewer's age, gender, social class, ethnic group, and level of education all could have an impact on respondents, and thus affect their reactions to a psychosocial instrument. For instance, young people might reveal more when interviewed by a peer, particularly if the peer is from another community and anonymity is maintained (Huygens *et al.* 1996). Similarly, a childless female interviewer might respond differently (or elicit different responses from the respondent) than an interviewer who has children during an interview covering reproductive issues (ibid.). The research team should question prospective interviewers thoroughly and become familiar with characteristics that could affect the quality of the information being gathered.

Does the Interviewer have Competence in at Least Three of the Essential Components of Communication: Linguistic Aptitude, Interactive Skills, and Cultural Knowledge (Anderson 1976; Prieto 1992; Saville-Troike 1989; Scott 1978)?

The importance of employing an interviewer who is both fully bilingual and culturally aware cannot be emphasized strongly enough (Vaessen *et al.* 1987; Bowen and Bowen 1990). Civic and Wilson (1996), for example, conducted focus group discussions among Shona-speaking females from Zimbabwe. Participants described vaginal drying agents as those that 'taste' sweet to men and used the Shona word for good-tasting: *kunaka*. However, further questioning revealed that the female respondents were not referring literally to taste. Because oral sex is uncommon among Black Zimbabweans, the description of agents as 'tasting good' was actually a figure of speech, implying a mutually satisfying sexual experience (ibid.). Should the interviewer be unaware of the subtle meaning of language, the intended meaning of a particular response will be missed and, more importantly, an erroneous conclusion could be drawn.

If the chosen interviewer is a member of the community, the protocol should specify whether or not he or she should have personal relationships with those who are being interviewed. A close relationship may allow some types of data to be collected that might not have been possible if the interviewer was unknown to the respondent. Conversely, as Wight and Barnard (1993) have noted, personal accounts may be *more* constrained when conversing with someone who is socially close than with someone who is socially distant.

Issues Related to the Respondent

Who is Represented by the Study Population and Will the Data be Used to Describe a Larger Population in the Country?

Is the sampled population an ethnic minority living within a city, a refugee community, an internally displaced population, or perhaps an elite subset of the community? Does the sample originate in the poorest sector of a wealthy city, the wealthiest of a poor but ethnically homogeneous city, or from the middle class? How many ethnic groups reside within a country's borders? Even in the anthropological literature, statements can be found that describe a country that may or may not be applicable to all segments of the population. When we write about

'Zambians', for example, are we referring to one or several of the more than seventy ethnic groups residing within Zambia? Similarly, Rwandans have been described as a homogeneous group with no mention as to whether research findings reflect the three major ethnic groups in the country: the Hutu, Tutsi or Twa. Finally, using such ethnic minority terms as Hispanic, Asian, or African provides little information with regard to country of origin or regional variations in ethnicity, and may reinforce stereotypic images of an entire continent or nation. Readers may not be informed of any variation in sexual practices within a particular ethnic group. If we design our materials to focus on a language or culture – one that is perhaps used by the majority of citizens – we may be promoting neo-colonialist preferences for one ethnic group over another.

Perceptions of a country can be formed from a small but influential group that represents only a fraction of the actual population. For example, in Haiti, a country with a largely rural population of six million, HIV transmission studies usually have been conducted in urban communities (Farmer 1995). Intra-social variability in sexual behaviour exists within all settings, however homogeneous they may seem, and representativeness cannot be assumed (Tuzin 1991). The researcher should choose the most representative and broad sample(s) possible in order to obtain the maximum data for a given population, and to provide assistance that is more culturally relevant. Above all, for the findings that are the most effective and the least harmful, authors must carefully describe or define their study population(s) in published reports and journal articles and avoid unwarranted generalizations.

Prior to Preparing and Translating an Instrument, What Information can be Gathered that will Provide Insights into the 'Emic' Perspective (the Perspective or Interpretation from Within a Culture)?

Are pre-existing materials available (e.g. dissertations, case studies, published or non-published documents) that might provide an indication of the emic perspective regarding sexual behaviour and contraceptive use? Can such materials be used to re-evaluate the questionnaire, survey, or scale prior to conducting the field pre-test? What social meanings are associated with concepts such as marriage and family within countries as diverse as Peru, Uganda, Rwanda, and India? What assumptions are being applied to the new setting?

Constructs pertaining to sexuality are laden with culturally specific meanings. For example, what is defined as 'extramarital sex' varies greatly according to cultural and ethnic affiliation. Parker *et al.* (1991) identify some of the definitions – premarital, extramarital, polygamous, serial enduring partner relationships – and emphasize that many of them can be used to define both heterosexual and homosexual relationships. Moreover, some forms of sex may be engaged in at the same time. Culturally specific sexual preferences strongly affect current and future HIV prevention technologies as well as advances in contraceptive research (Civic and Wilson 1996).

In another example, Taylor (1990) reviewed studies conducted in Rwanda in which female respondents were asked to indicate why they disliked condoms. Responses included diminished pleasure during intercourse, the possibility of disease, indication of mistrust of one's partner, fear that condoms were unsafe and/or that they could adversely affect fertility. Because information on ethnicity and cultural context (as well as responses from males) were not collected in the reviewed studies, Taylor wanted to understand Rwandan resistance to condom use in terms of Rwandan standards of meaning. Refuting the notion that 'Rwandans are an obdurate, irrational lot, impervious to the lessons of Western science,' Taylor found that Rwandan sexual practices emphasize reciprocal flow of secretions between partners and attach great importance to the female sexual response. Heterosexual sex involves reciprocity, whereby both partners derive pleasure from one another while their two 'gifts of self' fuse to produce a common product — a child. A single act of coitus, however, is not thought to be sufficient to bring about conception. Moreover, because bodily flows are considered healthful, Rwandan women have difficulty imagining any 'blocking' device – such as a condom – as good for the body (ibid.).

Many studies focus on contraceptive method use but fail to identify the associated sexual practices that are culturally sanctioned, e.g. wet or dry sex, and condom use (Civic and Wilson 1996). A study conducted in Zimbabwe revealed that agents were used to dry, tighten and/or warm the vagina prior to intercourse (Taylor 1990; Civic and Wilson 1996). Because a product containing both camphor and menthol was a highly favoured vaginal warming mechanism, study participants suggested that mint-impregnated condoms might provide a similar warming effect, thus alleviating the need for employing products that can damage condom efficacy (Civic and Wilson 1996). These sexual practices hint at the plurality of sexual cultures in Africa and in other parts of the world, and reveal similarities with, as well as differences from, practices among Western populations (Schoepf 1991). Although rarely investigated within a questionnaire or survey design, such preferences must be identified if we are to understand the contraceptive needs of the world's most underrepresented populations.

In an attempt to better comprehend the emic perspective, thirty interviewers, project counsellors, and health educators studied by Huygens *et al.* (1996) found it useful to identify, elaborate, discuss, and vote on community values regarding the safest and clearest terms for various body parts, sexual activities, and relationships. Devoting time to understanding the social, cultural and linguistic context in which sexuality takes place (the emic perspective) is critical if data is to be reliable (ibid.).

Are there Shared Characteristics of a Culture, Region or Country that Might Inform the Research Team, in a General Sense, that the Research Instrument Will Need a Different Structure?

Might the analysis of descriptors that generally describe a region or community allow one to more carefully structure a research project? This is particularly relevant with regard to instruments that are directed at understanding the benefits of contraception and the impact that use of methods might have on the community rather than the individual. For example, Triandis (1996) and Triandis *et al.* (1990) suggest that citizens in the USA, Britain, and some British-influenced countries such as Australia (Hofstede 1991) score high on 'individualism'. By contrast, citizens in many sample populations in Africa, Asia, and Latin America are characterized by a tendency toward 'collectivism'. Collectivist populations favour group over individual goals, emphasize the importance of hierarchy, and consider harmony to be an important attribute over 'saving face' (Triandis 1996; Triandis *et al.* 1990). In general, the group opinion is a homogeneous one. Collectivists offer more social responses when defining self and perceive themselves as closer to the in-group, but more distant from the out-group. Interdependence is emphasized and sameness is encouraged. Thus within a questionnaire, survey or scale, including the interviews of relatives may be more important than in cultures that are more 'individualist' in their approach.

Individualist cultures, by contrast, prioritize personal goals, value dissension, and emphasize independence and personal distinctiveness (ibid.). Although concepts such as collectivism and individualism take different forms around the world, such general population characteristics might allow one to conclude that dramatically different instruments will be needed to make the research process both worthwhile and meaningful.

The design of instruments that produce valid and meaningful data requires consideration of other general population characteristics. For example, can the population be described as mostly urban and educated or are the respondents from rural areas and less likely to be familiar with the kinds of information requested in the research design? Are there culturally appropriate ways to answer questions or to address sensitive topics? Are there certain culturally valued traits that might influence a response? These questions proved relevant when Cogan *et al.* (1996) examined perceptions of body size and beauty among male and female students in Ghana. In contrast to students from the United States, students from Ghana rated larger body size as ideal for both sexes (Cogan *et al.* 1996). For some cultures, large body size is not valued for either males or females. Thus, contraceptive methods that lead to weight gain or loss and thus alter the status of the body vis-à-vis its culturally determined image, may be positively or negatively perceived depending on the user's assessment of the side-effects of a given contraceptive.

What Impact Might the Research have on the Community?

Once data collection has been completed, some respondents may need additional familiarization with the questionnaire content and purpose, follow-up advice and/or counselling in order to mitigate negative impacts and remain comfortable with their participation. In some cases, reproductive health services may need to be identified for the community participants and access to additional information regarding both contraceptive methods and reproductive health in general provided. Researchers should continually monitor the impact they are having on participants (Preston-Whyte 1995).

For example, study participants have expressed fear of being identified as HIV positive once a research project has been completed (Huygens *et al.* 1996). Similarly, because communication style and content varies among cultural and ethnic groups (Gage 1995), participation in a research project could jeopardize the safety of the participant if it becomes known that the participant revealed information hidden from the partner, spouse, family, or local community. The research team should try to anticipate negative consequences that participation in a research programme could bring to a community, searching for strategies prior to the collection of data to minimize or eliminate any potentially harmful repercussions for participants.

What Setting Might Allow the Participant to Divulge Detailed Information Regarding Sexual Practices?

Is the home of a community leader the most comfortable setting in which discussions of sexual practices can be initiated? Is a respondent's own home more likely to provide a comfortable setting for sharing certain aspects of sexual practice? Is a medical clinic or local health post the best site for discussions, particularly if the sample is to be representative of the community, or is a local church, school building, market, coffee shop, or bar/pub a better setting in which to conduct interviews? The selection of the appropriate site often helps to elicit an emic perspective. Huygens *et al.* (1996), in a study of Ugandan citizens, discovered that informants who were interviewed in their own homes spoke more freely about their sexual behaviour than did those interviewed at a local clinic. Research findings from a study in Guatemala demonstrated the way in which respondents can alter responses based upon the setting: focus groups, for example, resulted in a general rejection, or feigned ignorance, of modern contraceptive methods. By contrast, individual home interviews encouraged admissions of contraceptive use and familiarity with modern methods (Terborgh *et al.* 1995). Prior to the onset of a new study, the researcher needs to give careful consideration to the selection of an interview site and to whether or not one is more likely to speak candidly in a group or in a solitary situation during the interview process. Each decision should be based upon the cultural context and the content of the material to be discussed.

Is the Topic Relevant to the Culture under Study?

A researcher must carefully consider the face validity (whether or not the document has meaning for the culture in question) of the question-naire, survey or scale. MacLachlan *et al.* (1995) suggest that researchers should determine whether the instrument appears acceptable to the respondents with respect to the stated objectives of the project. Some-times respondents simply have no information or opinion relevant to the question(s) asked (Hines 1993). This proved to be true when MacLachlan *et al.* administered the *Managerial and Professional Profiler* (MAPP) to a group of managers in Malawi. Developed in Britain for occupational settings, this 396-item personality questionnaire assessed respondents on four dimensions: people, tasks, feelings, and values. The Malawian managers indicated that while they clearly understood the questions, they were not sure that many of them had cultural relevance to their lives (MacLachlan *et al.* 1995).

Results of questionnaires, surveys and instruments often are admin-istered to a given population in the absence of pre-testing or focus group discussions. The results are interpreted and published but have no cultural application or validity. Similarly, while respondents in Guatemala answered survey questions about ideal family size, the concept of an 'ideal' family size did not have cultural significance. Respondents provided such answers as 'don't know' or 'God's will' (Terborgh *et al.* 1995). Clearly, such responses indicate lack of understanding and relevance to the study population of the concept in question.

Is the Topic of the Contraceptive-Related Study Routinely and Openly Discussed in the Culture?

Hines (1993) includes sex, religion, and income among those topics that can elicit markedly different responses around the world. In fact, many of the topics that might affect the impact of family planning methods (for example welfare status, citizenship categories, migratory experiences, previous political experiences, abortion or miscarriage, extramarital affairs and other kinds of sexual arrangements) are culturally taboo, too emotionally painful, or too sensitive to discuss (Hines 1993). Schoepf (1991) argues that most people, including commercial sex workers, are offended by requests to quantify and describe sexual behaviours in detail. Yet these types of data can dramatically impact the kinds of contraceptive methods that are developed and distributed.

Among some populations, for example South African Xhosa speakers, no direct references should be made to sexual activity. There is no comparable Xhosa phrase for the idiomatic English expression 'sleeping together', and consequently an archaic biblical phrase, a 'desire for flesh', had to be used in a questionnaire (Drennan *et al.* 1991). It is possible that for some questions a kind of preparatory or 'filter' question could be used to avoid the sensitive concept or phrase. For example, Huntington *et al.* (1996) used the notion of an unwanted pregnancy to prepare the participant for a discussion of abortion. The respondent did not have to discuss a particular pregnancy, but instead was asked if there was ever a time that she did not wish to be pregnant. If she responded affirmatively, then she was further questioned about the outcome of the pregnancy.

What Issues Might Constrain or Inhibit Accurate Responses to Questions in a Contraceptive Research Study?

Barriers might include fear or suspicion of the research process or of the interviewer, the stigma attached to a project or institution, the desire to hide or distort information, a lack of incentive to reconstruct experiences, or a misunderstanding of the questions (Mechanic 1989; Hines 1993). Young people questioned in Uganda, for example, were less likely to speak openly with interviewers who were the age of their parents because in Kiganda culture, parents are not supposed to speak to their children about sex (Huygens *et al.* 1996). Similarly, perceptions of the role of a funding agency, or institution hosting a particular research project, can alter respondent participation (Hines 1993). Answers provided in a research project actually might represent attempts to placate or sabotage a project or individual, or a host of other goals (Drennan *et al.* 1991).

The Research Instrument

How will the Psychosocial Research Instrument be Administered?

Should the participant be asked to self-administer the questionnaire, survey or scale? If the population is illiterate, is an audio administration possible? Is it essential that the interviewer be present to record answers? Each method of administration can affect differentially the nature and type of answers that a participant might provide. While self-administration might allow both study participants to share more concerning their sexual experiences, how might illiterate individuals be sampled so that each maintains his or her anonymity and privacy? Triandis (1994) alerts the cross-cultural researcher to the possibility that the culture being studied may or may not be familiar with a particular instrument format or administration method.

What Methods will be Employed to Translate the Psychosocial Instrument from one Language to Another?

Drennan *et al.* (1991) equate the use of a single diagnostic instrument with the 'clinical gaze' identified by Foucault (1973). The 'gaze' entails a range of evaluative behaviours: the mode of looking at patients, of interpreting signs and symptoms to signify disorders, and, most importantly, of establishing a power relationship between the person watched and the person watching. Translation makes the gaze more complex for the individual and for the social group (Drennan *et al.* 1991).

Based upon experience with the *World Fertility Survey*, Vaessen *et al.* (1987) suggest that prior to fieldwork in which surveys or questionnaires will be used, estimates should be made of the number of interviews to be carried out in each country as well as the number of languages involved. A specific study may need to be conducted preceding the actual collection of contraceptive-related data, simply to discover the number of languages spoken in a given country or region.

Numerous authors have discussed translation difficulties in a wide range of settings (e.g. Brislin *et al.* 1973; Drennan *et al.* 1991; Guillemin *et al.* 1993; Scott 1978; Vaessen *et al.* 1987). All conclude that the best translations are most likely to be achieved through the use of a combination of methodologies, the most important of which Drennan *et al.* (1991) have outlined as follows:

(a) Back-translation: The instrument is translated into the target language by an individual fluent in both the source and target languages. The translated instrument is then translated back into the source language by a person fluent in both languages. Subsequent comparisons are made between the original and back-translated versions. The instrument is modified and the procedure repeated until a satisfactory format is obtained. This method produces the best possible 'etic' instrument (the external interpretation or view from outside the culture).

(b) De-centering: This procedure does not require that the final version of the instrument matches the form or content of the original. Neither language is the standard by which the instrument must be measured. The conceptual arena, rather than language structure, determines the final content of the instrument. This approach introduces the emic perspective into the translation process.

(c) Bilingual approach: For this method, bilinguals receive the instrument in both languages or different groups complete the same sections of an instrument in the two known languages. Responses obtained using either option are examined to determine whether the translations are appropriate. Comparison between responses reveals whether versions in the two languages are tracking or covering the same areas.

(d) Committee approach: A group of bilingual individuals translates from the source to the target language. They discuss the translation and correction of mistakes among themselves. Participants may also work individually on translation, after which the discussion of the text is mediated through the researcher.

The complexities of translation must be taken very seriously. Brislin *et al.* (1973) have shown that if one cannot present the empirical evidence to validate an assertion that the different language versions of a single instrument are 'equivalent', then translation issues are plausible rival hypotheses for the study results. For example, Deutcher (1973) and Hines (1993) identify some of the back-translated equivalents of the English word 'friend' to be: *freund, ami, tomodachi,* and *amigo.* Although each is a reasonable translation of the word friend, and accurately reproduced by back-translation, important linguistic nuances in the levels of intimacy for each language version are not conveyed (Hines 1993). Similarly, administration of the *Beck Depression Inventory* (a tool to assess clients in developing country settings) to South African Xhosa speakers resulted in responses but revealed nothing of the cultural context (Beck *et al.* 1979). Item 21 in this inventory questions the respondent about change in his or her sexual activity and includes four response options: (1) any recent change in interest in sex, (2) less interest in sex, (3) much less interest in sex, or (4) a loss of interest in sex. While respondents could reply in a literal manner, the Xhosa language has no ungendered word or phrase for sexual desire equivalent to the English term 'libido'. Furthermore, Xhosa speakers do not decontextualize a loss of interest in sex without reference to a particular partner or specified practice. Issues of contextual reflexivity arise even in the use of English-language personality inventories with English-speaking subjects (Gergen *et al.* 1986; Semin 1987).

Similarly, determining changes in mental state is important because depression is a side-effect of some contraceptive methods – most notably oral contraceptives – and because oral contraceptives are often available to women in developing countries through development projects. The first item in the application of *The Beck Depression Inventory* illustrates the difficulty in the translation process. Drennan *et al.* (1991) ask the respondent whether or not he or she feels sad using four response options: (1) I do not feel sad, (2) I feel sad, (3) I am sad all the time and I can't snap out of it, and (4) I am so sad or unhappy that I can't stand it. The word 'sad' was translated into Xhosa as *khathazekile* by the Xhosa-speaking psychologist. Other back-translators translated *khathazekile* as 'worried', while still others produced the translation 'depressed'. As Drennan *et al.* (ibid.) discovered, the word *khathazekile* indicates worry with depressed overtones, the subtlety of meaning elicited through the speaker's tone of voice, inflection and gestures. Moreover, the psychiatrist indicated that the urban speakers of Xhosa had lost the subtle distinctions that rural speakers continue to use. This allows the urban speaker to assume that *khathazekile* has the same meaning as the English word 'sad'.

Although experimental research suggests that impromptu field translations from one language to another are directly responsible for a dramatic increase in the number of substantive errors committed in the language translation process, they continue to be used (Vaessen *et al.* 1987). This increase was observed for all types of errors, with major mistakes – a complete change in meaning or the entire omission of a qualifying phrase – noted most frequently. Many other problems can hinder the translation process. Among these are the lack of words or phrases to express an idea from another culture, translation of terms that might be socially offensive or insulting, and disregard of socially accepted ways that a culture communicates significant life events, e.g. death and pregnancy (ibid.). Additionally, dialect differences, scholarly versus vernacular language, regional differences in colloquial speech and use of idiom can be important (Anderson 1976; Bowen and Bowen 1990; Brislin 1976; Drennan *et al.* 1991; Morris, 1990; Prieto 1992; Prince and Mombour 1967).

Rarely does published literature include a thorough discussion of the translation procedures in the methods section. Rather, a statement is made that the instrument was back-translated and the reader is provided with no additional information. Yet translation-related problems can compromise the most basic results of questionnaire and survey research, and a complete explanation of the process is essential for both editors and readers to assess the merit or value of a particular research project.

Can the Topic be Fully Expressed Verbally, or is Written (or Other) Expression Necessary?

For topics such as HIV/AIDS and sexuality, Leap (1995) has shown that 'concealed or suppressed' factors can be more relevant than what is verbally expressed. This involves the language code itself, those concepts or issues embedded in the sentence structure and meaning, and the direction of the conversation (who says what to whom). In addition, the researcher must also understand the way in which a concept is expressed appropriately in a given situation (van Gelder 1996).

How Might Response Categories or Options within an Instrument be Interpreted?

Can the instrument be considered to possess scale equivalence across cultures? Baer (1996) noted that formal choice categories such as 'most of the time', 'some of the time', 'a little of the time' and 'none of the time' are not particularly useful because even native speakers of a particular language can define these categories differently. Not only is it difficult to distinguish among them effectively, but some overlap can occur based upon the amount of time associated with each category by a respondent (ibid.). Moreover, vague quantifiers usually imply 'a comparison to an implicit standard' with which the respondent may not be familiar (Schaeffer 1991).

Even basic indicators of health status might be defined differently by the researcher and the respondent. In a study of Mexican immigrants, Baer (1996) found that *good* and *bad* health were often described using characteristics that might be biomedically defined as good or bad *mental* health. Because the study population did not always separate mental and physical health into different categories, the health instrument used was a modified version of that administered to the broader population (ibid.).

In a study focusing on sexual behaviour, a variety of answers were given with regard to both 'steady' and 'casual' sexual partners (Huygens *et al.* 1996). Similarly, across cultures, abstinence can be defined in different ways (e.g. no contact, sex with one partner, coitus interruptus, using a condom, masturbation, and oral and anal sex) (ibid.). In many situations, a lack of specificity related to the use of general terms can compromise severely the reliability of the data, and hence invalidate results.

Within a Culture/Ethnic Group, are there Alternative Ways to Express the Same Concept?

If a language has a large number of synonyms for a given word, which one should be used (Prince and Mombour 1967)? In a study of Arab men, van Gelder (1996) distinguished among five distinct modes of reference corresponding to levels of decency: (1) a respectable, well-educated mode, (2) a socio-medical mode, (3) a less respectable but decent colloquial mode of reference, (4) an indecent mode, and (5) an impudent and abusive mode. For this particular Arab population, the levels of 'decency' were associated with varying degrees of openness and precision such that, in general, the more indecent the level, the more explicit and 'concrete' the speaker would be.

Parker *et al.* (1991) have emphasized that language not only constructs the domains of gender but is itself gendered. Therefore, even if the psychosocial instrument has been adapted for a new cultural setting, close scrutiny must be applied to the selection of individual words for instruments presented to men versus women. Overall, literacy in developing countries is likely to be higher among men than women (Terborgh *et al.* 1995). Moreover, men are more likely to speak more than one language and consequently, different instruments and/or different methods of administration may be needed for males and females in the same community. (For a thorough overview of linguistic issues and gender, see Burton *et al.* 1994.)

Are the Indicators Selected to Measure Each Topic Area Equally Useful Across Cultures?

Hines (1993) has reviewed the variety of indicators used to score marital satisfaction, (e.g. social role performance, intimacy, and time spent in conversation). In Japan, for example, social role performance might be more indicative of marital satisfaction than either intimacy or time spent in conversation (ibid.). Thus, the indicators of a particular state or concept for each application and setting should be outlined prior to the pre-testing of a specific instrument. In many cases, emic constructs might exist for the issue in question. Similarly, because there may be differences between males and females with regard to the specific indicators that measure each state, sensitivity to gender issues is critical.

Can Quantitative Study Results be Verified Using Qualitative Data?

Focus groups or discussion groups can be used to corroborate or elaborate on data obtained from a particular subset of respondents (Pickering 1988). In addition, results from quantitative studies can be replicated using a qualitative method like participant observation because 'it is unlikely that an unsound hypothesis will be supported with very different methods' (Triandis 1994). For instance, findings from a qualitative study of contraceptive method choice and birth spacing among Guatemalan women were compared to those of a quantitative study of a representative sample from the same region, but conducted several years later. The results using one method were shown to 'largely confirm' those of another (Terborgh et al. 1995). Parker et al. (1991) suggest that one should make efforts to locate secondary sources of information, conduct ethnographic observation and focus group discussions, and scour the host country for materials published and found only there. Although this additional data collection strategy may not be possible in each cultural context from which data is collected, one might select random samples from each region studied and gather data using an alternative strategy. The researcher should also visit census bureaus, health departments, medical departments, and ministries of health (ibid.). Where possible, sources of data on sexuality should include focus groups, in-depth discussion, sexual diaries, and linguistic analysis (Pickering 1988; Parker 1995; Parker et al. 1991).

Conclusion

As Schoepf (1991: 749) eloquently states, 'Policies based on inadequate research or misinterpreted findings often lead to unintended consequences which harm those they are presumed to benefit. In addition to failing to bring about improvements, such research may compound the errors by providing a cloak of apparent scientific validity which blames the afflicted for their misery.' In addition to ensuring that the highest quality psychosocial research is carried out, new approaches to the design, implementation, analysis and dissemination of such research in cross-cultural settings must be developed.

Anthropological methodologies and insights have long been under-utilized in development research, particularly in health-related areas. This is due, at least in part, to the perception that anthropological research is not scientifically rigorous – largely because many anthropological methods do not produce quantifiable results. However, the types of data needed to develop and improve methods of contraception and/or protection from HIV/AIDS and other STDs, and to simultaneously facilitate practical contraceptive choices, are precisely those that anthropologists are trained to collect. As Preston-Whyte (1995: 323) notes, 'It is anthropologists more than most social scientists who have developed and internalised the skill of listening to what people are saying, of sinking into the community and following the often tortuous web of cultural expression and behaviour.' It is time for anthropologists to claim their legitimate place in the scientific community, particularly in such areas as health-related research, where anthropological training and insight are so critical. In addition, the discipline should recant its own criticism of applied anthropology as a less rigorous sub-discipline and remove the stigma associated with those who work as applied anthropologists rather than academic anthropologists. At present, few new Ph.D.s can be assured academic posts upon completion of their graduate work. A 1993–95 survey conducted by the US Government's National Science Foundation indicated that a larger percentage of US-trained anthropologists (11.6 per cent in 1993 and 9.1 per cent in 1995) was employed in 'involuntarily out-of-field' or non-traditional (non-academic) positions than the percentage with Ph.D.-level training in any other biological or social science (National Science Foundation 1997). Although some anthropologists may choose to work in an applied setting, some have few career alternatives.

Health researchers from all disciplines need to create consistent standards for conducting survey and questionnaire work. This will allow more meaningful comparison of the results (and hence cultural groups and contexts) of contraceptive-related research. Moreover, publishing questionnaires, surveys and scales (as anthropologists often do) in dissertations, journal articles and reports will contribute to the establishment of standard approaches and refinement of related materials. Anthropologists must continue to embrace new areas of investigation, from health to sex behaviour research (Tuzin 1991). As they read journal submissions, evaluate grant proposals, and teach and influence government policy, anthropologists must continue to question everything, be intolerant of insufficiently rigorous work, and cast a wider theoretical net (Bolton 1995). Anthropologists should insist that the methods used to translate questionnaires, surveys, and inventories be thoroughly described in published material, and should look for and demand evidence that good research designs have been employed. We should conduct pretests of all psychosocial instruments and analyse both participant responses and interviewer behaviour in the process. We must publish beyond scholarly journals, use anthropological data to validate or invalidate quantitative methods and studies by other disciplines, publish our surveys and questionnaires for use by others, collaborate with other disciplines, and insist that those conducting cross-cultural research justify their methodology. Finally, we must discuss our research in communities before and after the research is conducted in order to encourage respondents to understand the work, ask questions, share in the results, and benefit from the study. Our best programmes will be designed to incorporate indigenous peoples into aspects of the project cycle: design, implementation, and monitoring and evaluation (Triandis 1994; Terborgh *et al.* 1995). Only this degree of effort will promote effective and practical contraceptive technologies and healthful approaches to sex for both men and women, allow new mothers and fathers to plan their families in culturally appropriate ways, and increase the likelihood that adolescents who have survived childhood will also reach adulthood.

References

Anderson, R.B.W. (1976), 'Perspectives On the Role of Interpreter', in R.W. Brislin (ed.), *Translation: Applications and Research*, New York: Gardner Press.

Ankrah, E.M. (1989), 'AIDS: Methodological Problems in Studying its Prevention and Spread', *Social Science and Medicine*, 29: 265–76.

Anonymous (1999), 'The Challenges Ahead', USAID: PHN Center, Family Planning Fact Sheet. Internet site: http://www.info.usaid.gov/pop_health/ infopack.htm#Introduction.

Baer, R.D. (1996), 'Health and Mental Health Among Mexican American Migrants: Implications for Survey Research', *Human Organization*, 55: 58–66.

Beck, A.T., A.J. Rush, B.F. Shaw and G. Emery (1979), *Cognitive Therapy of Depression*, New York: Guildford Press.

Bernard, H.R. (1998), *Handbook of Methods in Cultural Anthropology*, California: AltaMira Press.

Bolton, R. (1995), 'Rethinking Anthropology: The Study of AIDS', in H.T. Brummelhuis and G. Herdt (eds), *Culture and Sexual Risk: Anthropological Perspectives on AIDS*, Luxembourg: Gordon and Breach.

Bowen, D. and M. Bowen (1990), 'Materials Translation: Is That What You Really Want to Say?' *Conference Proceedings, 'Natural Family Planning: Current Knowledge and New Strategies for the 1990's'*, Georgetown University: Institute for Reproductive Health.

Brehm, S.S., S.M. Kassin and S. Fein (1999), *Social Psychology*, New York: Houghton Mifflin.

Brislin, R.W. (1976), 'Introduction' in R.W. Brislin (ed.), *Translation: Applications and Research*, New York: Gardner Press.

——, W.J. Lonner and R.M. Thorndike (1973), *Cross Cultural Research Methods*, New York: John Wiley and Sons.

Browner, C.H., B.R. Ortiz de Montellano and A.J. Rubel (1988), 'A Methodology for Cross-Cultural Research', *Current Anthropology*, 29: 681–702.

Brummelhuis, H.T. and G. Herdt (eds) (1995), *Culture and Sexual Risk: Anthropological Perspectives on AIDS*, Luxembourg: Gordon and Breach.

Burton, P., K.C. Dyson and S. Ardener (1994), *Bilingual Women: Anthropological Approaches to Second Language Use*, Oxford: Berg.

Civic, D. and D. Wilson (1996), 'Dry Sex in Zimbabwe and Implications for Condom Use', *Social Science and Medicine*, 42: 91–8.

Cogan, J.C., S.K. Bahlah, A. Sefa-Dedeh and E.P. Rothblum (1996), 'A Comparison Study of United States and African Students on Perceptions of Obesity and Thinness', *Journal of Cross Cultural Psychology*, 27: 98–113.

Deutcher, I. (1973), 'Asking Questions: Linguistic Comparability', in D. Warwick and S. Osherson (eds), *Comparative Research Methods*, Englewood Cliffs: Prentice Hall.

Drennan, G., A. Levett and L. Swartz (1991), 'Hidden Dimensions of Power and Resistance in the Translation Process: A South African Study', *Culture, Medicine and Psychiatry*, 15: 361–81.

Farmer, P. (1995), 'Culture, Poverty, and the Dynamics of HIV Transmission in Rural Haiti', in H.T. Brummelhuis and G. Herdt (eds), *Culture and Sexual Risk: Anthropological Perspectives on AIDS*, Luxembourg: Gordon and Breach.

Fluehr-Lobban, C. (ed.) (1991), *Ethics and the Profession of Anthropology: Dialogue for a New Era*, Philadelphia: University of Pennsylvania Press.

Foucault, M. (1973), *The Birth of the Clinic*, London: Tavistock Publications.

Gage, A.J. (1995), 'Women's Socioeconomic Position and Contraceptive Behavior in Togo', *Studies in Family Planning*, 26: 264–77.

Gergen, K., A. Hepburn and D.C. Fisher (1986), 'Hermeneutics of Personality Description', *Journal of Personality and Social Psychology*, 50: 1261–70.

Guillemin, F., C. Bombardier and D. Beaton (1993), 'Cross-Cultural Adaptation of Health-Related Quality of Life Measures: Literature Review and Proposed Guidelines', *Journal of Clinical Epidemiology*, 46: 1417–32.

Hines, A. (1993), 'Linking Qualitative and Quantitative Methods in Cross-Cultural Survey Research: Techniques from Cognitive Science', *American Journal of Community Psychology*, 21: 729–45.

Hofstede, G. (1991), *Culture and Organizations*, London: McGraw Hill.

Huntington, D., B. Mensch and V.C. Miller (1996), 'Survey Questions for the Measurement of Induced Abortion', *Studies in Family Planning*, 27: 155–61.

Huygens, P., E. Kajura, J. Seeley and T. Barton (1996), 'Rethinking Methods for the Study of Sexual Behavior', *Social Science and Medicine*, 42: 221–31.

Leap, W. (1995), 'Talking About AIDS: Linguistic Perspectives on Non-Neutral Discourse', in H.T. Brummelhuis and G. Herdt (eds), *Culture and Sexual Risk: Anthropological Perspectives on AIDS*, Luxembourg: Gordon and Breach.

MacLachlan, M., J. Mapundi, C.G. Zimba and S.C. Carr (1995), 'The Acceptability of a Western Psychometric Instrument in a Non-Western Society', *The Journal of Social Psychology*, 135: 645–8.

Mechanic, D. (1989), 'Medical Sociology: Some Tensions Among Theory, Method, and Substance', *Journal of Health and Social Behavior*, 30: 147–60.

Morris, N. (1990), 'Translation Issues in Survey Research: Confronting Linguistic and Cultural Variation', *Working Paper No. 126*, Philadelphia: Center for International Health, Development and Communication, The Annenberg School of Communication, University of Pennsylvania.

National Science Foundation (1997), 'National Science Foundation Survey of Graduate Students and Postdoctorates in Science and Engineering', Arlington, Virginia: National Science Foundation.

Parker, R.G. (1995), 'The Social and Cultural Construction of Sexual Risk, or How to Have "Sex" Research in an Epidemic', in H.T. Brummelhuis and G. Herdt (eds), *Culture and Sexual Risk: Anthropological Perspectives on AIDS*, Luxembourg: Gordon and Breach.

——, G. Herdt and M. Carballo (1991), 'Sexual Culture, HIV Transmission, and AIDS Research', *The Journal of Sex Research*, 28: 77–98.

Pickering, H. (1988), 'Asking Questions on Sexual Behavior . . . Testing Methods from the Social Sciences', *Health Policy and Planning* 3: 237–44.

Preston-Whyte, E.M. (1995), 'Half-Way There: Anthropology and Intervention-Oriented AIDS Research in KwaZulu/Natal, South Africa', in H.T. Brummelhuis and G. Herdt (eds), *Culture and Sexual Risk: Anthropological Perspectives on AIDS*, Luxembourg: Gordon and Breach.

Prieto, A.J. (1992), 'A Method for Translation of Instruments to Other Languages', *Adult Education Quarterly*, 43: 1–14.

Prince, R. and W. Mombour (1967), 'A Technique for Improving Linguistic Equivalence in Cross-Cultural Surveys', *The International Journal of Social Psychology*, 13: 229–37.

Saville-Troike, M. (1989), *The Ethnography of Communication*, Oxford: Basil Blackwell.

Schaeffer, N.C. (1991), 'Hardly Ever or Constantly: Group Comparisons Using Vague Quantifiers', *Public Opinion Quarterly*, 55: 395–423.

Schoepf, B.G. (1991), 'Ethical, Methodological and Political Issues of AIDS Research in Central Africa', *Social Science and Medicine*, 33: 749–63.

—— (1995), 'Culture, Sex Research and AIDS Prevention in Africa', in H.T. Brummelhuis and G. Herdt (eds), *Culture and Sexual Risk: Anthropological Perspectives on AIDS*, Luxembourg: Gordon and Breach.

Scott, C. (1978), 'Control of Data Quality in Developing Country Surveys: Experience of the World Fertility Survey (1)', in *Multipurpose Household Surveys in Developing Countries,* Paris: Development Centre of the Organisation for Economic Co-Operation and Development.

Semin, G.R. (1987), 'On the Relationship Between Representation of Theories in Psychology and Ordinary Language', in W. Doise and S. Moscovici (eds), *Current Issues in European Social Psychology*, Cambridge: Cambridge University Press.

Taylor, C.C. (1990), 'Condoms and Cosmology: The "Fractal" Person and Sexual Risk in Rwanda', *Social Science and Medicine*, 31: 1023–8.

Terborgh, A., J.E. Rosen, R.S. Galvez, W. Terceros, J.T. Bertrand and S.E. Bull (1995), 'Family Planning Among Indigenous Populations in Latin America', *International Family Planning Perspectives*, 23: 143–9.

Triandis, H.C. (1994), *Culture and Social Behavior*, New York: McGraw-Hill, Inc.

—— (1995), *Individualism and Collectivism*, Boulder: Westview Press.

—— (1996), 'The Psychological Measurement of Cultural Syndromes', *American Psychologist*, 51: 407–14.

——, C. McCusker and C.H. Hui (1990), 'Multimethod Probes of Individualism and Collectivism', *Journal of Personality and Social Psychology*, 59: 1006–20.

Tuzin, D. (1991), 'Sex, Culture and the Anthropologist', *Social Science and Medicine*, 33: 867–74.

Vaessen, M., C. Scott, J. Verrall and S. Coulibaly (1987), 'Translation of Questionnaires into Local Languages', in J. Cleland and C. Scott (eds), *World Fertility Survey*, London: Oxford University Press.

Van Gelder, P. (1996), 'Talkability, Sexual Behavior, and AIDS: Interviewing Male Moroccan Immigrants', *Human Organization,* 55: 133–40.

Van Willigen, J. (1993), *Applied Anthropology: An Introduction*, Connecticut: Bergin and Garvey.

Wight, D. and M. Barnard (1993), 'The Limits to Participant Observation in HIV/ AIDS Research', *Practicing Anthropology*, 15: 66–9.

3

Responding to Reality: The Efficacy of Anthropological and Participatory Methods for the Implementation of Sustainable Contraceptive Programmes

Joshua Levene

Reality and Contraceptive Acceptability

Dramatic population increase could be one of the greatest problems currently faced by the human race. Population growth, which is concentrated in, but not limited to, the southern hemisphere (Harrison 1993) has provoked richer nations to intervene on a global scale to introduce effective contraceptive programmes. However, population increase in many developing countries still continues at what many consider to be an unsustainable rate. Many attempts to introduce contraceptives have been largely ineffective in curbing population increase. This is perhaps because population increase stems largely from another of the developing world's ills: poverty. The persistent lack of an assured provision of adequate social security for many of its inhabitants has been linked with high fertility (Seabrook 1995). Unless people in the developing countries believe that they will be socially and financially secure throughout their lives, without the need for large numbers of children to provide for them, population increase is likely to persist.

However, even if people do have access to secure social welfare throughout their lives, as do many people living in industrialized countries today, they will still require acceptable forms of contraception. In addition to poverty, then, one of the most salient reasons for some contraception programmes' ineffectiveness, is the discrepancy between planners' perceptions of the acceptability of their contraception programmes and the perceptions of programmes and planners by the populations they target. In trying to develop acceptable programmes, planners and populations often seem in conflict rather than cooperation.

Within a basic reproductive health/human rights framework, which favours informed consent and freedom of choice, the degree of contraceptive acceptability depends broadly on three factors: the effectiveness of the contraceptive, a lack of side-effects, and ready access to the contraceptive in question (Family Care International 1995). Contraceptive programmes have therefore focused on providing and promoting ready access to reliable contraceptive devices that are free from side-effects. However, 'side-effects' have primarily been defined within a Western biomedical context. For example, Marshall and Polgar report 'that the Lippes IUD failed in India largely because it led to the unexpected increase in the amount and irregularity of menstrual bleeding. Such changes in menstrual patterns were usually not considered biomedically unacceptable, but in many cases they did exceed thresholds perceived as tolerable by Indian women' (1976: 209).

In addition to physical side effects unrecognized by biomedicine, there are multiple social side-effects to contraceptive devices or programmes that may hinder acceptability. Most commonly, these relate to conflicting religious beliefs, stigma attached to contraceptive use, or reduced sexual satisfaction (Harrison 1993). Such side-effects are rarely fully considered and compensated for in contraceptive programmes.

Yet, for a contraception programme to be successful, planners must realize that a contraceptive will only be used (if at all) in ways consistent with the beneficiaries' own perceptions of body, sexuality, reproduction, and family. In other words, biomedical or modern reproductive technologies will not always be used in ways consistent with population planners' perceptions of such. As Chambers notes, development planners need to ask '"Whose reality counts?" Ours? Theirs, as we think it should be? Or theirs as they freely express it?' (1992: 89). Contraceptive devices and programmes are only likely to be accepted if the perceptions (subjective reality) of the population planner and contraceptive technologist happen to coincide with those of their target population. Therefore the beneficiaries' perceptions of acceptability count. It is this perception of reality that must be researched and compared with population planners' perceptions if the problem of acceptability is to be suitably addressed.

Until preparatory ethnographic research into local acceptability becomes common practice for the planning of contraception programmes (or until contraceptive technologies are all designed in a culturally appropriate way) the degree of acceptability and the rate of contraception adoption will remain problematic. However effective, biomedically safe, or widely distributed a method may be, without first assessing and improving the cultural acceptability of a device or the programme meant to promote it, success or failure of that device or programme will lie beyond outside planners' control.

In order to determine cultural acceptability, anthropologists should be used to carry out preparatory research. Preventing problems that may arise from unacceptability is generally regarded as easier and cheaper than curing problems after they have arisen. However, in the recent past anthropologists have tended to be called in (if at all) to solve 'cultural problems' after the fact, as and when they arise. By this time there may be too many bureaucratic and symptomatic barriers in place within the programme for the anthropologist's recommendations to be effectively acted upon (Conlin 1985).

Why then, have planners tended not to employ anthropologists in formative acceptability assessment research? Marshall and Polgar (1976: 205) suggest that possible reasons may have to do with the inadequacy of current anthropological theories to satisfactorily and consistently predict or facilitate sustainable material and non-material cultural change. This chapter provides an example of how anthropologists, by adopting participatory development approaches and methods, can better facilitate such change in the realm of contraception.

The philosophy of participatory development arose from the ideas of Paulo Freire: that the poorest and most marginalized of peoples are able to analyse their own reality, and that this analysis can lead to 'conscientization' (or empowerment leading to social transformation) in which they feel empowered to make plans and negotiate with more powerful actors (1968). A family of methods and approaches that aim to facilitate this response have been developed (e.g. Chambers 1992). By incorporating these methods into anthropological inquiry, we can enable planners and target populations to bridge their differences and respond to each other's needs and world views. This chapter demonstrates the usefulness of a practical approach in which anthropologists, using participatory methods, engage the target community, as equal partners, in a dialogue concerning the nature of an intervention, and assist them in expressing their perceptions and concerns to the planners who would serve them.

The Ability to Respond to Reality

To explain my ideas about the need for participation in sustainable development, I find Sands' (1996: 65-8) visual representations helpful.

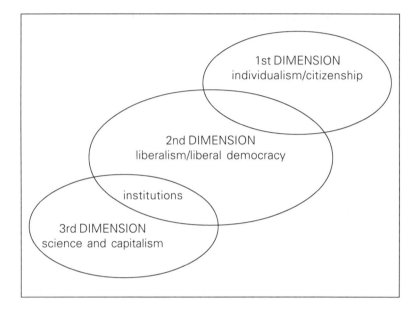

Figure 3.1 Diagrammatic representation of modernity

She suggests that the inability of planners to adequately respond to people's health needs is a result of a lack of communication between the two. She suggests that sustainable development is impossible without first addressing and correcting this problem. Sands offers a model of modernity (see Figure 3.1) to illustrate that, without direct communication between the people's reality (1st dimension) and scientific and economic reality (3rd dimension), people lose considerable control over how science and capitalism affects their lives. Their only means to respond to this is indirectly, through institutions.

Figure 3.1 is meant to represent modernity. The linear pattern of the first, second and third dimensions denies a direct mutual interaction between the first and third dimensions, i.e. between the individual and science and capitalism, although of course the effects of science and capitalism may be all to apparent in people's lives. This leaves the individual feeling powerless against 'the powers that be'. Institutions have control over what is filtered down from the third dimension through the second dimension to the individual (first dimension).

In this diagram institutions are seen to respond primarily to the reality of science economics and politics and this reality is filtered down through

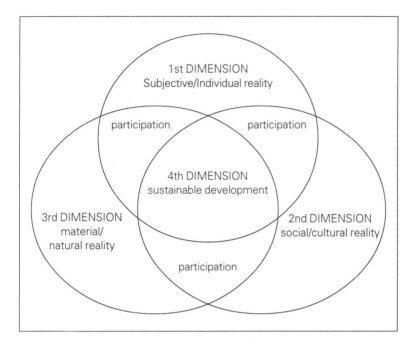

Figure 3.2 For sustainable development to be a reality, the diagram must present a notion of holism, where all the dimensions inter-link and interact

the mechanisms of liberalism and liberal democracy, to the individual citizens. The individual is only loosely able to respond, interact and control their material world. This means that science is not entirely reflecting people's needs. In such a top-down scenario, sustainable development is not possible. What is required is for all three dimensions to be brought closer together within a fourth dimension to interact with each other, to reflect each other's needs and fully participate with each other, as illustrated in Figure 3.2.

According to Sands, 'the fourth dimension represents both the objective and the outcome of human action. If health is the objective then health should be the outcome' (ibid.). Awareness of others' reality provides the common ground for a global sense of 'rights and entitlements on the one hand and responsibilities and obligations on the other' (ibid.). To convert this theoretical model into practice there must be the means for each dimension to be aware of the reality of the other and to respond and act on, or with regard to, that reality. The first step towards doing this, in the field of contraceptive provision, would be for both parties, planners and people, to increase their understanding of the reality of each other's perceived notions of acceptability. Both parties can thereby become more aware of their similarities and points of conflict. Increased awareness and understanding of each other's perceptions is a sound basis to work these points of conflict out and build on similarities.

A comparison between the perceived reality of the target populations and the perceived reality of the population planners requires an impartial third party. The third party – the anthropologist – can also investigate where the population planners' perceptions and target populations' perceptions do not coincide, and thus where contraceptive acceptability is likely to be low. In other words, anthropology that applies participatory methods can provide the means for establishing the fourth dimension. When the anthropologist mediates, both planners and target populations are in a responsible and influential position of informed choice regarding whether a programme proceeds, and if so, how. The planners should be able, based on an understanding of the reality of a situation, to justify themselves to their target population. Similarly the target population should be empowered with the ability to respond to the population planners based on an understanding of their own and the planners' realities.

The Role of the Anthropologist

Traditionally, the social anthropologist's primary methodological tool has been that of participant-observation. Participant-observation, which gained in popularity with the publication of Malinowski's research in the Trobriand Islands (1922), involves the anthropologist participating in the life of a society, learning about it much as a child would, through experience, listening and learning, and observing and doing (Haviland 1990: 40–56). Participant-observation does not necessarily involve 'going native'; most anthropologists prefer to keep some distance to maintain objectivity. The method, however, does entail the anthropologist building up a relaxed rapport with people, called informants, who supply him or her with data (Bernard 1995: 136; Chambers 1992). The anthropologist examines critically both the relationship that s/he establishes with the community and with his or her informants, and the manner in which the social status, positions and relationships of individual informants affects the data they supply (Seymour-Smith 1993). This relaxed rapport enables the anthropologist both to gain people's trust and to observe everyday life without people altering their behaviour. In researching a topic as sensitive as contraception, trust-worthiness and confidentiality are essential prerequisites to gaining valid data. According to Haviland, the anthropologist looks to draw data from three different viewpoints through participant-observation:

> First the people's own understanding of the rules they share – that is, their notion of the way society ought to be – must be examined. Second the extent to which people believe they are observing those rules – that is how they think they actually behave – needs to be looked at. Third the behaviour that can be directly observed should be considered. By carefully evaluating these elements, the anthropologist can draw up a set of rules that actually may explain [what is] acceptable behaviour within a culture (1990: 40).

In the context of contraceptive acceptability research the anthrop-ologist, through research on these three elements, is able to determine both what planners and target populations do and do not believe is acceptable. Perhaps more importantly, the anthropologist attempting to research the feasibility of implementing a contraception programme is able to interpret, by triangulating these viewpoints, what both parties are *prepared to believe*. In other words, s/he can define that area of convergence that could be acceptable to them both. With the knowledge of what is or isn't, could or couldn't be, an acceptable contraceptive programme for both planners and target populations, anthropologists are in possession of valuable knowledge regarding how best to facilitate and proceed with a programme.

But rather than simply dictating what needs to be done, the anthrop-ologist interested in sustainable interventions should encourage cross-party communication. This way, a programme can continue to evolve once the anthropologist has moved on. Such an anthropological praxis requires the development of a methodology that engages research participants from both parties in dialogue and action. A praxis is called for that involves co-operative activities that assist individuals, groups and organizations to make decisions and assume responsibility for planned change, rather than conceding that task to an outside expert. I contend that it is in participatory methods that anthropologists might be able to find a suitably engaging, ethical and empowering methodology.

The Role of Participatory Methods and Approaches

Rapid Rural Appraisal (RRA) was developed in the 1970s out of the desire for a more cost-effective method of learning than questionnaires, the realization of the value of indigenous knowledge to the planning process, and a dissatisfaction with what Chambers (1983) calls 'rural-development tourism', whereby development professionals make brief visits to non-representative sites (neglecting peripheries), at non-representative times of year (the dry more than the wet season) and speak to non-representative people, e.g. users more than non-users, elites more than the poor). RRA actively seeks the long-term inclusion of those most often marginalized from projects (e.g. the poor, minorities, women and youth), placing value on the capacity of local people and periphery communities to conduct their own analysis of their life conditions and actively inform the planning process. The outsider's role is thus that of facilitator rather than the extractive investigator. The information facilitated is owned, analysed and used primarily by local people, rather than outsiders (Chambers 1992) providing local people with some sense of stakeholding in the development activity – further increasing sustainability. Such participation further increases the chances of 'objectives and outputs being relevant to perceived need and greater efficiency and honesty of officials and contractors because they are under public scrutiny' (ODA 1995).

The focus of RRA is on cumulative learning, joint analysis and interaction by all participants – both outside professionals and locals in order 'to learn from rural people, directly, on the site, and face-to-face, gaining from local, physical, technical, and social knowledge. Learning rapidly and progressively, with conscious exploration, flexible use of methods, opportunism, improvisation, iteration, and cross-checking, not following a blueprint programme but being adaptable in a learning process' (Chambers 1994a). The parallels and borrowing between social anthropology and RRA in these approaches and techniques are clear although underlying principles may be different.

RRA methods often involve groups rather than individual interviews as it is thought that the full complexity and diversity of a situation can only be revealed through group analysis and interaction (Kronen 1997). Groups may be used to brainstorm, map and analyse topics, develop, rank and score variables, develop chronologies of local events, and conduct group transect walks to explore the local environment (Heaver 1992). On the other hand, while some applied anthropologists have used focus-type groups to facilitate data (for example Schellstede and Cizewski 1984), these have not been part of a sequence of methods based on the principle of empowerment.

The use of RRA methods in sequence enables cumulative learning about on a given topic. Results can be triangulated so that holistic knowledge may be built up. But it is not just the researcher who builds this knowledge or controls the methods used. To engender an even greater sense of ownership in the process, participants themselves are encouraged to invent new methods and sequences, and to use their own terms and names for criteria (Kronen 1997).

RRA methods rarely entail questionnaires because they are thought to be largely extractive rather than empowering (Pretty 1993). Questionnaires have other potential pitfalls. For instance, when language has not been adjusted to ensure validity, answers may not reflect the questions researchers had in mind. For example, whilst helping to analyse a knowledge, attitude and practice questionnaire in the Solomon Islands, I found data that over 70 per cent of Solomon Islanders had replied 'Yes' in response to the question 'do you use condoms?' No country in the world can claim that 70 per cent of the adult population uses condoms, let alone a country where they had only recently been introduced. In fact it was true that 70 per cent of Solomon Islanders do use condoms – for highly effective fishing lures!

RRA methods also have a large visual component. For example, participants often are asked to draw ideas rather than write them, or compare quantities rather than count them. Chambers' tabulation of some of the advantages of using visual over verbal methods is shown in Table 3.1.

The litmus test for participatory methods is whether they stimulate dialogue and analysis between all participants (especially those often marginalized such as women, children, minority groups and the elderly) that motivates the formulation of a plan for future action. Participatory Rural Appraisal (PRA) is a similar approach that has developed from RRA. The main difference between the two is that 'while RRA focuses more on the planning for people based on people's participation in the diagnostic stages, PRA aims at empowering people to manage their own affairs. Thus, RRA can be used to initiate a project while PRA can then be employed for local planning and implementation' (Kronen 1997). Previous research (see Chambers 1994b) has demonstrated that this is indeed an attainable goal. In the case study below it was originally intended that PRA would eventually be used. However, the disbanding of the implementing agency precluded this.

RRA and Anthropological Approaches Together

RRA methods can give anthropologists empowering, ethically sound, and perhaps more adequately representative methodological approaches

Table 3.1.   Contrasts between verbal and visual modes (adapted from Chambers 1992)

	Verbal (interview, conversation)	Visual (diagram)
Outsiders roles	investigator	initiator and catalyst
Outsiders modes	probing	facilitating
Insiders' roles	respondent	presenter and analyst
Insiders' modes	reactive	creative
The illiterate and innumerate can be	marginalized	empowered
Detail influenced by	etic categories	emic categories
Information flow	sequential	cumulative
Accessibility of information to others	low and transient	high and semi-permanent
Initiative for checking lies with	outsider	insider
Utility for spatial, temporal and causal information, relations, planning and monitoring	low	high
Ownership of information	appropriated by outsider	owned and shared by insider

to research and facilitate contraceptive acceptability. But RRA is not an absolute panacea (Wright and Nelson 1995). Much RRA methodology was developed in the Indian sub-continent, and some of the methods are suited to this environment and cultural context but not to others. For example, transect walks may work perfectly well in an Indian rural village, but they are impractical in some rural Zimbabwean communities spread out over five kilometres (Simon Stevens, Overseas Development Institute, personal communication). The importance of careful application of participatory methods, and in a suitable context, should not be underestimated. The anthropologist, with a holistic knowledge of the cultural and geographical environment, gained through prior participant-observation, should be able to identify the most suitable methodology.

RRA may pose problems above and beyond context and suitability of particular methods. Mosse (1994) suggests that one disadvantage is that the data arising from it emphasizes the general over the particular and the normative over the variant. However, when used in combination with more sensitive anthropological techniques, such as participant-observation, the anthropologist using RRA is able to attend to the various and the particular, as well as to highlight consensus where this exists. Thus, the anthropologist as participant observer is in a position to counteract the pitfalls of RRA and develop its strengths. As the following case study suggests, used together, RRA and participant-observation allow the anthropologist to research and bring together planners' and populations' views for them to collaboratively analyse and jointly plan sustainable programmes.

Case study: The Feasibility of Implementing Contraceptive Social Marketing in Tonga

Project Background

'Contraceptive Social Marketing' (CSM) is the use of commercial marketing techniques (such as market research, promotion, advertising and distribution) to achieve the social goal of improving reproductive health by increasing contraceptive use. It has proved a particularly useful strategy among lower income populations (Binnendijk 1986). There are generally three elements involved in CSM programmes:

1. The creation of an implementing agency with commercial marketing and management skills.
2. The selling of low-cost, generally subsidized contraceptives through commercial distribution and retail systems.
3. The promotion of contraceptive products through advertising campaigns and market research aimed at tailoring the contraceptive products to consumers' needs, preferences and desires (Binnendijk 1986).

From 1995 to 1996 I worked for twelve months for the South Pacific Alliance for Family Health's (SPAFH) regional strategy 'Project Excel', which was funded by AusAID (Australia) up until January 1996 (Levene 1996). Project Excel's aim was to improve reproductive health across the South Pacific region through the implementation of CSM programmes in the regions ten member countries (Samuel 1995). The 'Protector' condom and 'Secure' oral contraceptive pill' were judged by SPAFH to be the most appropriate forms of contraception to market in the South Pacific (Matangi Tonga 1995), and my remit was to investigate the feasibility of implementing a CSM programme in Tonga.

The Polynesian Kingdom of Tonga was one of the first countries to be selected for CSM for three reasons: its rising population, the presence of HIV, and the devoutly Christian population many of whom were considered to view condoms as promoting promiscuity. It was thought that successful implementation of a CSM programme in Tonga would advance and facilitate the implementation of CSM programmes in other Pacific nations (SPAFH 1993). A previous attempt by SPAFH to implement CSM in Tonga had failed as the extreme cultural sensitivity of the topic had not been adequately considered.

This time, Tongan attitudes towards CSM would be taken into account. This would leave SPAFH and other interested organizations in a better position to determine the feasibility of implementing a CSM programme in Tonga and, if at all, how best to go about promoting, distributing and advertising the programme. A major goal was to empower Tongans with the ability to analyse and respond to planners, and to bring their own perceptions of the problems of population increase and AIDS in Tonga and their solutions to the programme planning table.

Country Background
Tonga is made up of 170 mainly low-lying islands, thirty-six of which are inhabited. Tonga is the only nation in Polynesia not to have experienced colonial rule and as such has kept much of its traditional Polynesian and Tongan culture intact (During 1990). However, Christian missionaries in the last century converted Tonga into a devoutly Christian nation (Ward-Gailey 1987). Christianity is woven into all aspects of Tongan society and in the 1986 census 99 per cent of Tongans claimed to be adherents of a Christian church. Thirty per cent were Catholic, while the remainder were largely Methodist (Central Planning Department 1993).

In 1991 the Government Statistics Department estimated Tonga's resident population at 96,000 which makes for a population density of 132.5 persons per km². Most make their living agriculturally. A further 40,000 Tongans are thought to be living or working abroad. At 90 per cent, the literacy rate is high (Central Planning Department 1993). Tonga also has a low mortality rate as well as an increasingly large youth population – 37.7 per cent of Tongans are under the age of fifteen. Traditional Tongan culture values large families and the average *api* (household) size is 6.5 persons. The gradual increase in the population will further increase population density and further the already high demand for land (South Pacific Commission 1994). Only 60 per cent of the Kingdom is viable agricultural land (Central Planning Department,

1991) and in many places in this patrilocal society young men are already finding that there is no land available to them (Hau'ofa 1989).

In addition to the pressures exerted by population increase, HIV is a growing problem in Tonga which is also related to sex. The preliminary participant-observation phase of research revealed that with many male Tongans being migrant workers (either to the capital or abroad), there is plenty of opportunity for them to have illicit relationships. Similarly the spouses, with their husbands often away from their village and families for months at a time, have the same opportunity. Consequently, the majority of HIV infections have been among migrant workers and their spouses. However, because Tonga is a devoutly Christian country, condom promotion to prevent the spread of HIV was seen by the Ministry of Health as in conflict with Christian moral values, the topic of contraceptives and sex is supposedly a *tapu* (taboo) subject in Tonga (Van der Grijp 1993, McGrath 1993), chastity is promoted instead (Samuel 1995).

Pre-marital sex is publicly denounced by state, church and society. Participant-observation also suggested that although chastity for women is expected until marriage, unmarried male activities are not so tightly monitored and status is attached to male sexual conquests. Furthermore, for Tongan females marriage is often not only seen as a release from chastity and public virginity but also a chance to discretely explore unfulfilled pre-marital relationships. Of course, condoms can also protect against STDs like HIV/AIDS as well as conception. However, because condoms have been associated with promiscuity, Tongans, male and female, promiscuous or not, are often hesitant to be seen to go and get them from the current outlets (family planning clinics and hospitals). The SPAFH project's goal was to test the feasibility of instigating an effective CSM programme before the social and economic problems associated with population pressure and AIDS make an indelible mark on the Kingdom of Tonga.

Application of Methods

Ethnographic Data Collection

Detailed ethnographic data was collected over a preliminary five-month participant-observation and semi-structured interviewing phase and a comprehensive literature review. An analysis of this ethnographic data enabled firstly (through semi-structured interviews of SPAFH and Ministry of Health staff and a literature review) an understanding of what the planners' perceptions of CSM in Tonga were. Secondly, it gave an insight into Tongans' knowledge of, attitudes towards, and practice of contraception at that time (Levene 1996). Thirdly, a suitably culturally sensitive sequence of participatory methods for use in RRA sessions with communities were developed. With sex and contraceptives the subject of taboo in Tonga, culturally sensitive methods were vital. They had to be sophisticated enough not to compromise the Tongan sense of taboo and yet still elicit meaningful data. They also had to engage the target community as equal partners in a dialogue concerning the nature of the intervention, and allow them to express their perceptions and concerns to planners. Without the preliminary ethnographic research, I suggest that such sensitive methods could not have been devised.

For example *faka apa apa* is an incest taboo which makes it difficult for certain family relatives of the opposite sex to talk about such topics as contraception in front of one another. This applies primarily and most strictly to brothers and sisters although there are certain rules which also apply to other kin. In Tonga, where kinship lines may extend back to fourth or even fifth cousins (Grijp 1993) it can sometimes appear that almost everyone is related to each other in some fashion. Therefore, to avoid any confusion or embarrassment, appraisal sessions were either all male or all female with a moderator to match. Tongan culture also values respect for elders. In a session of mixed age, older people's views would be held in a higher regard as a matter of course and this would prevent younger people from speaking their minds. Hence participants and moderators for a given group were also matched for age. These breakdowns allowed attitudes to be compared between island groups, age groups and sex.

Implementation of RRA Research Sessions

Three-day workshops were conducted to train paid moderators to run the RRA sessions. Suitable moderators were identified from among community-based workers already employed by Tonga Family Planning, family planning nurses and other suitable Ministry of Health workers. The workshop was repeated in the three main island groups of Tongatapu, Ha'apai and Va'vau.

The main role of the moderator was to facilitate data collection rather than extract information from the community. To fit into this role the moderators had to be aware of their attitudes and be able to 'sit, listen and learn' (Chambers 1992). This was often hard for development workers who were more used to operating in the 'stand, talk and teach' mode. RRA is about allowing everyone to participate, respecting local knowledge and fully understanding their perceptions of that knowledge.

The onus was always on moderators to be flexible and to use their own best judgement and initiative in determining how best to facilitate the research sessions and which data were most relevant to record.

Moderators worked in pairs, one to facilitate the RRA session, the other to record data. It was vital that they built up a trust and rapport with the participants to ease the task of facilitation. Moderators were therefore usually either resident or extension community health workers, familiar with the community's social dynamics and aware of cultural sensitivities.

It was up to moderators to identify and recruit suitable participants for their research sessions. Anyone from the age of fifteen and over was encouraged to volunteer as a participant. To ensure a diversity of views moderators were asked to take care that there was a realistic distribution of contraceptive users and non-users.

Session locations were distributed over a broad area for each island group rather than them all taking place in the main population centre. From this a comparison of attitudes between rural and urban populations could be made. Moderators identified venues for the session. The venue of the research session had to be culturally neutral. For example a church hall (the common community meeting place in Tonga) would be likely to prejudice what people had to say about contraception. Many men's sessions occurred around the *kava* circles. *Kava* is a popular drink with a mild narcotic effect, ingested by men at *kava* clubs all over Tonga. Not only did the *kava* circle provide a relaxed social setting which encouraged voluntary participation but the *kava* also encouraged more open speech on the topic. Women's sessions commonly took place around a *tapa* board or similar handicraft setting. *Tapa* is a highly prized decorative cloth made from beaten woodbark and can often be tens of feet in length. This requires among other equipment, a large board of equivalent length to beat the strips of *tapa* together. This setting provided a similarly relaxed and practical setting for women's sessions. Furthermore, neither the *kava* circles nor the *tapa* boards interfered with the normal routine of the community.

In keeping with Tongan custom regarding all new ventures, RRA sessions would start and finish with a prayer to ask for divine guidance and give thanks. These prayers, always initiated spontaneously by a participant, would almost always state that what they were about to embark on or had done was for the good of Tonga as a whole.

The sessions normally lasted three to four hours and would conclude with participants presenting all of their results for cross-checking by everyone present. Moderators would record information during and immediately after the RRA sessions, on specially prepared report forms. These A4 size forms enabled moderators to leave the original (flipchart size) appraisals in the ownership of the communities who had drawn them and were also more manageable when comparing and contrasting similarities and differences between communities' appraisals. Both facilitator and recorder would go over the data recorded together to make sure that it was accurate and that all comments made by participants had been recorded. The completed forms were then returned to SPAFH.

RRA Sessions

RRA sessions thus formed the core phase of the project. Fifty sessions, with the participation of 604 people, were carried out over the course of two months throughout the four main island groups. Groups were homogeneous in terms of sex and age, because of the *faka apa apa* barrier revealed during participant-observation. Each RRA session contained a variety of exercises (summarised in Table 3.2). Together they formed an empowering sequence, each exercise building on the knowledge of the last. Participants began by analysing their own attitudes towards population increase and AIDS, and then planned solutions to these problems that they then analysed and appraised.

Brainstorming The RRA research sessions started with the participants brainstorming and listing on butcher's paper all of the problems associated with population increase in Tonga. They did this under the following headings: 'problems for society', 'problems for the family' and 'problems for the individual'. They were then encouraged to explore each of these in depth (often using the scoring system outlined below) and then to draw links of possible interconnections. On the reverse side of the butcher's paper they then drew a visual representation of these problems. From this exercise, people's knowledge and views of the problems of population increase and HIV/AIDS could be gauged. Participants then carried out exactly the same brainstorming exercise, except the topic this time was the problems of sexually transmitted diseases (STDs) with an emphasis on HIV/AIDS. One or two of the participants then presented the results of the brainstorming session to the rest of the group to make sure that they all agreed on what had been said. Any additions or subtractions were made as appropriate. This done, participants brainstormed, in the same fashion, their *solutions* to the problems of population increase and STDs.

Scoring and Ranking With their solutions laid out clearly before them, participants scored them individually according to their efficacy for implementation in Tonga on a rank of 1 to 10. This was done using locally gathered materials such as small shells or seeds. Each individual took ten counters and scored each solution according to their own preferences. This was done with a strict five-minute time limit and everyone scoring at once so they were not influenced too much by what other participants scored. The piles of shells or seeds were then counted up and each solution given a total group score. On completion, the shells or seeds gave a visual cue for innumerate participants about which was the most popular solution. By tallying up the number of times a solution was mentioned throughout the Kingdom its prevalence could be found out, and by taking an average of its score, the solution's perceived acceptability was quantified. These solutions were then presented to the group alongside the 'problems' to check that they were indeed practical solutions. Adjustments were made if necessary.

Impact Diagramming   If condoms or the pill were mentioned as possible solutions (which they were in all but one group) then the research session continued with 'impact diagramming'. In this exercise participants wrote and drew 'Condoms' or 'The Pill' in the middle of a piece of butcher's paper and then added two sub-headings off these – 'Advantages' and 'Disadvantages'. Under these they added four sub-sub-headings: 'society', 'family', 'individual', and 'the church'. They then brainstormed regarding all of the advantages/disadvantages of the pill or condom under these headings, adding lines to indicate links where appropriate. The end result resembled a spider chart illustrating all the advantages and disadvantages of the pill and condom. Participants then listed and scored these advantages and disadvantages, this time on matrices, and analysed these to see which were thought to be the greatest advantages, and disadvantages to using the pill and condom.

Pie Charts   Pie charts could be drawn and adapted to represent, proportionally, any given variable that participants saw as worth further exploration. For example, the disadvantages mentioned in the impact diagramming exercise (such as negative side-effects of the pill) could be divided up on a pie chart to demonstrate their relative impact.

System Diagramming   This exercise was intended to reveal the problems Tongans encounter in obtaining contraception under the present distribution system. Participants drew the hypothetical sequence of events and decisions made should they wish to obtain contraception. However many participants found this exercise too revealing and sensitive and it was soon abandoned in favour of individual semi-structured interviews conducted separately to the RRA sessions.

Sentence Completion   Men were asked to complete the sentence 'I would like to see condoms sold at'. Women were given the same sentence to complete and 'I would like to see the pill marketed in the following way'. The exercise provided data on potential retail outlets and methods of distribution for the pill and condom.

Poster Designing   In small groups, participants looked back at all of the information they had discussed in the session and used this information to design their own CSM poster for whichever contraceptive they desired.

Key Probes   These are basic and important questions – the what? why? how? when? where? ones – which motivate 'open space' forums and keep exercises on track. They were also the method used to explore certain ethnographic points which had arisen during the participant-observation phase of the research.

Portraits and Case Studies/Life Histories   Outside of the forum of RRA sessions, participants were asked to cite or construct a particular case study or portrait of a hypothetical situation or person. Portraits and case studies were also a useful method to use when building up a picture of fakaleiti (transvestites) and prostitutes' knowledge of and attitudes towards condoms.

Semi-Structured Interviews   Groups are preferable as they are able to cross-check and cross-reference themselves in all of the above methods, but when a research opportunity arose that dealt with just one individual a semi-structured interview was carried out using key probes. During RRA sessions they were useful in neutralising particularly vocal or dominating participants who could be taken to one side and interviewed. Subsequent to RRA sessions semi-structured interviews were also used to obtain information from various key informants such as church leaders and potential retail outlet managers.

Participant-Observation and Ethnography   Throughout all of this the researcher/moderator paid close attention to the outcomes of these exercises from an emic viewpoint and gauged their consequences for the research in hand.

Participants were asked to fill in evaluation forms immediately following the RRA sessions. These suggested that the participation of Tongans had, firstly, popularized some of the concepts and issues of CSM within communities. Secondly, it had provided a rare opportunity for free and open public discussion of the issues relating to contraception. For some

Table 3.2. Table of exercises and applications

Exercise	Application
1. Brainstorming	To gauge people's knowledge and views of the problems of population increase and STDs/AIDS, and the solutions to them
2. Matrices Scoring	To score the prevalence and acceptability of solutions to the above problems
3. Impact Diagramming	To show the participants perceptions of advantages and disadvantages of using the pill and/or condom
4. Pie Charts	For further exploration of various variables
5. System Diagramming	To hypothetically map the process of obtaining contraception
6. Open Sentences	To show the variety and popularity of potential retail outlets for the pill and condom
7. Poster Designing	To see how Tongans would like contraception advertised
8. Key Probes	To get open space forums motivated and to keep the research on track What? Why? How? Where? When? etc.
9. Portraits and Case Studies	Of people and situations
10. Semi-Structured Interviews	Of key informants such as church leaders and potential retail outlet managers
11. Participant-Observation and Ethnography	To understand Tongan notions of contraception from an emic viewpoint

it was clearly an emancipating experience: 'thank you notes' from participants attached to the back of forms were one such testimony to this. Sitting in as an observer and monitor at many of the RRA research sessions I always came across lively discussions and debates – one session lasted for eleven hours and, because every adult in the community wished to participate, expanded from twelve participants to thirty-four.

Results of the CSM Preliminary Research Project

The results of utilizing ethnographic and RRA methods provided information on the feasibility of implementing CSM in Tonga, and how condoms and contraceptive pills might be promoted, advertised and distributed throughout the Kingdom. Here I shall concentrate on describing the major findings of this research and shall do so in order to demonstrate the efficacy of the methods outlined.

Although CSM was an SPAFH initiative this was a 'bottom-up' or 'grass roots' project in the sense that the participants largely dictated how CSM should be implemented. The target population's opinions were obtained through anthropological research and culturally appropriate RRA methods. These were then analysed, and compared with those of the planners (SPAFH), to see where there were similarities, differences and points of conflict. These points of conflict were analysed in the light of holistic ethnographic data to see which were truly intractable problems and which were merely ill-conceived perceptions which could be worked through. The 'intractable problems' were vital to determining whether CSM could be implemented or not. The resulting report offered recommendations on how SPAFH could proceed with CSM in Tonga (Levene 1996).

Problems

The target population's awareness and perceptions of the problems associated with population increase largely coincided with those identified by the SPAFH (social and economic pressure due to lack of land and increasing urbanization). During all of the RRA sessions the consensus among participants was that, although they were aware of these problems and symptoms, only the RRA exercises had enabled them to see how they were all interconnected and to judge for themselves that population increase lay at the root of them. In the past they had not realized this and had tried to alleviate the symptoms rather than deal with the cause of the problems. They thus felt that with the holistic picture of population increase gained through the first RRA exercise they were better informed to identify holistic solutions to the problem. This RRA exercise also brought home the severity of the problems of population increase and the importance of finding a solution. Participants no longer saw population increase as simply a national problem that should be dealt with solely by the government, but that it was also an individual and community responsibility and challenge to solve it.

The participants' exploration of the problems associated with AIDS were also broadly in line with population planners' perceptions, but the planners had not anticipated the discussion of the socio-cultural ramifications of the disease. This brought out the intense stigma attached to the disease: because it implies promiscuity, it reflects not only on the individual but upon the family as well, as they are seen as having failed to bring the infected person up in a 'proper' Christian manner. This blame, responsibility and shame is in fact shared by the whole parish. AIDS' stigma, Tongans believed, would result in the isolation of the community from Tongan society, leading to serious social and economic repercussions. At the same time, however, discrimination would be unchristian. Participants therefore concluded that it would be best to prevent contraction of the virus in the first place.

Solutions

After the first exercises participants were, according to debriefings with moderators, eager to find solutions to all of the problems identified. The planners' solutions were to market the contraceptive pill and condom in alternative outlets to those currently available (hospitals and family planning clinics). These included pharmacies and, for condoms, possibly supermarkets and hotels as well. The contraceptive pill was perceived by participants in all RRA sessions as a potential solution to problems associated with population increase. However, female participants were unsure about whether the 'Secure pill' should be made available other than in clinics and hospitals because of physical side-effects they mentioned. Family planning advice and education was seen as vitally important and was a far more popular solution than abstinence and natural methods of birth control. The primary advantages of the pill were seen as protecting the mother's health through child spacing and providing a more manageable family size and hence the capacity to provide for the family.

One example of a problem identified with the 'Secure pill' through the preliminary ethnographic research phase was the planners' packaging design. The current package shows one happy, single young woman. Many Tongans saw this as implying that the woman is breaking the taboo of chastity before marriage, or that those who use the pill are promiscuous women. They said that this would put married women off using them for family planning. They recommended that the design show a 'happily married couple'. A persistent problem among all the RRA sessions was that people worried about the cost of the 'Secure pill' if procured at an alternative site. It is currently available free of charge from family planning clinics and hospitals and participants questioned why they should pay for them.

However, current outlets were not perceived as entirely adequate. In a place as small as Tonga, anonymity is a rarity and this further put people off from going to get contraception from clinics and hospitals.

For example a woman in Ha'apai complained to me that she once went to get some condoms from the hospital in Ha'apai and was told that there were no more left as they had been given to women whose husbands were overseas. This breach of confidentiality, as she saw it, put her off going to the hospital again. Furthermore, Tongans do not view hospitals in the same clinically efficient light as in Western countries. The literal translation of the Tongan word for hospital (*fale mahaki*) is 'house of pain' − one indication of their unpopularity compared to traditional healers. A CSM programme in Tonga would offer alternative, culturally appropriate, outlets where people could have unfettered and confidential access to contraceptives. However, marketing of the 'Secure pill' for sale at alternative outlets was not perceived by the target population, at this stage, as either necessary or desirable. Therefore, as a solution, SPAFH staff suggested that only current outlets would market the 'Secure Pill', but thorough training of staff would accompany it.

The 'Protector condom' was perceived by members at all but one of the RRA sessions as a potential solution for both population increase and AIDS. In fact of all the solutions identified (there were thirty-four in total), condoms consistently ranked in the top three. On average it was the secondmost popular solution, following widespread family planning/STD education in communities (of which there is currently little). The primary advantages of using the condom were seen firstly as protection against STDs and, secondly, protecting the social and economic health of the family as a whole by preventing unwanted pregnancy.

But the participants also perceived significant disadvantages to using condoms. Condoms were apparently perceived to promote promiscuity. As condoms have never been proved to encourage promiscuity this was not the view held by SPAFH. Was this an 'intractable fact' or merely an ill-conceived perception? The participant-observation and interview phase of research revealed that few individuals believed that the use of condoms would encourage them personally to be more promiscuous. It was merely seen to be promiscuous by Tongan society's public social mores. What was seen as difficult, according to those interviewed, was not necessarily using condoms, nor buying them, but rather being *seen* to use them or *seen* to buy them. The government's current policy of promoting abstinence is actually preventing Tongans who would otherwise use condoms from going to obtain them from family planning clinics and hospitals because of the embarrassment of being seen to obtain them. In ranking participants' suggested retail outlets, hospitals and family planning clinics were low on the list for this very reason.

The high demand in RRA sessions for alternative discreet outlets for condoms confirms this.

Those condom retail outlets suggested by participants that ranked highest varied in form but not in content, i.e. they needed to be discreet. One of the most popular forms of retailer was an informal, confidential, trained salesperson. Participants regularly asked RRA moderators and town officers whether they could fulfil this role. Vending machines in hotels, night-clubs, dance halls, *kava* clubs, bars and gas stations were the other most popular suggested retail outlets. Many of these places are also frequented by tourists and therefore are seen as more culturally appropriate for the sale of condoms (as tourists of European descent are seen as promiscuous).

Participants' conclusions at RRA sessions were that condoms should be promoted through advertising that highlights their role in protecting women's health. Additionally, and in keeping with participants' statements about male gender-role expectations, stress should be placed on the responsibility of the male (the traditional head and chief provider for the household) to protect his family and society from the socio-economic problems associated with population increase by using 'Protector condoms'. SPAFH and participants in the sessions alike saw posters, newspapers and the radio as the most efficient forms of advertising. I recommended several of the posters, designed by participants and fulfilling their marketing criteria, for inclusion in the advertising campaign. The current packaging design of 'Protector condoms' also needed changing because the couple illustrated were clearly of an ethnic origin other than Polynesian.

Variations

Variations between island groups were largely related to differences of lifestyle. Tongatapu, with its large urban population in Nuku'alofa, is more socially and economically Western in its outlook and more used to Western-influenced change. Therefore, Tongatapu was most in favour of CSM. The type of retail outlets proposed on each island group naturally depended on what outlets were available. For example 'Eua (an island in the Tongatapu group) has no night-clubs or tourist facilities so these were never suggested.

Condoms and the pill were most popular with those males and females between the ages of twenty-one and forty, and second most popular with under 21-year-olds. There was less enthusiasm for CSM from males over the age of forty, but females of this age remained largely enthusiastic. Male reticence may have reflected Tongan male elders wanting to preserve *faka Tonga* (the traditional 'Tongan way'), in order to maintain their status within the family and wider community. On average, men were also slower at carrying out RRA exercises. This was only partly due to the length of time *kava* drinking ceremonies take, since male sessions that did not involve *kava* drinking were still more lengthy than female sessions. Rather, I believe that male groups took more time because, prior to the RRA session, they had not considered family planning issues in as much depth as women who, in the past, have been the primary target for contraceptive programmes. Also, male prestige as heads of households means that they are often slower and more reticent about admitting to socio-economic problems than are women. Therefore more time was required to discuss the issues and implications of contraception with men.

Conclusions

If family planning development is to occur at all, it has to be sustainable. For this to be the case, target populations have to be empowered to analyse their own problems, and to plan solutions for them. This does not necessarily mean that people should be left alone to sort out their problems. What it does mean is that government programmes meant to serve the people need to take the people's perceived needs into account. If an effective dialogue were to occur prior to any programme implementation, both planners and people would be in a better position to respond based on an understanding of the other's 'reality'. Planners could more easily design new technology or programmes for their constituents, rather than trying to fit those people to previously conceived technology or programmes. Similarly, by participating and contributing to the planning process people can make a more informed choice of whether or not to partake in new programmes or technologies.

Trained to gain both a holistic and emic perspective of the realities of planners and target populations, the anthropologist is in a unique position to mediate, arbitrate and communicate similarities and differences between the two and to identify intractable facts and ill-conceived perceptions. The mediating anthropologist can help both parties to acknowledge and build upon their collective reality, to shed light on ill-conceived perceptions and work with their 'facts'.

But anthropologists currently lack a routinized way to engage target populations in this process. For their vital contribution to development work to be fully acknowledged and utilized, anthropologists should respond to the current demand by development organizations for an empowering, participatory approach to development. Participatory techniques and approaches have proved helpful here. Although RRA also has its drawbacks, the anthropologist is in a position to counteract these and, furthermore, develop RRA's strengths.

The case study and applied anthropological methods described here demonstrates how the anthropologist can contribute to assessments of contraceptive acceptability prior to programme implementation. It is possible that this process can increase contraceptive acceptability, as seems to have been the case in the RRA sessions held in Tonga. Firstly, they facilitated an increased awareness in the target population of how contraception directly affects their lives. Secondly, they empowered people to design their own culturally appropriate solutions to problems related to use or non-use. Last but not least, they connected planners and target populations, aiding communication and action, so that each could co-operatively respond to each other's reality in ways that should lead to more sustainable development.

Postscript

In February 1996, due to internal politics within SPAFH, AusAID withdrew its funding for Project Excel from SPAFH and all CSM activities, apart from my own research (which was funded by the UK Voluntary Service Overseas' Overseas Training Programme), were terminated. CSM of the 'Protector condom' and the 'Secure pill' was thus not implemented in Tonga by SPAFH. To date AusAID are considering other organizations to implement Project Excel in the South Pacific.

References

Bernard, H.R. (1995), *Research Methods in Anthropology (2nd edition)*, London: AltaMira Press.

Binnendijk, A.L. (1986), *AID's Experience with Contraceptive Social Marketing: a Synthesis of Project Evaluation Findings*, US Agency for International Development.

Central Planning Department Nuku'alofa (1991), *Kingdom of Tonga; Sixth Five Year Development Plan 1991–1995*, Nuku'alofa: Government Printing Department.

Central Planning Department Nuku'alofa (1993), *Kingdom of Tonga, National Report on Population and Development*, Nuku'alofa: Government Printing Department.

Chambers, R. (1983), *Rural Development: Putting the Last First*, England: Longman Group.

—— (1992), 'Rural Appraisal: Rapid, Relaxed and Participatory', *Discussion Paper 311*, Sussex: Institute of Development Studies.

—— (1994a), 'The Origins and Practice of Participatory Rural Appraisal', *World Development*, 22(7): 953–69.

—— (1994b), 'Participatory Rural Appraisal (RRA): Analysis of Experience', *World Development*, 22(9): 1253–68.

Conlin. S. (1985), 'Anthropological Advice in a Government Context' in R. Grillo and A. Rew (eds), *Social Anthropology and Development Policy*, London: Tavistock.

During, K. (1990), *Pathways to the Tongan Present. 'Uuni Hala ki Tonga he Kuonga ni*, Nuku'alofa: Government Printing Department.

Family Care International (1995), *Commitments to Sexual Reproductive Health Rights for All*, New York: Family Care International.

Freire, P. (1968), *Pedagogy of the Oppressed*, New York: The Seabury Press.

van der Grijp, P. (1993), *Islanders of the South. Production, Kinship and Ideology in the Polynesian Kingdom of Tonga*, Leiden: KITLV Press.

Harrison, P. (1993), *Inside the Third World*, London: Penguin Books.

Hau'ofa, E. (1989), *Our Crowded Islands*, Suva: Institute of Pacific Studies of the University of the South Pacific.

Haviland, W.A. (1990), *Cultural Anthropology (6ᵗʰ edition)*, Fort Worth: Holt, Rinehart and Winston.

Heaver, R. (1992), 'Participatory Rural Appraisal: Potential Applications in Family Planning, Health and Nutrition Programmes', *RRA Notes*, No.16, Special Issue on Health (University of Sussex).

Kronen, M. (1997), *Participatory Methods*, Suva: Pacific Regional Agriculture Programme.

Levene, J.M. (1996), *The Feasibility of Implementing Contraceptive Social Marketing in the Kingdom of Tonga*, Tonga: South Pacific Alliance for Family Health.

McGrath, B.B. (1993), *Making Meaning of Illness: Dying and Death in the Kingdom of Tonga*, Michigan: UMI Dissertation Services.

Malinowski, B. (1922), *Argonauts of the Western Pacific*, New York: Dutton.

Marshall, J.F. and S. Polgar (1976), 'The Search for Culturally Acceptable Fertility Regulating Methods', in J. Marshall and S. Polgar (eds), *Culture, Natality and Family Planning*, Carolina Population Centre Monograph No.21. Chapel Hill, North Carolina Population Centre.

Martin, J. (1991), *Tonga Islands, William Mariner's Account*, Tonga: Vava'u Press.

Matangi Tonga (1995), *'Putting Condoms in the Market Place'*, Nuku'alofa, Tonga: Matangi Tonga (January–March).

Mosse, D. (1994), 'Authority, Gender and Knowledge: Theoretical Reflections on the Practice of Participatory Rural Appraisal', *Development and Change*, 25(3): 497–525.

Overseas Development Administration (1995), *A Guide to Social Analysis for Projects in Developing Countries*, London: HMSO.

Pretty, J.N. (1993), *'Criteria for Trustworthiness'; A Note for the Joint IIED/ IDS Meeting on Alternatives to Questionnaires, October 26*, London: Sustainable Agriculture Programme, IIED.

Samuel, S. (1995), 'SPAFH's Initiative in Social Marketing of Contraceptives in the Pacific', *Fiji General Practitioner*, 2(2): 173–4.

Sands, R. (1996), 'Creating a Global Community Through Citizenship', *The Journal of Contemporary Health,* Issue 4: 65–9.

Schellstede, W.P., and R.L. Cizewski (1984), 'Social Marketing of Contraceptives in Bangladesh', *Studies in Family Planning*, 15(1).

Seabrook, J. (1995), 'Third World Resurgence' in Instituto del Tercer Mundo (ed.) *The World : a Third World Guide 1995/96*, Montevideo: Instituto del Tercer Mundo.

Seymour-Smith, C. (1993), *Macmillan Dictionary of Anthropology*, London: Macmillan Press.

SPAFH (1993), *South Pacific Alliance for Family Health Information Booklet*, Nuku'alofa: Government Printing Department.

South Pacific Commission (1994), *Pacific Island Populations*, Noumea: South Pacific Commission.

Stanley, D. (1993), *South Pacific Handbook (5th edition)*, Chico: Moon Publications Inc.

Tupouniua, P. (1991), *A Polynesian Village – the Process of Change*, Suva: South Pacific Social Sciences Association.

Ward-Gailey, C. (1987), *Kinship to Kingship – A Gender Hierarchy and State Formation in the Tongan Islands*, Austin: University of Texas Press.

Wright, S. and N. Nelson (eds) (1995), *Power and Participatory Development*, London: Intermediate Technology.

PART 2

Contraception in its Political and Economic Contexts

4

Fertility Running Wild: Elite Perceptions of the Need for Birth Control in White-Ruled Rhodesia[1]

Amy Kaler

Introduction

In this chapter, I question some assumptions about women, men, race, families and human nature which bolster theory building in relation to family planning. My subject is discourse about black fertility and overpopulation in Rhodesia, now Zimbabwe, in the 1960s and 1970s, a setting where a small wealthy white electorate coexisted uneasily with an impoverished, disenfranchised and increasingly restive black majority, whom they had ruled and attempted to manage since the advent of white colonists in the 1890s.

By the 1970s, the contradictions and tensions inherent in this political and economic structure had produced a plethora of laws and socio-economic conditions defining the second-class citizenship of black Africans under the government of the Rhodesian Front.[2] Within this context, concern about African reproductive behaviour was part of the intellectual apparatus of colonialism, whether framed as concerns about the labour-supply implications of a too-low birth rate (Vaughan 1989), or as concerns about the political instability of a growing African population in the century's later years. By the 1960s and 1970s, as political tensions climbed, stemming African fertility became a national white obsession because of the threat it was thought to pose to white political security and the challenge it posed to the benevolent white stewardship of a 'backward' African population. By examining the way whites talked about African fertility, I show how the creation of know-ledge about population in Rhodesia was conditioned by a specific set of political concerns.

Since 1957, the promotion of family planning to Africans had been in the hands of the Family Planning Association of Rhodesia (FPAR). The FPAR was funded by the central government, which supplied 98 per cent of the FPAR's income by 1979 (*Annual Report of the Family Planning Association of Rhodesia* 1979). The Rhodesian Front government was unwilling to be openly associated with family planning, fearing (correctly) that government family planning programmes would be tainted by African suspicions that family planning was a political tool to keep their numbers down or if it was seen as a government programme.[3] While the FPAR ran a few of its own clinics, and in the 1970s trained some of its educators to distribute pills and injectable contraceptives, it concentrated on stimulating demand for contraception. Because I am concerned here with issues of discourse and representation, I will not engage the question of the extent to which Rhodesia, with a population of approximately 6.74 million in 1977, and an annual rate of increase of 3.6 per cent, was actually overpopulated or whether its growth rate was too high, and I will not try to gauge the gap between political rhetoric and demographic reality. Rather, I will first describe how the problem of African over-population and excessive fertility was framed by white Rhodesian academics and social engineers in the 1960s and 1970s; and then reconstruct the pseudo-anthropology of 'the African personality' that underlay this framing. My concern here is with the characteristics of the population crisis as it was constructed and understood by the Rhodesian governmental and para-governmental elites.

The foundations and outlines of this construction can be found in the published writing of highly educated white Rhodesians who worked for the government, the University of Rhodesia, and the Family Planning Association of Rhodesia (FPAR) between the late 1950s and 1980.[4] Unfortunately, biographical details about specific authors are not readily available. They published in both local and regional journals. Local journals such as the *Rhodesia Science News* and the *Rhodesian Journal of Economics* were intensely provincial in focus, written by and for the colonial white intelligentsia. Papers dealing with Rhodesian family planning and overpopulation, written by white Rhodesians, were also found in regional professional journals, especially the *Central African Journal of Medicine* and the *South African Medical Journal*. None of them published in standard international demographic journals, such as *Studies in Family Planning* or *Population and Development Review*, although their ideas show some affinities with ideas current in population journals in the rest of the world at the time of publication, as described in Watkins (1993) and Wilmoth and Ball (1992).

The gap in rhetoric and audience between these Rhodesian publications and popular media such as the *Rhodesia Herald* was not as pronounced as the difference between academic journals and mass media in present-day North America or Europe. The Rhodesian publications that I cite are analogous to *Psychology Today or Popular Mechanics*, filling a niche between academic discourse and the (white) mass media. The people who wrote the editorials and the letters-to-the-editor in the *Rhodesia Herald* about population issues were also, in their academic and professional capacities, the contributors to the *Rhodesia Science News* and its fellow publications. The group of texts I am concerned with here occupies a zone in between popular magazines (Wilmoth and Ball 1992) and academic journals (Watkins 1993).

Benevolent Development in a Colonial Context

Cooper and Stoler assert that human reproduction was a central part of the 'tensions of empire': 'At different times, colonial regimes had to come to grips with how people – colonizers and colonized – reproduced themselves, ... where they did so, ...with whom, ... under whose eyes, ... and with what degree of success' (1989: 613). However, the terms in which most historians and other social scientists discuss reproduction are predominantly those of sexuality. This emphasis produces many studies of concubinage, 'miscegenation', metis (mixed race) populations, and black, white or yellow perils. 'With what degree of success' – reproduction defined in biological terms, as the production of increasing numbers of human beings and the tensions that attend this process among colonizers and colonized alike – has not yet received this degree of attention, and this chapter is an effort to redress that omission.

Concerns about African reproduction in Rhodesia is one example of the 'tensions of empire' in a particular time and place, in which white anxiety about the continued survival of the racial oligarchy coexisted with and masqueraded as 'modernization'. The Rhodesian construction of a population crisis and of a generic African population prone to overpopulating is located within the history of colonial projects intended to reshape African sexual and reproductive practices. Although the Rhodesian state provided very little in the way of health services for Africans, Rhodesia in the 1970s had many programmes, both governmental and non-governmental, aimed at 'socializ[ing] African women as biological reproducers', such as women's homecraft clubs and religious institutions (Hunt 1988: 430; see also Kaler 1998). These, in turn, can be traced to the establishment of 'scientific' programmes to improve the practice of mothering and domestic hygiene in early twentieth-century Britain and the United States (Davin 1978). The existence of such projects was tied to wider waves of development, modernization and rationalization of domestic life as they coincided, in the early and mid-twentieth century, with the time when home economics, nutrition and child psychology were becoming 'scientific' enterprises in Europe and North America.[5]

The set of Rhodesian colonial projects aimed at African sexual and reproductive practices can be divided into two subsets – those dealing with concerns that the whites perceived as 'immoral' or 'perverted', such as polygamy, child marriage, or the 'black peril' (the sexual threat African men were said to pose to white women), and those dealing with domesticity, attempting to reshape African home and family life in the pattern of European ideals (including, in the aftermath of the European fertility transition, the production of fewer children). Jeater (1993: 261) argues that concerns of immorality or perversion were the focus of condemnation and prohibition by colonial authorities, especially early in the colonial period in Rhodesia. In contrast, the latter subset were the focus of persuasive, rather than coercive, attempts to 'civilize' Africans, relying on campaigns of education, and exhortations to civilized behaviour rather than the punitive power of the state. This is the category into which family planning fits, as the introduction of new means of fertility regulation in Rhodesia was brought into the African rural and urban areas through persuasion rather than by coercion. The operation of colonial power was thus less overt and confrontational here than it was when controlling 'perversion'.

Other projects of domestication and persuasion included courses in child care, home economics, tailoring and homecrafts, often run by Christian missionaries. While these projects might appear to have been aimed at superficial changes in dress and diet, the Comaroffs (1992) argue that their deeper intent was to urge Africans to adopt a 'moral' social and economic order, founded on European notions of gender-specific propriety and disciplined sexual and reproductive relations. In Rhodesia, Schmidt argues that these projects were linked to efforts to create a suitable family life for an African elite based on Europeans models. A well-regulated family was not merely an adjunct to a 'civilized' Christian African man, but an essential part of his life. This necessitated the existence of 'wife-training' courses at missions for women about to marry African Christians, and homecraft and women's clubs in rural areas to keep women abreast of new techniques for managing modern homes and families, and to keep them cognisant of their position as part of the drive to recreate African home life in the

European image (e.g. Ranchod-Nilssen 1992 and other contributors to Hanson 1992).

By attempting to organize and rationalize processes of African family life, white Rhodesian discourse on family planning was part of this grander project. The racial structure of the Rhodesian state and economy generated imperatives for the whites to define the 'other' – the African – in such a way as to justify the perpetuation of benevolent white superiority. Within this discursive field, discussion of family planning took two forms.

It was possible for white family planners to express concern for the development and betterment of both individual families and the nation as a multiracial whole and to speak of family planning as the means to achieve a higher, more modern standard of living. At the same time, the discourse about population was characterized by anxieties and fears for the survival of the racial hierarchy under the pressure of a growing African population. The fear of an uncontrollable demographic threat reflected the fear of an uncontrollable political threat. White Rhodesia could be submerged by the sheer mass of black bodies, or, calmer voices argued, African population growth could sharpen the pains created by the racially asymmetric economic organization of the country, and could thereby lead to a political crisis. Containing the African population was thus a matter of long-term political strategy, a consideration which co-existed with expressed concerns for the well-being of the African population.

How Does Population Matter?

In this chapter, I seek to determine *how* overpopulation mattered to Rhodesian social engineers. Wilmoth and Ball (1992) undertake a parallel task in their survey of population debates in popular United States magazines. They describe five argumentative 'frames' that pre-dominated in the American popular media after the Second World War, three of which can be detected in Rhodesian discourse on overpopulation in the same era. These include the 'limits to growth' frame,

> a mild version [of which] asserts that an excessive rate of growth threatens the ability of a nation's economy to absorb additional people. The perceived harm of growth in this case is retarded economic development, unemployment, or an economically burdensome child dependency ratio (1992: 640).

A second salient frame was the 'overcrowding' frame, which focuses on the ways in which population growth and population density produce 'various forms of social pathologies, ranging from street crime to domestic violence and sexual deviance' (1992: 641). However, Wilmoth and Ball's 'race suicide' frame is most resonant with the ways in which African fecundity and fertility were viewed by the white elite. In Rhodesia, where the white population feared that they were already under threat by Africans on political and military fronts, this frame describes the most prominent fears of Rhodesian social engineers:

> The central premise . . . is that population growth among some other group is too rapid in comparison with the growth of our group. However the notion of 'us versus them' is defined, the argument deplores the . . . perceived prospect that we are being outbred by them, or that they are invading, now or eventually, our space. . . . The argument builds on a perception that one population (or sub-population) is losing, or will lose, control over some vital aspect of social and political life because of its relative decrease in numbers. (1992: 642)

In the 1960s and 1970s, Rhodesian writing on overpopulation was permeated by a sense of urgency. According to the rhetoric emanating from the Ministry of Health, the Family Planning Association of Rhodesia, and white intellectuals within the University of Rhodesia, African overpopulation was a massive problem. Consciousness of this supposed threat was manifested in many unexpected places, suggesting a generalized concern among the white population. For example, a report on the birth of quadruplets in an African township hospital concluded 'while this sort of thing presents problems in its sudden contribution to the population explosion, it no doubt provided the hospital staff with an interesting exercise in pediatrics' (Ministry of Health (Rhodesia) 1966: 24). The *Rhodesia Science News* sponsored a school essay competition on the topic 'What changes do you think might occur in this country as a result of increases in numbers of people? Do we have the natural resources to cope with four extra people per hundred of existing persons *every year*?'(*Rhodesia Science News* 7: 256, emphasis in original). In 1975, the Rhodesia Scientific Association sponsored a conference on increasing yields of protein in Rhodesia, at which the opening address by the president of the Association took as its theme 'Population and Protein'.

Alongside these manifestations of awareness of a population crisis were frequent warnings about the growing urgency of the crisis, both domestically in Rhodesia and internationally. A prominent Salisbury (now Harare) educationalist, Kathleen Rea, questioned whether conditions in the future were likely to be such that life could be lived 'in a manner worthy of human beings'. Multitudes were born, lived and died in the roadside mud and dust of the exploding cities of the Third World. In contrast, a tribe inhabiting the borders of Kenya and Sudan had 'scarcely human' outlooks. Did the world have a future? 'The best I can say is – perhaps,' Mrs Rea said. 'Man has the intelligence and the ability to pull himself out of the mess, but will he?' ('Population growth must cease,' *Rhodesia Herald*, 28 March 1977).

On the domestic front, the leaders of the FPAR obviously had a great deal at stake in perpetuating this idea of impending national catastrophe,[6] and the tone of a 1971 article by K.E. Sapire, the medical director of the FPAR, is typical:

> For many years there has been an ostrich-like attitude and an ominous silence about the population problem, but recently demographers, economists, world organisations and responsible governments have been uttering dire warnings about its consequences . . . The problems are vast and urgent, and to quote Dr Roger Bernard, of the Pathfinder Fund, Boston, who visited us recently after going to India: 'In India the time has run out, but in Rhodesia you have five minutes more!' (Sapire 1971: 104, 108)

Peter Dodds, the third director of the FPAR, contributed to this sense of emergency in 1977 by arguing that hormonal contraceptives should be available to African women without prescriptions and without medical supervision because the need to spread contraceptives as widely as possible overrode any minor health concerns (Dodds 1977: 315). At the same time, Alfreda Geraty, a research fellow attached to the FPAR who appears to have been concerned primarily with humanitarian rather than racial rationales for promoting family planning amongst African women, expressed concerns that an exaggerated sense of crisis was warping Rhodesian population control efforts:

> an element of panic has crept into the situation which could defeat more carefully considered plans which take into account all the variables that influence dynamics in a multicultural society. (Geraty 1974: 8)

But Geraty's opinion was a minority one. Concern with excessive fertility among rural Africans intersected with concerns about ecological degradation and agricultural inadequacy in the Tribal Trust Lands (TTLs). These lands, set aside for African occupation like the 'homelands' of South Africa, held over 60 per cent of the African population, and were the most concentrated pockets of African poverty in Rhodesia. The

TTLs included some of the poorest agricultural land in the country, yet 'they carry over three times as many people as the land is safely able to carry, given current levels of capitalisation (Gilmurray *et al.* 1979: 8). In 1969, 57 per cent of African land fell into the categories 'overpopulated' and 'grossly overpopulated' (Hanks 1975: 174). The overcrowding of the TTLs was reflected in the declining nutritional status of the inhabitants.

The Natural Resources Board and the Ministry of Native Affairs had been wrestling with the problem of the TTLs for years, concentrating on what they considered the 'primitive and destructive methods of husbandry [which] have placed an intolerable burden on the soil, water, and vegetation resources of nearly half the land surface of Rhodesia' (cited in Hanks 1975: 173). Measures to regulate traditional agricultural practices, such as the Land Husbandry Act of 1951, met with active resistance or non-compliance. Given this history, it is not surprising that in the 1970s, these concerns were adopted by the backers of family planning and integrated into the discourse of betterment and modernization of rural Rhodesia. Sister McCarthy, head of nursing for the FPAR, explicitly linked intervention in population matters with intervention in agricultural ones:

> 1975, say the experts, is the year when the Stork passes the Plough [i.e., when natural increase outstrips food cultivation]. But I hope that over the next four years family planning will clip the wings of that overworked bird – and that scientific progress will push the plough faster (McCarthy 1971: 8).

When overpopulation was discussed in relation to urban settings, particularly the spectre of rising urban unemployment, concerns for the uplifting of Africans dovetailed with fears for the stability of the racial hierarchy. Sapire extrapolated the existence of a high dependency ratio from the fact that 58 per cent of the Rhodesian population was under nineteen years-old, putting pressure on wages and harvests produced by adults (Sapire 1971: 104). Unemployment, especially urban unemployment, would be exacerbated by increasing population.

Clarke (1971) explicitly linked African unemployment to the future of white rule in Rhodesia. The percentage of African males aged fifteen to fifty-nine in some kind of waged employment had declined from 78 per cent to 58 per cent from 1956 to 1968, although the total number of employed African males had increased. At prevailing rates of employment and population growth, Clarke estimated that by the year 2000 only 29 per cent of African males would be employed (Clarke 1971:

14, 16). The consequences of this decline might be felt by Rhodesian society as a whole, as well as by the families of the men involved, as the number of 'idle' young people, who could not be absorbed into the overcrowded rural areas or the paid workforce, grew. Those who did not have a stake in the survival of the political and economic system that a job might provide could easily become politically volatile.

Population and White Security: Racial Ratios

The political volatility of the black population and the possibility of being overrun by Africans were themes frequently sounded by writers who framed the population explosion as a matter of national security for whites. Discussions of the African fertility crisis usually turned on comparisons between the demographic characteristics of the European and African populations, as opposed to discussions of absolute numbers, or of the impact of both numbers and production/consumption patterns on the carrying capacity of Rhodesia.[7] In 1964, Paddy Spilhaus noted that 'there were 19 African children born to one European child in Southern Rhodesia' (' 14,000,000 Africans in Southern Rhodesia by 2000 AD', date unknown, *Rhodesia Herald* 1964). The framing of the over-population problem as a problem of racial ratios was also evident in the efforts by the FPAR to attract outside funding. General William Draper, head of the International Planned Parenthood Foundation, wrote in a 1966 press release that '[FPAR] needed much more outside financial help in order to meet the needs of the Bantus or Africans, who outnumber the whites in Rhodesia sixteen to one'.

This concern with racial ratios occurred in the context of the shift in overall black:white proportions. Most Rhodesians would have been very much aware, although they may not have known the exact figures, that the white share of the total population was shrinking. Until 1959, the white share had been slowly increasing because of white immigration; after 1960, it shrank (Weinrich 1982: 119).[8] The rate of natural increase among whites was also declining. In 1968 it was 'close to the levels experienced in economically advanced countries' at 1 per cent per year (Clarke 1971: 13). Africans, however, had a natural increase of around 3.6 per cent per year (Hanks 1973: 250). The very public release of the 1969 census, the first moderately accurate population estimate, confirmed to the white public that they were indeed a shrinking minority (Hooker 1971).

Indeed, whites were outnumbered by blacks, even in areas officially designated for whites only, by a factor of 8:1. In the urban zones of

Salisbury and Bulawayo, where in theory no blacks were supposed to reside, there were four times as many Africans as whites (Hooker 1971: 2). In 1969, only 4,004 white children were born as opposed to about 215,000 Africans, so that 'there are nearly as many African babies as there are Europeans in the entire country' (ibid.). Even worse, in Hooker's opinion, of the 4.8 million Africans in Rhodesia, 52.6 per cent were born after 1952, as opposed to only 38 per cent of the Europeans, so that Africans were not only more numerous but were also younger and presumably stronger.[9] Based on these ratios, Hooker called for a programme of birth control to limit African population growth. His concerns were shared by white government members:

> The demographic contrast between African and European reproductive styles was expressed by a white Rhodesian Front backbencher who introduced a (failed) private member's bill in 1966, urging a national campaign to reduce the African birthrate, through aggressive promotion of family planning to Africans. His supporters contextualised the motion by denouncing 'the appalling tendency on the part of the European to limit his family' and urged tax breaks for large white families (Parliamentary Debates vol.63 (1966), cited in West 1994: 18).

Similar concerns were expressed in another letter to the editor of the *Rhodesia Herald* by Mrs B.C. Gadd:

> At present, [Europeans] are somewhat restricted by our own laws and customs and [are] losing out matching the African wife for wife and child for child, in order to secure a corresponding increase in population on the European side . . . Is it cricket [i.e. is this a sportsmanlike way to compete with an opponent]? (*Rhodesia Herald,* 2 July 1970).

The keen interest of many Rhodesian Front backers for family planning was an awkward issue for the FPAR to handle. While white support for the programmes of the FPAR was essential, white enthusiasm for reducing the number of Africans could be an embarrassment when the FPAR tried to present family planning as a disinterested health and welfare measure for Africans. In public, this embarrassment had to be muted, but Dodds did allow himself the grumble that 'we could well have done without the contributions of certain politicians who chose to involve themselves' ('Let the population pessimists beware', *Rhodesia Herald,* 27 December 1974).

White fears about African population growth were exacerbated by the gradual decline in numbers among the European population due to emigration. Net emigration figures were consistently reported in the

Rhodesia Herald and the *Sunday Mail,* often on a monthly basis.[10] With a white population hovering at the quarter-million mark, the fact that the whites lost 10,908 of their number to emigration in one year alone had a considerable psychological as well as demographic impact, especially as those most likely to emigrate were young and affluent (*Sunday Mail,* 22 January 1978). According to some, the outlook for the cultural survival of white Rhodesia was even worse than the demographic figures indicated, since many of the remaining whites were 'sojourners' or 'immigrants', rather than true 'Euro-Africans' (*Rhodesia Herald,* 19 May 1977).[11]

Pathogenic Fertility and the White Man's Burden

These concerns for the future security of the white oligarchy shaped white fears of African reproduction. White writers constructed theories to explain, in sociological terms, why African fertility had increased to such alarming levels and, in ethical terms, why whites should do something about this. Overpopulation was presented as a problem afflicting Africans that required white intervention, in the form of the FPAR or the unrestricted distribution of the pill. Underlying this presentation were two ideological constructs – the idea of white responsibility, in the sense of both causal responsibility and a welfare responsibility for their less-developed African wards; and the idea of a generic African personality and culture possessing subtle deficiencies which allowed unrestrained fertility to reach a crisis point.

The white Rhodesian intellectual establishment drew on Weberian and Durkheimian ideas about cultural change, stasis and the production of anomie. This gave them the intellectual foundation for building an equation according to which the atavistic personality of the African, plus the pathological effects of the collision between African backwardness and European modernity, added to white benevolence and compassion equalled a problem of pathogenic African hyper-fertility. The stage was thus set for another application of European problem-solving techniques and know-how on the bodies of Africans, in the form of the promotion of contraception and family planning.

Rhodesian writers did not assume that uncontrolled fertility was innate to African cultures. Instead, they painted a strong picture of the population crisis as a white man's burden, engendered by the whites' own altruistic effort to 'uplift' the blacks.[12] A long history of benevolent white social engineering, according to this view, was producing the unintended consequence of high fertility. In particular, they claimed the advent of white medicine and health services had bred a population explosion:

> White Rhodesians have been trapped, ironically, by their own civilisation. Having built hospitals and clinics, they brought a standard of health to Rhodesia unknown among Africans north of the Zambezi. They eradicated or severely curtailed killing and wasting diseases . . . the authorities have underestimated the efficacy of their public health efforts . . . now that they have begun to understand, their consternation is both serious and apparent. (Hooker 1971: 2)

> Our problem is not in the birth rate, which has only risen from 45 per 1,000 to 52 per 1,000 since the turn of the century; the problem stems from the impact of preventive and curative medicine, which, over the same period of time, dropped the African death rate dramatically from 38 per 1,000 to 16 per 1,000. (Dodds 1977: 314)

Africans themselves were largely absent from these accounts of the genesis of the population crisis. They are the bodies on which the miracles of preventive health and medicine are worked, but they are not described as people actively seeking health or interacting with the new technologies of health appearing in their villages or townships. They respond to white medicine, as if to new fertilizers or weedkillers applied to agricultural crops:

> Nature is delicately balanced and our manipulations might have results we never bargained for. We treated whole tribes for tropical yaws with massive penicillin campaigns only to find that syphilis, which had been held in check by cross-immunization from yaws, now became rampant. . . . Those of the technologically advanced nations of the world have brought their new knowledge to the developing nations and are therefore in part responsible for the population explosion. (Philpott 1969: 3, 5)[13]

The image of a benevolent, albeit fallible, white colonialism was complemented by the construction of an African personality and culture that was essentially incompatible with white civilization. In its most benign form, this meant asserting the existence of a 'cultural lag' according to which the Europeans had already begun to regulate their fertility in 'modern' ways and have small families, while the Africans, languishing in ahistorical stasis until colonialism jump-started their economic development, followed generations or centuries behind.

In its most overtly racist form, this construction took the form of positing biological differences between Africans and Europeans which made the former incapable of understanding the need for fertility regulation and family planning. Few Rhodesians, by the 1970s, would express this as baldly as did the South African-born van Rensburg, speaking about the problem of African overpopulation confronting the entire region of southern Africa:

> Black and White races have quite distinct traits in their brain formation which influences very significantly the output and character and modes of thought as well as their quality in each of these stocks. One of the many . . . is 'foresight' . . . The African enjoys the present, the white cannot beat him at that. The future exists for the African in a lesser degree than it does for the white. It is as if the African's time arranges itself closely around the present. He makes few plans. He also has little history. (van Rensburg 1972: 116)

The ascription to Africans of fatalism, passivity and a distorted sense of time is also present in Spilhaus' address to prominent white mining executives to enlist their support for her nascent family planning association, although she does not carry biological determinism to such crude extremes:

> How can we gain the co-operation of the African people with whom we are mainly concerned? I cannot over-emphasize the difficulty of this task. The African, through no fault of his own, has, even to-day, little consciousness of the forces at work beyond the limited sphere of his own interests. They are certainly unaware of global population pressures and the problems that confront the government due to rapidly increasing numbers. Generally speaking, these problems are beyond their comprehension . . . Also to be considered in some ways is the fatalism with which many of them take the so-rapid increase in their families. (Spilhaus 1961: 4)[14]

Elizabeth Still, writing for other health professionals, attempted a slightly more nuanced explanation for these personality traits as they afflicted the 'unspoiled' African who had not yet come into contact with white technology. Such a person was culturally conditioned to produce large numbers of children, conditioning which exacerbated the tendency towards irresponsible procreation once these people did come into contact with white social welfare:

> [P]eople who have never known much more than a hand-to-mouth existence and are only now coming into contact with the rigours and possibilities of a

cash economy have not looked on their lives as being other than 'natural' and not of exceptional hardship. The climate is ideal, thought droughts occur. The men hunt or clear the bush, but enjoy village life, go visiting, gossip, and drink home-brewed beer. . . . I am told that if the maize crop is exceptionally good one year, the truly rural African sees no need to plant a similar acreage the following year. And he sees no reason to limit the number of children he has either. There is always enough to feed an extra mouth, the children are much loved and cosseted, especially while they are babies, and all the female members of the family help with their upbringing. (Still 1973: 93)

These ideas about African traits as related to fertility were part of a wider construction of an African personality and culture at odds with white values, white society and white technology. Many Rhodesian writers held that the cultural discontinuities between rural life in a subsistence economy and urban life in the orbit of the European cash economy generated psychological stress for individual Africans, which led to socially undesirable phenomena, including drunkenness and crime as well as overpopulation. This belief led them to recast political problems of oppression and exploitation as 'cultural' issues, generated by the collision of two unfortunately incompatible cultures. Urbaniza-tion and the recruitment of men into waged labour, while necessary for the growth of Rhodesian industry, produced other unintended consequences:

[Africans] have relinquished the high moral standards of their own customs, they have given up the idea of ancestor worship, but they have found nothing to take the place of these foundation pillars of their society. This must surely be a lesson to those who seek to lead people into a new way of life. (Philpott 1969: 13)

Pathogenic fertility was the by-product of psychopathological anomie. According to Hooker, for the African woman who came into closer contact with European amenities in towns,

there is little of importance she can accomplish in town. Traditional village tasks, though perhaps performed in the new setting, are done so in a distorted form. There is a communal water tap rather than a distant stream; there is charcoal to buy instead of wood to be cut or gleaned. There is no stock to feed and so on – a litany of boredom. So little to do, and so much to buy. Having children in such circumstances might prove one's existence, might demonstrate that one does indeed have a job to do. Whatever is responsible, the babies are certainly produced. (Hooker 1971: 6)

On the macro level, this tragic cultural clash was manifested as a fertility explosion.

> The incompatibility of traditional Black African values, concepts and institutions on the one hand and the way of life embodied in Western technology on the other is the cause of conflicts and problems of which we can only perceive the outlines. The explosive rate at which the formerly stationary Black African populations are increasing today is a striking example of this incompatibility. (van Rensburg 1972: 22)

Even among those few Africans who successfully 'modernized' themselves, the collision between 'traditional' and 'modern' worlds could produce disturbing fertility behaviour:

> An article in the January *African News* showed a picture of an 'enterprising man' who owned a boat in which he ferried people across the Sabi River. So successful was he that he earned 30 to 50 [pounds] in a good month, and had ten wives and 80 children. Tribally, he was a great man with many descendants, relatives and potential rememberers of his spirit. In terms of the cash economy, he would certainly have another status! (Davies 1970: 81)

Some white writers were aware of the instrumental reasons that Africans might choose to have many children, such as concern for old age security or the need to send more children out to work to compensate for declining agricultural productivity. However, even these reasons were defined as purely 'cultural', thus robbing them of the justification of economic rationality. Geraty, one of the more liberal FPAR workers, acknowledged that 'the man who can see security for his old age in the ground he is cultivating or in the job he is doing will not need to look to his children for old age support [and therefore will not have so many]' (Geraty 1974: 15). However she concluded in the same article that the main reason why Africans were not flocking to the FPAR clinics was that they were not 'cognitively ready' to understand birth control (ibid.). Lack of a modern mind-set, rather than a reasoned cost-benefit analysis, was the real reason for high African fertility, according to the accepted wisdom of white Rhodesia.

This view of African fertility as primarily a manifestation of cultural, and, to a lesser degree, psychological, pathology, led to many silences in the Rhodesian discourse on population. One of the most striking empirical silences is the lack of research into factors that by the 1970s were well known as determinants of fertility, such as the infant mortality rate. According to most mainstream thinking on population in the 1970s, obtaining such information was an essential precondition to mounting a national family planning campaign. However, I believe that most whites in Rhodesia had a vested interest in upholding the idea that overpopulation was the result of innate cultural and psychological deficiencies among Rhodesian Africans. If high fertility was ultimately the result of 'primitive' culture, pathology, and an uncontrolled biological imperative, research into proximate social and economic determinants of birthrates would be a waste of effort.

Rhodesian family planners argued that it would not be necessary to improve Africans' economic and political status in order to see a decline in the African birth rate. If such changes had been undertaken on a large enough scale to produce an appreciable national effect, they would have threatened the racial inequalities on which Rhodesia's political and economic structures were founded; a politically unwise stance for the FPAR to take. Two administrators of the FPAR explicitly stated that their work was intended to 'challenge the hypothesis that only antecedent social and economic development can produce a decline in the birth rate' and then proceeded to do so through a survey of family planning clinic attendees (Castle and Sapire 1976: 965). Dunlop (1975) concurred with this, describing as 'positively dangerous' the findings of another social scientist, R.J. Thiesen, that 'there is a simple causal relationship between socio-economic status and family size (cited in Thiesen 1977: 161). Peter Dodds, director of the FPAR, described Thiesen's findings and the beliefs of other development experts that 'the best population policy is a development policy' as a 'dangerous dogma' (Dodds 1977: 314). He later warned that those who 'urge the socio-economic prerequisite [i.e. that birth rates will fall as a result of increased standards of living]' are 'harmful to Africa's future' and can undermine national family planning programmes (Dodds 1978: 162). This as also the opinion of Rowan Cronje, the Rhodesian Front Minister of Manpower, Social Affairs, Health and Education, who stated that 'economic development or international aid is not going to help us control the birth rate' (*Rhodesia Herald,* 'Rhodesia's public enemy No. 1', 20 May 1978).

This perspective might have been justified by the demographic research of the day, as the causal relationship between socio-economic development and decreasing birthrates was not (and is not) clear. However, it also fit into the status quo very well, and it is impossible to rule out the possibility that family planners' viewpoints were produced in conformity with the colonial status quo, rather than through independent assessment of existing research.

Conclusion

In this chapter, I have concentrated on two aspects of the ideology of fertility and population among white Rhodesians — the definition of why overpopulation is a problem; and the assumptions about the causes of this problem. White writing on family planning was linked to the intellectual imperatives created by the specific political structure of Rhodesia, according to which white sovereignty was a necessary and benevolent institution. The particular predicament of intellectuals in Rhodesia, in terms of the constraints that the political environment imposed on their work, differs from that of most present-day intellectuals, but I believe that the relation between political environment and ideas about fertility (especially the fertility of 'the other') holds firm, as the historians of the 'population movement' cited by Wilmoth and Ball (1992: 632) confirm. The way intellectual communities think about population and fertility is closely related to the communities in which they live, and to normative ideas about the innate nature of different types of people, such as men, women, adults, children, whites, and blacks.

However, such constraints cannot wholly determine fertility theory. In this chapter, I have considered the effects of political structure and historical circumstance on the production of knowledge. In choosing this focus, I have neglected the issue of intellectual resistance to dominant ideas, and have slighted the works of Rhodesian intellectuals who did not subscribe to the dominant ideas about race, civilization, modernity, and their roles in shaping individual and aggregate fertility patterns. The question of resistance to the forces that shape the social production of knowledge is one that should be taken up by future researchers who want to understand how structures and circumstance affect what we know about fertility and population crises.

Notes

1. This research was supported by an International Predissertation Fellowship from the Social Science Research Council and the American Council of Learned Societies with funds provided by the Ford Foundation, and the Anna Welsch Bright Fellowship from the Department of Sociology, University of Minnesota.

I would also like to acknowledge the helpful comments provided by Guy Thompson and Susan Cotts Watkins.

2. As of 1976, when over half the population of approximately 6.6 million was under the age of 15, only 846,260 were enrolled in school, and less than half of one per cent of all African children could expect to complete high school (IDAFSA 1977: 22). The earnings of white Rhodesians averaged $R5,583 per year, while those of Africans averaged $R517 (and Africans employed in agriculture, which absorbed most of the waged African labour force, averaged only $R201) (IDAFSA 1977: 15). African associations were circumscribed by repressive laws aimed at preventing African political expression and economic mobility, such as the Vagrancy Act, the Masters and Servants Act, the African Registration and Accommodation Act, the Industrial Conciliation Act, and the notorious Law and Order Maintenance Act.

3. Rhodesia was not unique in this. In colonial Kenya, the white government refused for many years to consider setting up state-sponsored family planning clinics for Africans on the grounds that such clinics would be too controversial with the African population, who would assume that the clinics had been established to shrink the African population, so that whites could take over the land (Susan Watkins, personal communication). However, more research is needed to establish the extent to which the ways in which population issues were framed, and the operational understandings of native populations differed among different colonial regimes.

4. I have concentrated on publicly circulated texts that were available to the white elite who were involved in making policy decisions and implementing pro- grammes for governing the black population. These journals and newspapers can be found in public archives and libraries in Zimbabwe and abroad. I have excluded texts that were produced for a circumscribed readership only, such as private correspondence between members of the elite, memos that were internal to specific organizations, or confidential letters and minutes.

5. These projects to reshape African women as biological reproducers coincided with similar projects directed at men, aimed at escorting them into the rational world of modern scientific agriculture, again in imitation of foreign models. Scientific agriculture and domestication represent respectively the public and private faces of attempts to 'modernize' Africans.

6. Within the leadership of the FPAR, this tendency towards catastrophism coexisted with assertions of the efficacy of social engineering and a con- structionist view of human evolution, under the stewardship of benign technocrats. Peter Dodds, third director of the FPAR had to walk a line in his public pronouncements between pessimism and optimism, propounding the idea that the population crisis was indeed a looming disaster, but that the means – family planning – existed to avert it, and that therefore all that was needed was a commitment of will and resources by the white public.

7. Gilmurray et al. estimated each peasant farmer to require 385 pounds of maize per year. In 1962, 352 pounds of maize were available per person; by 1977 this amount had fallen to 231 pounds (Gilmurray et al. 1979: 18). In 1969, 'on

average each European family has two servants, 76 per cent of European homes
have telephones and 97 per cent have refrigerators'. Whites had universal
free education up to Secondary IV, and had a death rate of 8.2/1,000 (compared
to 11.2/1,000 in the United Kingdom) and an infant mortality rate of 17/1,000
(compared with 16/1,000 in the United Kingdom (ibid: 14–15).

8. Ratio of black to white population:

    1904 – 46:1
    1911 – 31:1
    1941 – 20:1
    1959 – 12:1
    1966 – 17:1
    1975 – 22:1
    1977 – 25:1 (Weinrich 1982: 119)

9. Hooker overstates the case in implying that white Rhodesians had been
    oblivious to African population growth before the census – the long history
    of attempts to regulate African life belies this. But he is correct in saying that
    the census provided irrefutable proof that Africans were increasing in numbers
    and were advancing on the margins of white society.

10. Demographic figures on white emigration were faithfully reprinted in the
    official organ of the Zimbabwe African People's Union (ZAPU, one of the
    two major liberation organizations), as evidence that the war was being won
    by Africans.

11. The author of this piece came to the depressing conclusion that the 'White
    African' could never integrate and live harmoniously with the 'Black African'
    – implying that some form of racial dominance was inevitable, leaving only
    the question of which race would dominate.

12. A letter to the editor from 'Hopeful', in Umtali:

    [T]he whites of Rhodesia are not on trial, the whites are not the ones needing
    to respond. . . . They have already proved themselves. Rhodesia is their
    proof. The whites are responsible for keeping the peace between the various
    black tribes, and through their integrity are responsible for the country's
    orderly development, which has been brought about by the predominance
    of sound judgement, honest endeavour, goodwill and leadership based on
    Christian values. (*Rhodesia Herald*, 8 April 1978)

13. Other aspects of white colonialism, in addition to preventive health care, shared
    some of the blame for creating an African overpopulation problem. Mission-
    aries, who promoted monogamy instead of polygamy, are blamed for
    increasing the number of children per woman; as are urban development
    policies which reserved urban African housing for married couples, thus
    forcing men to marry and have children in order to live in town (Geraty 1974:
    14; Hooker 1971: 6).

14. The construction of 'the African' as being absent from historical time and
    having little sense of causality pervaded Rhodesian popular anthropology. In

this excerpt from *The Man And His Way*, a booklet put out by the Rhodesian Ministry of Information in 1975 to encourage 'understanding between the races' and to help whites relate better to their servants and employees, the following description of African 'timelessness' is tinged with amused benevolence:

> During generations of endurance, he [the African] has acquired a passive fatalism . . . There was nothing he could do to avoid it [misfortune], so he gave no thought for tomorrow. He conserved his energies and blamed everything bad on something else. How often do we hear 'I was failed by the examination' rather than 'I failed'! . . . The African loves laughter. His needs are few and when he has satisfied them he is inclined to sit back. After all, time is given to men for nothing. It has no value, so why do today what can be put off to tomorrow? Land and water have also been put here for the free use of mankind, so they, like time, can be wasted. Let tomorrow take care of itself! . . . How then should we deal with this man? We should remember his background and treat him with patience and courtesy. (Rhodesia Ministry of Information 1975: 4–5)

References

Castle, W.M. and K.E. Sapire (1976), 'The pattern of African acceptance of family planning facilities in relation to social class', *South African Medical Journal*, 50: 965–8.

Clarke, D.G. (1971), 'Population and family planning in the economic development of Rhodesia', *Zambezia*, 2: 11–22.

Comaroff, J. and J. Comaroff (1992), 'Home-made hegemony; modernity, domesticity and colonialism in South Africa', in K.T. Hanson (ed.), *African Encounters with Domesticity*, New Brunswick: Rutgers University Press, pp. 38–74.

Cooper, F. and A. Stoler (1989), 'Tensions of empire: colonial control and visions of rule', *American Ethnologist*, 16: 601–40.

Davies, C.S. (1970), 'Tribalism and economic development' *Native Affairs Department Annual*, 10(2): 78–83.

Davin, A. (1978), 'Imperialism and motherhood', *History Workshop*, 5: 9–64.

Dodds, P. (1977), 'The community and family planning', *Rhodesia Science News*, 11: 314–16.

—— (1978), 'Family planning in Africa', *Rhodesia Science News*, 12: 160–3.

Dunlop, H. (1975), 'The publications of the Tribal Areas of Rhodesia Research Foundation', *Zambezia*, 4(2) (unpaginated).

Geraty, A. (1974), 'A population policy in a multicultural community', *Rhodesia Science News*, 8: 8–17.

Gilmurray, J., R. Riddell and D. Sanders (1979), *The Struggle for Health: From Rhodesia to Zimbabwe Vol.7.*, Salisbury (Harare): Mambo Press.

Hanks, J. (1973), 'The population problem in Rhodesia and the consequences of unlimited growth', *Rhodesia Science News*, 7: 249-56.

—— (1975), 'Population problems in Rhodesia', *Rhodesia Science News*, 9 (pagination unknown).

Hanson, K.T. (ed.) (1992), *African Encounters with Domesticity*, New Brunswick: Rutgers University Press.

Hooker, J.R. (1971), 'Population planning in Rhodesia 1971', *American Universities Field Staff Reports: Central and Southern Africa*, 15(6): 1–9.

Hunt, N.R. (1988), 'Le bébé en brouse: European women, African birth spacing and colonial intervention in breastfeeding in the Belgian Congo', *International Journal of African Historical Studies*, 21(3): 401-32.

IDAFSA (International Defense and Aid Fund for Southern Africa) (1977), *Zimbabwe: the Truth About Rhodesia*, London: IDAFSA.

Jeater, D. (1993), *Marriage, Perversion and Power: The Making of a Moral Discourse in Southern Rhodesia 1894–1930*, Oxford: Oxford University Press.

Kaler, A. (1998), *Fertility, Gender and War: The 'Culture of Contraception' in Rhodesia 1965-1980*, Ph.D. thesis, Department of Sociology, University of Minnesota.

McCarthy, E. (1971), 'Communications and family planning', Address to the Rhodesia Science Congress.

Ministry of Health (Rhodesia) (various years), *Annual Report of the Ministry of Health*, Salisbury (Harare): Ministry of Health.

Ministry of Information (Rhodesia) (1975), *The Man and His Ways*, Salisbury (Harare): Ministry of Information.

Philpott, R.H. (1969), *Motives and Methods in Population Control: An Inaugural Lecture Given in the University College of Rhodesia*, Salisbury (Harare): University College of Rhodesia.

Ranchod-Nilssen, S. (1992), 'Educating Eve: the women's club movement and political consciousness among African women in Southern Rhodesia 1950–1980', in K.T. Hanson (ed.) *African Encounters with Domesticity*, New Brunswick: Rutgers University Press, pp. 195–217.

Sapire, K.E. (1971), 'Family planning', *Rhodesia Science News*, 5: 104–10.

Schmidt, E. (1992), *Peasants, Traders and Wives: Shona Women in the History of Zimbabwe 1870–1939*, Hanover: Heinemann.

Spilhaus, P. (1961), 'Family planning', address to Anglo American Corporation medical and welfare officers, Ndanga, Northern Rhodesia (Zambia) October 1961.

Still, E. (1973), 'Problems of family planning in Rhodesia', *Family Planning*, 21(4): 91–5.

Thiesen, R.J. (1977), 'Variables of population growth'. *Zambezia*, 5(2): 161–8.

van Rensburg, N.J. (1972), Population Explosion in Southern Africa. Pretoria: self-published.

Vaughan, M. (1989), 'Measuring a crisis in maternal and child health: an historical perspective', in M. Wright, Z. Stein and J. Scandlyn (eds), *Women's Health and Apartheid: The Health of Women and Children and the Future of*

Progressive Primary Health Care in Southern Africa, Frankfurt: Medico International, pp. 130–42.

Watkins, S. (1993), 'If all we knew about women was what we read in *Demography*, what would we know?' *Demography*, 10: 551–77.

Weinrich, A.H. (1982), *African Marriages in Zimbabwe and the Impact of Christianity*, Harare: Mambo Press.

West, M. (1994), 'Nationalism, race and gender: the politics of family planning in Zimbabwe 1957–1990', *Social Science and Medicine,* 7(3): 447–71.

Wilmoth, J. and P.R. Ball (1992), 'The population debate in American popular magazines, 1946–1990', *Population and Development Review*, 18: 631–48.

Rhodesia Herald, various articles.

5

A Clinic in Conflict: A Political Economy Case Study of Family Planning in Haiti

M. Catherine Maternowska

> Perhaps the most critical transaction of all in family planning programs is that between the program and the client, for all others ultimately revolve around that nexus. If this transaction fails, the program will fail with it. Warwick (1982: 183)

There had been no electricity in Haiti for month-long stretches during the embargo of 1994; 30 March was no exception. I am visiting clients and staff at a family planning centre built for the residents of *Cité Soleil*, a desperate slum community in this, the poorest country in the western hemisphere. Inside the clinic it is a typical afternoon: hot, sticky and very still. The staff sit on their metal folding chairs, staring blankly, waiting for the doctors to arrive. The nurse, preparing cotton balls and alcohol, exclaims that it's too hot to move. Nine women from the community, referred to by the staff as *kliyan* (clients), sit on hard wooden benches in the waiting room. Some are dressed in clothes reserved for Sunday mass and doctor's visits. Others are too poor and they wear rags. All have come to the clinic for more pills, another DepoProvera shot, or relief from irregular bleeding or itching and burning 'down there'. Each hopes that the doctor will allay her discomfort.

Upstairs is where the doctors see clients. The two Haitian doctors are tall and heavy by national standards. They always look neat and cool when they arrive in their crisp clothing and inevitably they too comment on how hot the clinic is. They speak impeccable French. Their Creole, unlike that of the poor women who attend the clinic, is studded with French phrases, confirming that they are both urban-born and educated. One of the doctors marks his clients' charts with a fancy gold pen.

The two examining rooms are small and sparse. The rooms are filled with the din from *Route Nationale 1*, Haiti's major thoroughfare.

Sometimes when the articulated lorries honk, it is so loud that both the doctor and client wince. The stifling rooms are coated with a layer of dust from the *Cité* that seeps in through the window slats. Since electricity is not a constant on *Cité Soleil*'s grid, the old examining lamps have been pushed into the corner. For light, the doctors crank open the slatted windows, positioning the rays of sunlight on their clients' groins.

I am poised in my anthropologist-researcher role: observation form in hand, a tape recorder perched on the desk. Conversations are recorded and actions noted during each interaction I observe.[1] Individual family planning clients shuffle in and out of the doctors' room, sometimes as many as sixty per doctor per afternoon. Today, Yvonne enters, with some hesitancy. She is 24 years old, unemployed, and the reproductive history scribbled on her chart indicates she has four children. She has come to the clinic for more birth control pills. She stands, nervously clutching her big vinyl purse.

Doctor:	Enter! Have you seen your period?
Client:	Yes.
D:	When did it come?
C:	It comes every twenty-eight days.
D:	It came today?
C:	No it hasn't come yet.
D:	Because – you were supposed to come on the 16th and you didn't come.
C:	I couldn't come, I was busy that day.
D:	But if you don't have your period, I can't give you the pills.
C:	But it will come anyhow.
D:	It's not an affair of waiting, *madame*. It must be here for me to give you the pills. It's been fourteen days since you have taken the pills, and where is your period?
C:	I took them. It was two packets of pills that you gave me.
D:	It wasn't two packets, it was only one, *madame*.
C:	Well, maybe you didn't mark it, I took two. I still had pills, that's why I didn't come earlier.
D:	[Mumbling to himself] She took one packet in January, one packet in February, I marked it.
C:	I took two packets in January.
D:	But if you took two packets – I'll tell you a little thing. If you took two packets in January, you should have come in early March. So where do you fall now? On your head or what?

C: I haven't fallen. It seems like you didn't mark it because you gave me two packets.

D: [Throwing the chart at her] Where do you see that? Where do you see that?

C: Then – [shaking, she reaches into her purse, for an empty packet].

D: Well, it's finished. For that matter – are you taking them at home, where's the other packet? Where is it, huh? If it's two you have, huh?

            So, you don't have your period, you missed your appointment and you're not taking your pills. I'm giving you condoms, *madame*. When you have your period come here again. If you don't want condoms, tell me rapidly that you're not OK with this.

C: You can give them to me.

D: When your period arrives you'll come here.

C: Yes.

D: OK.

In the last minute of the transaction, with the client still present, the doctor, exasperated, writes on a tiny piece of paper, '*The Black Jacobins* by C.L.R. James' and slides it over to me, asking if I have read this definitive account of the Haitian Revolution of 1791–1803. I nod yes, perplexed by the reference to the book during the encounter. He raises his finger and says, 'one minute'. He finishes with the client and sends her from the room, then looks to me. He says,

'Do you remember in the book, there is a slave, those slaves they were stupid and they lied, they could easily keep you in their lies. The slave he stole a pigeon, he put it in his shirt and his master catches him. His master says, "You stole that pigeon!" The slave denies it, saying "I don't know how that pigeon got underneath my shirt!" and the pigeon is flapping wildly inside his shirt.

Do you understand? Their mentality hasn't changed. It's the same thing with this woman, she's so stupid that – that she says she took two packets of pills but she didn't. Oh! It's all the same, they're still stupid, they still lie and they're still slaves! That woman, she can't read, she's nothing.

The referenced passage in *The Black Jacobins* varies slightly but significantly from this doctor's version. In the historical account, the master who accuses the slave of stealing is the same man who had minutes before *sent* the slave to steal the pigeon; without warning, 'the master orders him a punishment of 100 lashes to which the slave submits without a murmur' (James 1989: 15). The doctor's insights are uncanny. Later, when I check a daily register of clinic data, I see that the doctor had in fact prescribed two packets of pills for Yvonne. In the consultation, as in the paraphrased passage, the doctor fails to account for his own mistake and punishes the client for it, denying her her preferred method of contraception or a reasonable alternative.

Yvonne's encounter, like the 153 others I observed, encapsulates how the doctor-client relationship is a domain where ideology — ideas and doctrines of a distinctive perspective — is reproduced. The asymmetrical relationship, including an infallible and therefore blaming doctor and the initially challenging client who, in the end, had no choice but to agree with the accusations made against her, reflects and replicates the dominating structures that reverberate throughout Haitian society. In this way, as Waitzkin contends, 'Medical encounters become micropolitical situations that reflect and support broader social relations, including social class and political-economic power' (1991: 9). Treatment such as Yvonne received is not unusual in Haiti. It conforms to the society's dominant expectations about appropriate behaviour towards the poor, behaviour that the majority of Haitians have endured for nearly 300 years.

Doctors generally represent a small slice of Haiti's privileged class. Clients in the clinic I studied are primarily landless peasants who migrated to this waterlogged urban community for lack of other choices. To challenge what goes on during the doctor-client encounter inside the family planning clinic is, ultimately, to challenge the social conditions in Haiti, including a vast class disparity, social hierarchy and, primarily, poverty.

Moving beyond the conventional ways of assessing family planning practice, this chapter applies a political economy of fertility framework to situations observed within the clinic setting. Viewing reproductive behaviour within the wider context of Haiti's political economy brings a grounded perspective to the clinical encounter revealing reasons for resistance to contraceptive use that transcend traditional public health issues.

A Political Economy of Fertility

Employing anthropology's use of the term political economy, Greenhalgh (1990, 1994: 17) was the first to propose a political economy of fertility: a demography that 'contextualize[s] reproductive behaviour not only in the social and economic terms of conventional demographic theory, but in political and cultural terms as well'. This framework is expanded here to analyse family planning practice *in situ*. I examine the Port-au-Prince community of *Cité Soleil* and its family planning programme as they interact and respond to national and international forces. In this way, what happens to poor women and men in *Cité Soleil* is directly linked to international health and development policy makers' decisions in places such as Washington, D.C. This union of global and local perspectives highlights what Ginsburg and Rapp (1991: 313; also see 1995) call the 'politics of reproduction' and explicates the multiple levels on which reproductive practices, policies and politics so often depend. This framework views reproduction – including gender relations, fertility strategies and efforts to control birth – as a process determined by larger forces and constantly in flux.

There are several elements central to a political economy of fertility analysis, all of which have generally been considered separately in demographic analyses of societies and communities, and rarely as the syncretic mix proposed here. They include history, culture and power. History, and all of the political nuances that shape it, plays an important role in a political economy analysis because it raises the question of the relationship of fertility and family planning practice to colonialism, neocolonialism and the powerful international institutions that have resulted from these periods. The historical evolution and implications of a unidimensional reproductive health policy in Haiti, with family planning as its sole intervention, have shaped the contours of what is now a faltering sector. Examination of the policy over time reveals how international medical and political ideologies have suppressed and deformed national – and local – interests and needs.

Culture, or the socially transmitted behaviour patterns, beliefs, institutions, and processes of a given population or community, is also central to this political economic analysis. A notable trend in evaluation and survey reports and general assessments of fertility and family planning programmes written by field experts is to cite 'culture' as a largely indefinable and problematic notion.[2] Cultural barriers, cultural attitudes, cultural preferences, cultural practices, and cultural traditions are all noted as obstacles and yet most demographic theory, policy or evaluation does little to explain these processes or how they impact women's lives. Even less is known about the medical culture that determines how programmes function. Greenhalgh (1994) suggests it is essential to 'untangle' these cultural processes.

Power, a third crucial variable in political economic analysis, is generally absent from most demographic theories of fertility. One main reason for demographers' failure to acknowledge power has been the inability to standardize measurement of this seemingly abstract force. Yet an understanding of the meaning, articulation and impact of power relations can shed light on previously misunderstood fertility strategies. Research in medical anthropology has shown that people who live in oppressive situations (i.e. people who lack power) devise undermining strategies to survive in a system that oppresses them (Martin 1987; Morgan 1987; Rapp 1988; Singer et al. 1988; Farmer 1995). One way to examine the effect of power differentials is to investigate their expression in the micro-context of the medical world, for example in studies of how doctors exercise power over patients (Waitzkin 1979, 1991; Taussig 1980; Zola 1985; Fisher 1986; Todd 1989). Inversely, patients too can exert power over doctors by refusing to use the method prescribed, or by seeking the help of indigenous healers who often successfully treat fertility, infertility or side-effects in ways that the clinic cannot. As this chapter will show, the clinic can serve as the microcosm for the analysis of power relations as they are played out in society.

Methods and Analysis

Ten years (1985–1995) of observing clinical procedure and practice in the family planning centre provides the basis for this in-depth clinic analysis.[3] Participants in the study included the two doctors working at the clinic, women between the ages of 15 and 45 years attending the clinic as new or continuing clients and the clinic's other staff members. Sampling for the interactions was done by designating every third client who entered the doctor's office as eligible for observation. This was the most efficient alternative to strict random sampling since it was impossible to assign random numbers to an undetermined number of clients daily. Over half (eleven) of the staff members – the director of the clinic, two doctors, two nurses and six family planning promoters – were also interviewed using a loosely structured interview guideline. Considerable time was spent talking informally with staff members, asking questions about values, attitudes and practices, thus gaining a sense of the social world of the clinic. Two staff meetings were attended and tape-recorded.

The doctor-client interactions cited in this chapter were also tape-recorded over a period of four months and transcribed for later analysis. Observation forms based on the work of Simmons (1991) were used to assist in the standardization of data collected during the interaction. Information on the form included participant's names, the client's clinic number (for follow-up and verification of data), method(s) used/requested,

reason for the visit, interpersonal relations during the exchange, physical
setting, procedures and duration of the visit. With the assistance of
family planning promoters, reproductive and contraceptive histories
were recorded while the client waited for her appointment.

A total of 108 transcripts of medical interviews, blending taped
discourse with more impressionistic ethnographic data, were gathered.
Forty-six additional observations of doctor-client interactions were
completed, without the benefit of tape-recording but with observation
notes, making a total sample of doctor-client interactions of 154.

In the clinic, both manifest and latent dimensions of observed medical
encounters (Simmons and Elias 1994) were analysed. The line that divides
that which is 'readily apparent' – the manifest dimensions – and that which
is 'relatively hidden' – the latent dimensions – is not clear-cut. For
example, when a doctor ignores a client's complaint and/or a voiced desire
to change methods, we may note the manifest dimensions of courtesy
and choice. At the same time, we may note a latent dimension, such as a
doctor's backhanded use of power or authority to control a client, the
information supplied to her, and her choice of method.

In this analysis, manifest dimensions considered are courtesy during
the encounter, duration of the exchange in the clinic, and choice. Latent
dimensions are considerably more difficult to operationalize. Unlike
manifest dimensions they cannot be quantified. Here they are defined as
indicators of power such as status, authority, the control of information
and knowledge within the socio-economic, cultural and medical contexts
of an encounter. Latent dimensions creep into encounters in very subtle
ways and, as this analysis shows, rarely appear as sole indicators of power
differentials.

Cité Soleil and the Family Planning Centre

The setting for this local analysis, *Cité Soleil*, is a large urban neighbour-
hood on the northern border of Port-au-Prince, the capital of Haiti. The
population is densely packed into an area covering 5 km^2 (de Zaluando
et al. 1995). Although health and social services including religious
organizations, international non-governmental organizations and even
US-funded university public health research have been provided to this
community since the 1950s, its residents remain locked in absolute and
abject poverty (de Zaluando *et al.* 1995).

In 1998, per capita GDP for Haiti overall was $231, a figure that has
decreased since the mid-1990s when this family planning research was
completed (UNDP 1998). A lack of infrastructure, including the most

basic amenities such as potable water, latrines and electricity, adds to the generally deplorable conditions. Residents suffer – and die – from chronic and often untreated ill-health. Surveys show that the principal causes of mortality in *Cité Soleil* include diarrhoea and AIDS (Lerebours and Canez 1992). In 1994, maternal mortality in the capital of Port-au-Prince was recorded at 1,210 per 100,000 births, making it one of the highest rates worldwide (UNFPA 1994).

The Family Planning Centre of *Cité Soleil* first opened its doors to the area's poor in September 1983. At that time illegal abortions were on the rise, and family planning was a relatively new concept to this community. Family health surveys done in 1981 and 1983 indicated that residents, particularly women, wanted access to modern methods of birth control (Boulos 1985). The clinic relocated twice during its history. Although the clinic under study is now defunct, its final location was a spacious split-level building, well located next to the busiest entrance to the community. The clinic was extravagant by local standards with running water, an occasional flicker of electricity and large, imposing metal gates to protect it from vandals.

The Clientele

During my fieldwork, in the mid-1990s, the population of *Cité Soleil* was estimated to be between 180,000 and 200,000 (Despagne 1994). Based on an estimated 10 to 15 per cent use of contraception among women of reproductive age countrywide (CHI/CDC 1991), the clinic should have been providing services for approximately 4,500 to 6,500 women. In fact, the numbers attending were considerably lower, with less than 1,500 regular users. Fewer clients were attending than in previous years, when the family planning centre was located in a nearby house in much more cramped quarters (Burton 1993). The actual number of users countrywide was no more encouraging, the contraceptive prevalence rate of 10 per cent in Haiti (up 4 per cent since 1981), comparing to 56 per cent in the Dominican Republic, 55 per cent in Jamaica, 59 per cent in Peru, 30 per cent in Bolivia, 41 per cent in Honduras, and 47 per cent in El Salvador (UNICEF 1994: 76; UNFPA 1994: 2).[4]

The International Planned Parenthood Federation (IPPF), an international agency that helped fund clinic activities, claimed it was 'unclear' whether a lower proportion of women in *Cité Soleil* actually practised family planning than the 10 to 15 per cent rate reported nationally by the CDC, or whether women were going elsewhere for services (Burton 1993). Either way, it was clear that services were not filling the said 'need' in *Cité Soleil*.[5] Yet more money was poured into this clinic, and IPPF reported that the cost per user in *Cité Soleil* was one of the highest among programmes they funded.[6] IPPF investigated the problem and attributed the low number of users to declining quality of services and 'in particular very poor patient/provider interaction' (Burton 1993: 2).

Quality of Care and the Medical Encounter

The provider-client interaction is one element of what is now a widely accepted quality of care framework (Bruce 1989), and rightly so since such interactions generally form the centrepiece of any programme's activity (Simmons 1991). Yet research addressing the actual doctor-client encounter in the family planning setting, particularly in developing countries, has been curiously avoided, although this is where patients often bring their most intimate and troubling problems. A close-up look at the dimensions of these encounters, however, uncovers reasons for low rates of contraceptive use, dissatisfaction and poor communication. All of these are issues central to the quality – and failure – of medical care (Lazarus 1988) in this clinic.

The Manifest Dimensions in the Encounter

Courtesy, Time and Choice: Respect or Neglect? Greetings are an implicit part of Haitian language and are very basic *politesse*, expected of everyone in every setting. Yet they do not occur in the medical encounter in this clinic. Greetings from the doctors of 'hello' (*bonjou/bonswa*) or 'how are you' (*ki jan ou ye*) were given six times in the entire sample of 154 encounters. In many encounters the doctor would merely shout out 'Enter!', thus ordering the next client to the consultation room. The majority of encounters began like this: 'When did you get your period?', 'Have you seen your blood?', 'How many days has your blood been flowing?', 'Did your period come?' Most of the time the doctor would ask these questions without ever glancing at the client.

Time, another manifest dimension, is costly in Haiti. For women, time at the clinic could be time at the market selling, or in the factory producing, or at home tending to the multiple needs of family and extended kin. All these activities are crucial to maintaining the fragile balance in a poor Haitian household. And yet, the average wait before seeing the doctor in this clinic was approximately one hour and four minutes in contrast to the average doctor visit which lasted approximately two minutes.[7] The consultation presented at this chapter's opening was actually 2.4 minutes longer than usual, although very average in tone.

Much of the time expended in the encounter was spent by the doctor writing in the chart, not conversing with the client. For women who had pap smears, the logistics, such as putting on and taking off gloves or smearing a mucus sample on a slide followed by a spray of fixant, involved more time than conversation between doctor and client. First-time visits that included a breast exam and manual pelvic exam averaged only three minutes. Visits that included a pap smear in addition to a resupply[8] of a birth control method were on average four minutes in duration. Overall, clients spent only 3 per cent of their clinic visit time with the doctor. This corroborates Gay's (1980) research in Latin America, which found that time spent with clinicians was often measurable in seconds.

Choice, another manifest dimension, is in the Western view an important indicator of quality of care, so much so that it stands as a separate element in Bruce's (1989) framework. Because several contraceptive clinical trials have occurred in Haiti, Haitian women, particularly in urban areas, have been able to choose from an array of contraceptives long before most North American women have had the equivalent choice.[9]

In the *Cité Soleil* family planning centre, birth control methods are supplied, but at a 'small' cost to the client. As of 1993, methods were priced as follows: condom (H1g), pills (H1g), IUD (H15g), injectables (H5g) and Norplant (H15g).[10] Population planners in Haiti insist that when clients are asked to pay for a method they consider it more valuable.

Haitian women are the first to explain that no cost is a small cost. Once the initial fee is charged, follow-up fees can be even more expensive, particularly when they entail treating side-effects related to method use, getting pregnancy tests if there is fear of method failure, seeking other laboratory procedures requested by the physician, or purchasing antibiotics for STDs. All these costs – both the direct cost of method purchase and the indirect costs of staying on a method – are relatively huge financial burdens and do not constitute true freedom of choice. Simply put, poverty in *Cité Soleil* reduces choices.

Although many methods may be available in the clinic this does not automatically enhance overall quality of care. Meaningful choice is also bound up in a clinic's ability to offer more than just multiple methods and depends equally on clinic capabilities to respond to clients' method-specific needs (Simmons and Elias 1994: 510). While doctors in the family planning centre would usually let a woman state her preferred method, they were typically deaf to these requests, and ultimately they would choose her method. An example of this occurred with Solange, who was 34 years old with five children. This was her first visit to the clinic and she was excited about meeting the doctor. She was smiling when she entered, standing tall, dressed in clean, crisp white blouse, a mid-calf length skirt and second-hand high-top tennis shoes. Her smile quickly faded as the doctor began speaking.

D: When did you have your period?
C: I got it Saturday.
D: It's still there?
C: Yes.
D: Do you get it normally, every month?
C: Yes.
D: When it comes, how many days does it usually last?
C: Five, sometimes six days.
D: Have you ever had family planning from another centre?
C: No.
D: Go downstairs and they will give you the injectable and return on April 25th. Did they explain the method to you?
C: No.
D: Ok, go downstairs and tell them that.
C: Yes, thank you.

Overall, in this sample, the pattern varied little during the course of observation: choice of method was generally determined by the doctor. Some women knew what method they wanted, based on a friend's experience or a conversation with a family planning promoter but the doctors were quick to override any suggestions or options women would present. Although doctors' choices might often have been medically mandated, there was little, if any, discussion with the patient. A curt '*ou pa kapab*' ('you can't') was the typical response to an expression of choice. Deleting choice of contraceptive from the discussion, or failing to elicit information regarding a client's preferred choice, served to reinforce doctors' opinions and thus their authority.

If choice of methods is limited for medical reasons then counselling and providing clear, simple information to clients takes on pronounced importance. However, sending clients away from the clinic without their chosen method of birth control, even if only temporarily, and without an explanation as to why the choice was denied, happens frequently in this setting. New clients are particularly susceptible to this clinic practice. For example, women who are not menstruating (and therefore, due to clinic protocol, cannot begin a method[11]) are often sent from the clinic, typically defeated, with a stack of condoms in their hand.[12] Although they are told to return when they are menstruating, clients are rarely counselled as to why.

Choice, in this clinic and most others in Haiti, is typically quantified, measured through inventories of contraceptive stock and commodities. But the observed encounters show that, as a variable, choice is equally qualitative, and failing to address it may lead to client dissatisfaction.

The Hidden Dimensions in the Encounter

The Class Divide: The Socio-Economic Context of Encounters   Power, or lack of it, in an encounter can be viewed in relation to status, authority and knowledge, all latent dimensions that imbue almost every aspect of doctor-client interactions in this family planning setting. Divides between doctors and clients appear in different guises – social, economic and cultural – and stem from a general failure of doctors 'to criticize the social structural roots of their clients' distress, especially the sources of suffering in class structure' (Waitzkin 1991: 22).

Witness the encounter of Desermite, who came to the clinic for an injection of Depo-Provera. Carrying her baby on her hip, she entered the examination room with a sad air about her. Frail and worn looking, an angular face framed her large eyes. Her worn dress was limp, hanging off her bony shoulders and fastened with a loosely knotted rope. She was 24 years old, and returned to the clinic following the birth of her child. Her baby, visibly thin with splotches of hair, clung to her skinny arm.

D: Have you seen your period?
C: A little bit of blood came.
D: A small amount?
C: Correct.
D: Are you breastfeeding, you are taking vitamins, right?
C: Well, I don't want to breastfeed anymore.
D: You must breastfeed.
C: But, it makes me thin.
D: You're eating, taking vitamins?
C: If you find vitamins, but if you don't have money?
D: But you can't just leave him, when you have a child, especially if he's not yet vaccinated, you have to breastfeed to protect him from diarrhoea, to stop the *mikrob* [microbes, germs] from attacking.

C: I'm resigned, I'll take the injectable again.

D: But, but no.

C: I'll take him off the breast, so that I can take that thing.

D: You have to start feeding him, give him lots of liquids, mash up some vegetables and beans and you, eat an egg a day.

C: Where am I going to find these things?

D: How much money do you have?

C: I have five *gourdes*, I have to pay for the injectable and then I am left with nothing.

D: They'll ask for five *gourdes*, but you should make a case for only one [*gourde*]. Go downstairs.

The woman had come, looking for support, wanting to halt her own fast demise brought on by the strains of breastfeeding, hunger and poverty.[13] She also tried to contextualize her condition: her baby that appeared to be dying from malnutrition, she feared another pregnancy and was worried over her wasting body. She received advice that had little to do with her immediate reality; her circumstances were reduced to a biological event. She worked to bring the conversation back to her reality: 'If you find vitamins. But if you don't have money?' and her even more resolute question about the expensive foods recommended – 'where am I going to find these?'

What was particularly poignant about this encounter was that it occurred in the midst of the devastating economic embargo that had, in addition to increasing the poverty of clinic clients, financially-speaking wiped clean almost every market vendor in *Cité Soleil*, a community normally jammed with vendors vying for space, selling everything from herbal medicines to underwear. Many types of food simply were not available – at any price. Almost all women in this study were lucky if they had three meals weekly, not daily. To suggest vegetables, beans and eggs daily was preposterous even for an elite doctor who at some level also had to be feeling the pinch of the embargo. For a poor woman to 'make a case' (to pay less than the staff were asking), as the doctor suggested, was equally absurd since clients, like most Haitian citizens, do not own such rights.

Hermite, another client, entered for a consultation. She was experiencing side-effects from the injectable. A large and commanding market woman, she looked directly at the doctor, even though he looked at her only at the end of the encounter when he gave her directions to the nurse's station. During the encounter Hermite almost immediately launched into the subject of persistent bleeding, clearly affecting her ability to market: 'But the injectable, it gave me bad cramps and my period flowed and flowed and flowed, it wouldn't stop, I couldn't sit, I couldn't do anything, the other doctor he gave me pills to take and they did nothing for me'. Writing in the chart, the doctor responded, 'It [the injectable] can make your period flow more but it doesn't give you cramps.' The client pressed, recounting her experience with the method, although she was ignored. This type of situation occurred repeatedly during observations. Indeed not all clients are entirely diminished in the presence of the physician and some, like Hermite, will challenge their power. But clients rarely win in this situation. Typically, clients who do not receive answers upstairs with the doctors will try again downstairs with the nurses, who are less elite than the doctors, but still educated and experienced enough to preserve their standing in the social pecking order of the clinic. Though the nurse's response is slightly more informative, clients are still met with a measurable degree of contempt and leave the clinic with unresolved problems, or worse, misunderstandings regarding their health.

The implications of heavy bleeding for many Haitian women are unsettling, particularly in the context of an economy that offers so little. A Norplant user, for example, explained her excessive bleeding in terms of too many costs: physical costs because it made her weak and the economic costs due to time spent washing her undergarments (which therefore lasted half as long) which, in turn, cut into valuable market selling time and drained daily finances just to pay for soap. Finally there were serious social costs because her husband refused to tolerate the bleeding and left her for another woman.

What was clear from the observed encounters was that authority, medically and technically informed, took precedence over the patients' concerns or reality. Fisher and Todd (1986: 8) state it well: 'Patients rely on medical practitioners as authorities and medical providers act like authorities.' Responding in a technical way, or not at all, is much easier than confronting the real problems women bring to the encounter. As Waitzkin (1991: 76) argues: 'The structure of medical discourse tends to marginalize the contextual sources of personal distress.'

The Cultural Divide: Belittling Beliefs   Women's economic, physical and time concerns had little currency for the doctors. When clients brought in concerns related to indigenous cultural beliefs and practices the divisions grew even more vast. Repeatedly, a whole array of beliefs and fears related to menstruation, birth and birth control were dismissed by physicians.

Marie Marthe entered the consultation room. She was holding a large straw hat and clutching the brim nervously as she spoke to the doctor. She was 32 years old and had been a client for over two years. She came to the clinic to resupply her pills but expressed considerable concern about a condition called *move san*:

C: Well, when I have *move san* I feel bad and I can't eat.
D: You don't have *move san, madame.*
C: I wasn't sure. I thought maybe the pills were giving me that.
D: It's not the pills. So, is it one packet of pills you'll take this time?

Move san, literally 'bad blood', 'Begins as a disorder of the blood, but may rapidly spread throughout the body so that head, limbs, eyes, skin and uterus may all be affected. It most frequently strikes adult women . . . Although considered pathological, *move san* is not an uncommon response to emotional upsets. The disorder is seen as requiring treatment, and this is often effected by locally prepared herbal medicines. Untreated or unsuccessfully treated, course and outcome are reported to be dismal.' (Farmer 1988: 62)

In another encounter, a client expressed concern with her incessant bleeding caused by *tay ouvè*, literally translated as 'open waist'.[14] *Tay ouvè* is, according to informants, closely associated with blood loss so severe that it prevents women from being able to bear children, a deeply damaging social stigma among Haitians. Low back stress from carrying heavy loads or excessive work can lead to this condition. Treatments with local 'leaf doctors' consist of massages with macerations made of sour oranges followed by wrapping the waist to 'close' it. Left untreated it is said to render women incapable of carrying a child to term. Immediately, the doctor dismissed her self-diagnosis as impossible: '*Tay ouvè* never makes you bleed like that.'

During another encounter, a client made several excuses to avoid a pelvic exam, which the doctor found amusing: 'It's an excuse! She's scared a cold wind will enter inside her!' he said to me, smirking. When a Haitian woman gives birth, as this client did only six weeks earlier, she is 'opened up' and takes great care to not *pran fredi* ('take in the cold'). In addition to special diets, dress and bathing vapours, only certain kinds of activities are warranted until closure is complete. A cloth covers the vagina and the vaginal region is washed twice daily for forty days. To open oneself up to any other elements is extremely dangerous.

Generally, cultural concerns, much like clients' socio-economic plights, were dealt with by interruptions, cut-offs, shifts in tone of voice, or silence. Doctor's negative or mocking reactions are critical as they determine whether these clients will return for more family planning. When doctors fail to understand women's difficulties, let alone acknowledge women's concerns, then the family planning process becomes a deeply disem-powering one.

The Reality of Side-Effects

Side-effects range from merely bothersome to severely debilitating for women everywhere and typically lead to low rates of contraceptive use. In this realm, the discrepancy between what doctors heard and/or diagnosed and what clients said was striking. According to what the doctors in *Cité Soleil* recorded in their charts, only 12 per cent (13 out of 108) of the observed women reported side-effects. Yet, the actual transcriptions revealed that 40 per cent (41 out of 108) had actually reported and enquired about them – often at length – though returning to the clinic for more contraceptives was the main reason recorded for the visit.

Irregular bleeding was the side-effect most frequently cited by clients. In this clinic, dismissal of irregular bleeding as a meaningful problem was common and did little to encourage clients. Repeatedly, during the collection of data, clients brought their fears, complaints and concerns to the doctor, only to be met with scorn. The rules of social hierarchy in Haiti dictate that those from the *klas pòv* ('poor class') do not normally ask questions of a *moun rich* ('rich person').[15] Frequently, clients worked around this by citing examples or mentioning concerns related to methods, though even this tactic yielded little in the way of a response or information.

When Ginette, a 27-year-old new client with five children, came to the clinic, her anxiety about using Norplant was totally disregarded.

> C: I won't be 'emptying out'? [reference to her blood] I know another woman and she bled for eighteen months straight! Without stopping! She had the five-year method, it emptied her entire body.
>
> D: OK, when you return Monday. You will see the nurse downstairs, for Norplant.
>
> C: Please, excuse me?
>
> D: For the five-year method. Go see the nurse downstairs. OK.

Sonite, 22 years old, a continuing client using pills, visited the doctor because she hadn't had her period in over four months. She was visibly nervous during the consultation, shifting from side to side, hoping the doctor would offer some resolution to her problem. Her pleading inquiries evoked a stern, paternalistic response.

C: What I am saying is, if a person doesn't have their period, can you give that person pills to make the period flow?

D: *Madame.* Look, let me ask you a question: what is a period?

C: [laughing nervously] No, I think it can be a real problem, if someone used to get their period and 'Plap!' it's gone.

D: OK, let me ask you this, when you were a child and you didn't have a period, did it do anything to you?

C: It didn't do anything because I hadn't yet arrived at the proper age.

D: OK, when you become an old person, fifty or so, you're not twenty anymore, how come you don't have a period?

C: I really think that if you don't have your period it's a problem.

D: There are people who have an operation and remove the entire uterus, you have heard of it? And they don't have a period. Do you see that they die from that? What method do you want, pills again?

In both cases, Ginette and Sonite challenged the doctors' authority and yet, doctors were unable to cope when problems could not be technically fixed.

Sexually Transmitted Diseases

Sometimes, what are perceived as side-effects from contraceptive methods are actually due to sexually transmitted diseases (STDs). STDs are common in this population, as they often are where poverty forms the grid of life. Normally, STD screening was not part of the regular service provided to women in the clinic. However, an STD prevalence study was underway during part of the fieldwork period and so the clients in the family planning centre benefitted from the temporary change in protocol.

Preliminary results of the study showed a high prevalence of many STDs, greater than 60 per cent in the community (CDS 1993). STDs are a grave health risk for men and women in *Cité Soleil* (de Zaluando *et al.* 1995) and yet the approach in the family planning centre to the research was perfunctory at best. During each exam, the language was elliptical. In one instance, the doctor explained the STD study like this,

Tuesday you come here and I will do an exam for you. I'll pass a small stick over your country [vagina[16]], to examine, because they are doing research on the sick and things like that. You understand?

Sometimes, although not always, the doctor named what he could see – *ti sèvesit*, a 'little cervicitis', for example. No information about the disease, its severity, outcome or treatment options was ever provided. More often he stated, '*Madame*, you have an infection.' The clients always responded 'yes', though they appeared confused, frightened and notably anxious. In follow-up interviews, some clients said they neither understood the origin nor meaning of their STD, which could have serious – even deadly – consequences in the long run. Doctors rarely addressed the implications for the other sexual partner, except to say 'don't have sex' or 'have your husband wear a condom.'

> D: What to do. Take tetracycline. If you buy eighty tetracycline you take two in the morning, at noon you take two, in the afternoon you take two – are you listening to what I am telling you? – and in the evening you take two.
>
> C: In the morning I take two?
>
> D: Like I have written here. Just buy it. The other thing is a cream that you put inside. There are six suppositories in a box. You buy it in the pharmacy. At *Pharmacie Valliere* you can find it.
>
> C: What's it called?
>
> D: You get it wet and then you put it inside. If you have your period don't use it. And when you put it in, don't have any sexual relations, no sex.
>
> C: Yes, if I have, wait until my period? Before I . . . ?
>
> D: You'll look to see how many times to take it.

Similar in content to countless other encounters, the doctor failed to identify the STD (this client had candida and gonorrhoea) and he did not take the required time to explain the treatment effectively. The doctor also assumed that the woman could read instructions, forgetting that most of his clients are illiterate. Even more disturbing, filling the prescription was nearly impossible. The cost of a single Tetracycline prescription – approximately $US48 – at the time was as high as half an average household's yearly income.

Both of the other recommendations – not having sex or demanding the use of a condom – assume that women have control and rights within the reproductive and sexual realms of their lives. But they do not. As the following quote shows, STDs, like problematic side-effects, function as symbols of social incapacity, bringing to the foreground how disease undermines poor women on so many fronts. Marie Ange, a resident in *Cité Soleil*, clarified this, describing what is a 'right' for women:

Oh sure, you've got the right to ask them to put on a condom, and when they don't want to, then you don't want to. It's not a matter of insisting because they beat you, this is the progress that women have made. They beat you, they sleep with you, they *mawon* you [literally 'maroon', to flee into hiding], and you are left pregnant.

Even more telling were the comments the doctor made after the patient left the room. I asked:

CM: Do you always choose tetracycline for gonorrhoea?

D: Not always because there are lots of choices for STDs. It depends on their economic means. Tetracycline is the best buy. You give it as necessary, between 80 and 120 pills per treatment.

CM: Is that the normal dose, eight pills a day for ten days or more? Are there side-effects?

D: Well you can have side-effects but you have them eat when they take it, out of necessity. Or you can give them Canistotine [unclear] 250 mg a one-time shot and you're finished. But it costs $45 a box plus the syringe. It's all a choice.

It was all a choice in the doctor's mind, but for poor clients, there is very little, if any, choice at all.

Life in *Cité Soleil* for a woman with a reproductive or sexually-related infection is infinitely more complicated than the way doctors saw it. Emilienne reminded me of how the poor cope with their severely limited options. Twenty-six years old, with two children and no steady partner, she visited the clinic for what she thought might be an infection. She looked frightened, twisting a pink plastic shopping sack around her hands as she spoke to me. 'Are you a doctor?' she asked, her eyebrows tightly knit. She showed me how a poor household tries to manage sickness: 'I have no money and I am sick, that's why I am selling these.' Inside the dirty bag were her four year-old daughter's little shoes. 'They're used,' she said, looking down.

Revisiting a Political Economy of Fertility

This chapter has shown how low contraceptive use is far more than a simple 'quality of care' or 'contraception uptake' issue. When critically analysed, medical encounters show how contraceptive behaviour is influenced by a myriad of forces. Attempts to improve this clinic have centred almost exclusively on the technology and its most efficient delivery. But more flipcharts, speculae or family planning promoters will do little to change the complex and deeply embedded structural issues that give shape to women's contraception-related experiences.

In the clinic, the micro-politics of reproductive medicine reveal how the family planning process is an entirely alienating and disempowering experience. The small percentage of women who withstand community and household pressures and decide to use family planning are not rewarded for their perseverance. The power that providers claim in the encounter reminds clients that they are unworthy, even 'animals', a descriptive used to castigate one client who wanted to discontinue her method. Because doctors' directive power is so forceful, clients are systematically denied information they need to participate actively in their reproductive health. If anything, these encounters serve to remind poor Haitian women of their marginalization. Confirming my claim to the strength of a political economy analysis, addressing power, culture and history, Marguerite summed up her reasons for quitting the pill: '*paske li te esklave m*' ('because it enslaved me').

One of the great claims of family planning is that it empowers women and men to make choices and control their own fertility. In *Cité Soleil*, the quality of the programme and its relationship with the community do little to support that claim. Rather than helping clients gain control of their reproductive lives, this programme has effectively prohibited the poor from broadening their base of power or gaining social support for their decision to use contraceptives.

Family planning use in this community, however, is not confined to the clinic but bound up in power relations that extend far beyond those between doctor and client. Many women oppressed in the clinic setting became vocal community organisers, with the support of their partners, once outside the clinic doors. Their collective acts of resistance, including public forums denouncing family planning, and the publication of a booklet criticizing unethical Norplant acceptability trials, garnered significant attention. The results were negative opinions and general distrust regarding the programme, dissuading residents from attending the clinic, and confirming suspicions that the programme was working against the poor. The community's resistance, in reaction to exclusion from decisions that effect their lives, is another potent indicator of why this family planning programme failed to succeed.

This chapter highlights the impact of a family planning programme, in terms defined by the poor, while showing how deliberate contraceptive-related interventions are resulting in an ineffective and dangerous programme of neglect. Applying a political economy framework to assess traditional family planning issues helps analyse programme impacts, situating care-givers and receivers in their larger social, political and economic contexts. When the programme is presented as a political organism, it becomes clear that relations of power in the clinic and the community shape the manner in which health care is both provided and perceived. Incorporating and analysing the multiple layers of power, struggle and resistance clarifies why contraceptive use is so low in this community. The public health challenge is first to acknowledge this reality in its multiple aspects and then to offer family planning and other health programmes that respond as appropriately and humanely as possible.

Notes

1. An interaction, or encounter, in this study is defined as beginning when the client entered the doctor's office and ending when she left.
2. For example, many Haitian men claim they prefer a dry vaginal environment during intercourse. Programmers saw this as a 'cultural barrier' to condom use, yet only lubricated varieties of condoms were made available in the *Cité Soleil* clinic.
3. A more comprehensive study that includes the international, national and local-level power relations that directly affect family planning practice in this community will be contained in a book in progress: *Coups d'Etat and Contraceptives: The Politics of Family Planning in Haiti*. The research for this initial fieldwork was funded by the Interamerican Foundation (1992–1993) and the Rockefeller Foundation (1993–1995).
4. Although representatives from Haiti signed on to the 1994 Cairo declaration, agreeing to establish guidelines for population and reproductive health pro-grammes to be accessible to all by the year 2015, officials admit that 'there is no official mechanism [in place] to implement the Cairo recommendations' (Cooney, personal communication 1999). Simply put, Haiti has no population policy.
5. 'Need' here is defined by population planners – not by poor women – and is based on reaching national contraceptive prevalence targets.
6. As no experts could tell me the actual cost per user in *Cité Soleil*, I made a conservative estimate (based on previous clinic budgets and the current number of users) of approximately US$50 per client – about half the average annual income in *Cité Soleil* at the time of the study.
7. Todd (1989: 15) notes that studies in the United States reveal that the average doctor visit lasts 15.4 minutes, more than seven times longer than the average

visit in the *Cité Soleil* clinic. Still, Todd argues, this does not allow considerable amounts of time to deliver a diagnosis, prognosis and treatment – or to elicit a patient's views on his or her problem.

8. The clinic generally provides women with one packet of pills and asks them to return each month in order to continue with the method, this is commonly referred to as 'resupply'.

9. Several phases of clinical and/or acceptability trials have been completed in Haiti: on pills (1957), Norplant (1985-86) and Quinacrine (allegedly in the 1990s, though not verified first hand by the researcher). The issue of whether an untested or non-FDA approved method is really a 'choice' is questionable where information is generally withheld from clients and clinical research participants.

10. References to currency are based on the Haitian *gourde*. Calculations used throughout the chapter are based on H15g = US$1.00,whereby H1g is approximately equivalent to US$ .067.

11. The clinic protocol requires women to be menstruating when they receive their packet of pills so that doctors can tell women the exact date to begin taking the cycle of pills. Doctors have told me they do not 'trust' women enough to be able to calculate this on their own.

12. Whether the condoms are ever used is another issue. Women indicate that even broaching the topic of condoms could put them at risk, since condoms are associated with sexually transmitted diseases. Haitian men are known to refuse responsibility for carrying infectious diseases and implicating them (by requesting to use a condom) frequently leads to domestic violence or the break-up of a conjugal union.

13. Desermite's references to her health coincide with Farmer's (1988) informants' descriptions of *move san* (bad blood) – a chief cause of *lèt gate*, or spoiled milk, syndrome. The syndrome makes it impossible for a nursing mother to provide her infant quality milk and is commonly cited as a motive for early weaning, generally disastrous for infants who have no other nutritive sources.

14. The waist refers to that region of a woman's body that encompasses her reproductive organs and thus her ability to reproduce.

15. There is an ongoing international controversy around the issue of race in the social sciences, and more recently in public health debates, which I deliberately do not address in this analysis. In Haiti, I would argue that issues of both colour and class have been prominent forces, historically and presently. This study is driven, in part, by a class analysis because participants, especially the poor women, always spoke of class distinctions typically referring to the elite as educated and powerful.

16. Reference to women's genitals as an 'asset', 'land' or 'country' is common in Haiti, suggesting the vital economic importance associated with reproduction.

References

Boulos, R. (1985), Operations Research to Improve Access and Continuation of Family Planning Through Community Based Outreach in Cite Simone, an Urban Slum of Port-au-Prince, Haiti, Final Report, New York: Center for Population and Family Health, Columbia University.

Bruce, J. (1989), 'Fundamental Elements of the Quality of Care: A Simple Framework', *Working Papers,* No. 1, New York: The Population Council.

Burton, N. (1993), 'Memo: CDS Family Planning Program: Recommendations for Consolidation of Activities', Port-au-Prince: Centres pour la Développement et la Santé/USAID.

CDS (1993), 'Preliminary Results: STD Study', Port-au-Prince: Centres pour la Développement et la Santé.

CHI/CDC (Child Health Institute and the Center for Disease Control, Division of Reproductive Health) (1991), 'Haiti National Contraceptive Prevalence Survey 1989', Atlanta: US Department of Health and Human Services.

Cooney, K. (1999), Electronic mail communication with Senior Population Policy advisor, Port-au-Prince, Haiti: United States Agency for International Development.

Despagne, P. (1994), 'PF rapport d'activités du centre de PF', Port-au-Prince: Centres pour la Développement et la Santé.

Farmer, P. (1988), 'Bad Blood, Spoiled Milk: Bodily Fluids as Moral Barometers in Rural Haiti', *American Ethnologist,* 15: 62–83.

—— (1995), 'Culture, Poverty, and the Dynamics of HIV Transmission in Rural Haiti', in H.T. Brummelheis and G. Herdt (eds), *Culture and Sexual Risk: Anthropological Perspectives on AIDS,* New York: Gordon and Breach.

Fisher, S. (1986), *In the Patient's Best Interest: Women and the Politics of Medical Decisions,* New Brunswick: Rutgers University Press.

—— and A.D. Todd (1986), *Discourse and Institutional Authority: Medicine, Education, and Law,* New Jersey: Ablex Publishing Corporation.

Gay, J. (1980), 'A Literature Review of the client-provider interface in maternal and child health and family planning clinics in Latin America', paper prepared for the Pan-American Health Organization/World Health Organization.

Ginsburg, F. and R. Rapp (1991), 'The Politics of Reproduction', *Annual Review of Anthropology,* 20: 311-43.

—— (eds) (1995), *Conceiving the New World Order: The Global Politics of Reproduction,* Berkeley: University of California Press.

Greenhalgh, S. (1990), 'Toward a Political Economy of Fertility: Anthropological Contributions', *Population and Development Review,* 16(1): 96–106.

—— (1994), 'Anthropological Contributions to Fertility Theory', *Working Papers,* No. 64, New York: The Population Council.

James, C. (1989), *The Black Jacobins (3rd edition),* New York: Vintage Books.

Lazarus, E. (1988), 'Theoretical Considerations for the Study of the Doctor-Patient Relationship: Implications of a Perinatal Study', *Medical Anthropology Quarterly,* 2(1): 34–58.

Lerebours, G. and Canez, M. (1992), 'Migration à la Cité Soleil', Port-au-Prince: Institut Haitien de l'Enfance.

Martin, E. (1987), *The Woman in the Body*, Boston: Beacon Press.

Morgan, L. (1987), 'Dependency Theory in the Political Economy of Health: An Anthropological Critique', *Medical Anthropology Quarterly*, 1(2): 131–54.

Rapp, R. (1988), 'Chromosomes and Communication: The Discourse of Genetic Counseling', *Medical Anthropology Quarterly*, 2(2): 121–42.

Simmons, R. (1991), 'Methodologies for Studying Client Interactions. Seminar on Client Relations and Quality of Care'. New York: The Population Council, unpublished manuscript.

—— and C. Elias (1994), 'The Study of Client-Provider Interactions: A Review of Methodological Issues', *Studies in Family Planning*, 25(1): 1–17.

Singer, M., L. Davison, and G. Gerdes (1988), 'Culture, Critical Theory, and Reproductive Illness Behavior in Haiti', *Medical Anthropology Quarterly*, 2(4): 370–85.

Taussig, M. (1980), 'Reification and the Consciousness of the Patient', *Social Science and Medicine*, 14B: 3–13.

Todd, A. (1989), *Intimate Adversaries: Cultural Conflict Between Doctors and Women Patients*, Philadelphia: University of Pennsylvania Press.

UNDP (United Nations Development Programme) (1998), *Human Development Report 1998*, Oxford: Oxford University Press.

UNICEF (United Nations Children's Fund) (1994), *The State of the World's Children*, Oxford: Oxford University Press.

UNFPA (United Nations Fund for Population Activities) (1994), 'New Study Finds 50 Percent Abortion Rate Among Haitian Teenagers' in Fonds des Nations Unies pour la Population, *Briefing Paper* No. 1, Port-au-Prince: 25 aout.

Waitzkin, H. (1979), 'Medicine, Superstructure and Micropolitics', *Social Science and Medicine*, 13A: 601–9.

—— (1991), *The Politics of Medical Encounters: How Doctors Deal with Social Problems*, New Haven: Yale University Press.

Warwick, D. (1982), *Bitter Pills: Population Policies and Their Implementation in Eight Developing Countries*, Cambridge: Cambridge University Press.

de Zaluando, B., J. Bernard and the Culture, Health and Sexuality Project Team (1995), 'Meanings and Consequences of Sexual Economic Exchange: Gender, Poverty and Sexual Risk Behavior in Urban Haiti' in R. Parker and J. Gagnon (eds), *Conceiving Sexuality: Approaches to Sex Research in Post-Modern World*, New York: Routledge.

Zola, K. (1985), 'Structural Constraints in the Doctor-Patient Relationship: The Case of Non-compliance', in L. Eisenberg and A. Kleinman (eds), *The Relevance of Social Science for Medicine*, Dordrecht: Reidel.

PART 3

Contraceptive Policy and Practice: User Perspectives

6

'Weak Blood' and 'Crowded Bellies': Cultural Influences on Contraceptive Use Among Ethiopian Jewish Immigrants in Israel[1]

Jennifer Phillips Davids

Introduction

In this chapter I examine the ways that culturally informed notions about the body, sexuality, and health influence contraceptive practice. The analysis presented here challenges certain assumptions underlying much international family planning research:

1. that the main barrier to successful fertility control in many traditionally high fertility populations is access to contraception.
2. that the main priority of people adopting family planning methods in these populations is to limit their total fertility rather than space their children.

Using data collected from three years of anthropological research among Ethiopian Jewish immigrants in Israel I show that, despite a stated desire to have fewer children and virtually free access to Western contraceptives, the majority of Ethiopian Jewish immigrants do not use family planning methods regularly or consistently. Concerns about the long-term fertility-depressing effects of contraceptives and the cultural preoccupation with proper blood flow during menstruation (believed to be disrupted by the birth control pill, in particular) lead women to reject long-term use of such products. Most women who use birth control, do so without the desire to limit total fertility; instead, contraceptives are used primarily to control the timing of their pregnancies and to mimic the normal and culturally acceptable birth spacing found in Ethiopia. I show that reproductive ideologies have had a profound impact on beliefs about female modesty, proper sexual behaviour, and female body function, and these in turn influence contraceptive practice.

I begin by outlining relevant literature on the use of contraception in Ethiopia and other countries in sub-Saharan Africa, and show how the targeting of family planning programmes in this region is based on the assumption that local people will use contraception for the same purpose for which it is supplied to them. Following a discussion of the study population and research methods, I describe aspects of Ethiopian Jewish ethnophysiological beliefs as they relate to pregnancy, breast-feeding, and birth spacing. I then show how these beliefs directly affect contraceptive use. I argue that delineating the ways that cultural beliefs and practice influence reproductive behaviour are essential to understanding overall fertility patterns.

'Unmet Need' and the Purpose of Contraception

Since the 1950s, the global increase in population has been a central concern of demographers, health planners, and aid organizations. Population increase in Asia and Africa, in particular, has been decried because of the fears that 'continued rapid population growth will cause such irreparable damage to the environment that the world's capacity to support its inhabitants at a reasonable standard of living will be imperiled' (Caldwell and Caldwell 1994: 355). Population growth rates in much of sub-Saharan Africa seem particularly stubborn: in 1990, 23 nations had growth rates above 3.0 per cent per annum (Lesthaeghe and Jolly 1994), with an estimated tripling by 2025 (Caldwell and Caldwell 1994). As a result, there is great potential for environmental degradation leading to poverty and disease. Moreover, reducing fertility rates in developing countries is believed to lead to reduced infant mortality, improved maternal and child health, and enhanced quality of life, particularly for women (World Bank 1993).

In light of these concerns, the primary focus of many aid organizations has been the funding of family planning programmes that offer modern contraceptives. Access to low-cost contraception is seen by many to be the most important factor influencing fertility decline in developing nations. To this end, billions of dollars worldwide have been targeted towards the acceleration of global fertility decline. The World Bank estimates (1993) that in 1990 total expenditure on family planning programmes was between four and five billion US dollars per annum.

This expenditure is expected to increase to 8 billion US dollars by the year 2000.

Two central tenets have governed these programmes. First, researchers have assumed that there is a great latent demand for contraception, such that family planning is acceptable and desirable to many people, but the appropriate service delivery systems are not in place to provide it (see Lesthaeghe and Jolly 1994; Wawer et al. 1991). This perspective emerged from the analysis of data collected in the KAP ('Knowledge-Attitude-Practice') studies in the 1970s which revealed an inconsistency in women's stated desired family size and actual use of contraception (Bongaarts 1991). In Bongaarts' review of the issue (ibid.), he estimates that the total unmet need for contraception averages about 17 per cent (i.e. demand for contraception/prevalence of use) in developing countries. In sub-Saharan Africa, where fertility rates are among the highest in the world, researchers estimate that contraceptive demand far exceeds availability (ibid; see Wawer et al. 1991). For instance, one study found that in sub-Saharan Africa desire for family planning ranged from 34 to 86.5 per cent, while actual use ranged only from 1 to 11.6 per cent (Wawer et al. 1991).

The disjuncture between desire and practice has been interpreted to mean that access to family planning is the primary barrier to fertility limitation. Thus, the researchers cited above concluded that the 'establishment of broader service delivery systems to bridge the gap between stated desires and contraceptive use represents one urgent challenge' (ibid: 285). In light of these findings, it is not surprising that addressing the worldwide 'unmet need' for family planning is among the explicit policies of many of the international aid organizations, including USAID and the World Bank (World Bank 1993; Wawer et al. 1991).

A second assumption made by some international family planning programmes is that those who utilize contraception do so for the purpose of limiting pregnancies and overall fertility. In the developing world, contraceptive innovators are thought to be a group apart: more educated, less fatalistic, and more sophisticated in their understandings of Western medicine (Bledsoe, Banja, and Hill 1998). This is supported by data from a number of international settings that show a strong relationship between female education and fertility decline (see Martin 1995, Lesthaeghe and Jolly 1994; Handwerker 1989), as well as associations between rising socioeconomic status, lowered desire for children and declining fertility (see Ross and Mauldin 1996, Mauldin and Segal 1988).[2]

Several lines of evidence suggest that these two central assumptions may be faulty, however. First, researchers continue to be perplexed at the low prevalence of use in many international settings where family planning services are now more accessible. Pritchett (1994a) argues that the availability of contraception has had little impact on fertility rates in developing nations and that contraceptive prevalence has had an empirically small effect on fertility variation across nations. Although this perspective has been disputed (see Bongaarts 1994, and rejoinder by Pritchett 1994b), other evidence lends credence to his view. In Ethiopia, for instance, family planning programmes increased fivefold between 1972 and 1982 (Ross and Mauldin 1996), but total fertility rates during the same period actually increased (Hailemariam and Kloos 1993).

Other evidence also calls into question the idea that the main barrier to successful fertility control is access to contraception. For instance, researchers have noted the lack of 'compliance' or consistency of use among those who state that they want no more children and who seek contraceptive services (e.g. De Silva 1991, see below). Other studies have indicated that a large group of women who use contraception are those who are actually seeking to enhance their fertility (e.g. Bledsoe *et al.* 1998).

The research presented in this chapter serves to clarify some of these issues. Ethiopian Jewish immigrants come from a country with high fertility (mean completed fertility of women in my study was 7.3) and virtually no access to contraception in the more rural areas. Their move to Israel is to a country with relatively low fertility rates[3] where modern methods of contraception are readily available for low or no cost and are promoted by health care providers. The contraceptive prevalence rate (that is, women currently using birth control) among the general population of Israeli Jews is nearly 70 per cent (Okun 1997). And while the contraceptive prevalence rate among Ethiopian Jewish immigrants in Israel is probably at least five times greater than it was in Ethiopia (see below), it still falls far below that of their non-Ethiopian counterparts.

Thus this chapter addresses two questions that have been central to population research and planning: (1) Is access to modern contraception the primary limitation on effective use? and (2) Do women that use contraception do so for the purpose of limiting lifetime fertility, or simply to space their children? Here I use the case of Ethiopian Jewish immigrants in Israel to show how the delineation of cultural beliefs and practices relating to reproductive behaviour and contraceptive use can shed light on these issues.

Study Population

Ethiopian Jews[4] are an Ethiopian ethnic minority that inhabited the highland plateau in the Gondar and Tigre regions of Northwest Ethiopia. Most were rural craftspeople (smiths, weavers, and potters) that were tenant farmers upon lands owned by the dominant ethnic group in the area, the Christian Amhara. While religiously and economically distinct from the Amhara, the Ethiopian Jews (or Beta Israel, as they were known in Ethiopia) were otherwise culturally very similar to their Christian counterparts (Pankhurst 1992).

Although their modern contact with the international Jewish community only extends to the late eighteenth century, Beta Israel liturgy, which is based on the Pentateuch, is filled with references of the return to Zion and Jerusalem. Thus, after the founding of the State of Israel in 1948, members of the Beta Israel community longed to emigrate to what they felt is their homeland. Before 1975, however, they were not recognized as Jews by the State of Israel and were not permitted citizenship. In 1975, a ruling by one of the Chief Rabbis of Israel found that they were descendants of the Lost Tribe of Dan,[5] and thus had ancient links to the Jewish community (Kaplan 1988). Since that time, they have qualified for immigration according to the 'Law of Return' which grants full Israeli citizenship and rights to all Jews.

While accepted into Israel, leaving Ethiopia did not prove easy for most emigrants. Following the Yom Kippur war in 1973, diplomatic relations between Ethiopia and Israel were severed, and exit visas were denied to the Beta Israel. Until 1985, the majority left via Sudan where they lived for months and even years in refugee camps while they waited to be transferred to Israel (Karadawi 1991). Between 1977 and 1983, over 5,000 Jews were brought from Sudan to Israel.[6] Civil unrest in the late 1970s and the famine of 1983–84 led to increased numbers arriving in Sudan in 1984. In November of that year, Israel began a covert airlift known as 'Operation Moses' and in one month more than 7,000 Ethiopian Jews were transferred from Sudan to Israel (Gruber 1987). The mission was cut short when the news of the covert operation was leaked to the press (Parfitt 1985). Several thousand Jews still trapped in Sudan were rescued during the following year.

Starting in 1989, a slow trickle of Jewish emigrants was allowed to leave Ethiopia after diplomatic relations between the two countries were restored. Family members were eager to be reunited with their relatives in Israel and increasing political tensions and fighting between Ethiopia and Eritrea pushed others to leave their homes. However, the unrest and political upheaval surrounding the overthrow of leader Mengistu Haile Mariam in 1991 made it difficult for Jews to leave, despite the fact that thousands had amassed in Addis Ababa to await emigration. In May of that year, Israel again launched a massive airlift, this time bringing 14,000 Jews out of Ethiopia in a mere 72 hours (Kaplan and Salamon 1998).

Ethiopian Jews from 'Operation Soloman,' as the second airlift was known, were initially settled in hotels that served as makeshift absorption centres for the thousands of new immigrants. Following nearly a year in hotels, the majority of the Ethiopian immigrant population was moved to temporary housing facilities. Known in Hebrew as *caravanim*, these resembled American mobile home parks. Most immigrants have now moved into permanent housing in Israel's central region (Kaplan and Salamon 1998). There are now over 60,000 Ethiopian Jews living in Israel, of which nearly 20 per cent are Israeli-born.

While a small number of immigrants had attained higher education in Ethiopia, the vast majority of immigrants were subsistence farmers and craft workers; as such, they had no marketable skills in the industrial-capitalist Israeli economy. Today economic problems are a chronic concern for Ethiopian immigrants in Israel. Recent figures, for example, indicate that in some areas, more than 30 per cent of households have no primary breadwinner; among single heads of households (predominantly women), this may be as high as 85 per cent (Kaplan and Salamon 1998). Nonetheless, Ethiopian Jewish men between the ages of 20 and 40 tend to be consistently employed, although they tend to work as unskilled labourers in low-paying jobs (Noam *et al.*1993). For example, while in one study over 75 per cent of Ethiopian Jewish men were employed, 53 per cent were employed as unskilled workers, 44 per cent as skilled workers, and only 3 per cent were employed in professional capacities (ibid.). By contrast, in 1995 only 9 per cent of Israeli men in the general population were unskilled labourers, 42 per cent skilled workers, and 49 percent were professionals (Central Bureau of Statistics 1996).

Ethiopian Jewish women are consistently under-employed compared to their Israeli counterparts, and those that do work also tend to be employed in menial jobs (Kaplan and Salamon 1998). In my study, for instance, only 25 per cent had ever worked in either the formal or informal sector, and only 13 per cent of women were currently working at the time of the survey. By contrast, official figures estimate that approximately 50 per cent of Israeli women in the general population participate in the labour force (Goldscheider 1996), with a great deal more working in unreported work in the informal sector (Kaplan and Salamon 1998). Ethiopian families, particularly single mothers, rely heavily on government assistance for their day to day survival.

Economic pressures are not the only problems facing Ethiopian Jewish immigrants. Changes in the family have been profound. As with most new immigrants, Ethiopian Jewish parents find that they are no longer 'cultural experts' in Israel and therefore have little to offer their children who are navigating new arenas of school, work, and relationships with non-Ethiopian peers. Religious leaders and elders have no recognized authority in Israel and they no longer function as mediators of family strife.

Gender conflict is also marked. While young, single Ethiopian Jewish women in Israel have more freedom of self-determination than they would have had in Ethiopia, married women who immigrated with their husbands have had some of their activities curtailed. In Israel, there are no more gardens to maintain, no more pots to make and sell, and thus very little personal money for women to control. Men try to maintain their traditional positions of authority, although at times it is undermined (so men believe) by social workers and community members who try to encourage Ethiopian Jewish women to be 'liberated'.

Divorce in the community is as commonplace in Israel as it was in Ethiopia. In my study, for example, approximately 25 per cent of Ethiopian Jewish women surveyed had been divorced. While divorce was traditionally followed by a second or even third marriage in Ethiopia, rates of remarriage appear to be declining in Israel (Phillips Davids 1999). Researchers estimate that a single mother heads between 30 and 40 per cent of Ethiopian Jewish households with children (Weil 1991; Noam *et al.* 1993).

Methodology

Research for this project was conducted over the course of three years, from September 1993 to August 1996. The majority of the research was conducted in Jerusalem with immigrants from Operation Soloman (1991), while five months of fieldwork was conducted in the Israeli coastal city of Ashkelon with a mixture of immigrants from both immigration cohorts (all of those interviewed immigrated between 1980 and 1991). Both cities have large concentrations of Ethiopian Jewish immigrants located in dense population clusters, making them ideal sites for urban research.

In Jerusalem, research was conducted in a *caravan* absorption centre, where I made daily visits or stayed overnight with one of two families that became my 'home base'. As people moved into permanent housing in 1995, I made weekly rounds to visit the families from the caravan and to follow their progress. From November 1994 to March 1995, I spent three days a week in Ashkelon (a one-hour bus ride from Jerusalem) where I worked in conjunction with the Israeli Ministry of Health conducting a survey of health-related behaviour of Ethiopian Jewish women. In Ashkelon, I lived with two different Ethiopian families who had been in Israel since the early 1980s.

The research combined quantitative and qualitative approaches to the study of fertility change in the population. Participant-observation in the community was the primary methodology, providing the fine-grained material on which my interpretations are based. I was a member of the *caravan*, joining in family meals and celebrations, local holidays and festivities, births and funerals. Most of my research was conducted in Hebrew (which I had studied before commencing fieldwork), although I used more and more Amharic as the fieldwork continued.

In addition to participating in the day-to-day lives of the *caravan* families, regular, informal discussions with approximately twenty women (alone and in groups) were directed toward several key areas. Women were asked to reflect on their lives in Ethiopia and the changes that have occurred since immigration. Changes in daily activity, in economic status, in relationships between men and women and between parents and children were the focus of many conversations. During conversations with groups of women, I was able to gather information on women's understandings of conception and pregnancy, religious prescriptions regarding fertility, fertility ideals, and sexuality.

Following six months of fieldwork, I developed a survey instrument that was designed to gather quantitative data on immigration, residence, education, employment, and fertility. Between May 1994 and March 1995, I conducted hour-long semi-structured interviews with nearly 150 Ethiopian Jewish women in Jerusalem and Ashkelon (see Table 6.1 and Table 6.2 for sampling details). All interviews were conducted in Hebrew, Amharic, or Tigrinnya by myself with the aid of local field assistants. A survey form was used, and answers were coded as they were given. In addition, space was left on the form for comments to the open-ended questions to be recorded. In particular, a number of qualitative and open-ended questions were asked regarding the 'moral economy of childbearing', following the methods of Handwerker (1989). These included questions on obligations between parents and children, the best life course trajectories for women, the ideal age for marriage, for childbearing to commence and terminate and ideal family size. To support the findings of my survey, population data were collected from the Central Bureau of Statistics in Jerusalem. This provided raw data on population

Table 6.1. Number of women who participated in semi-structured interviews, by age and immigration cohort

	Sample Distribution by Age and Cohort[7]			
Age	Moses	Interim	Soloman	Total
15–19	4	3	12	19
20–29	20	11	25	56
30–39	14	9	16	39
40–49	5	2	6	13
50+	6	3	11	20
Total	49	28	70	147

Table 6.2. Number of women who participated in semi-structured interviews, by residence and marital status

	Sample Distribution by Residence and Marital Status			
	Currently Married	Never Married	Divorced or Widowed	Total
Ashkelon	87	13	16	116
Jerusalem	23	4	4	31
Total	110	17	20	147

distribution and births, deaths, and immigration. Analysis of all data was conducted with the JMP statistical software package (SAS Institute).

While my sample represented a wide range of Ethiopian Jewish women with varied experiences, my discussions in this chapter concern primarily those women who immigrated as adults from villages rather than cities, the majority of whom were already married when they arrived in Israel. Women who arrived as young girls and grew up in Israel, particularly those who spent much of their schooling in Israeli boarding schools, have a different reproductive trajectory (for details, see Phillips Davids 1998b).

The Availability and Use of Contraception

In rural Ethiopia, contraception was not readily available and women in my study report having used no traditional methods of contraception per se. There are no demographic data and few health statistics specific to the Ethiopian Jewish community in Ethiopia. Thus, we are dependent on retrospective reports from women in Israel and comparisons with studies of Amhara Christians who lived in the region where the Jews had lived. For example, in a study of the socio-cultural determinants of fertility in the Gondar region in 1982, Haile (1990) reports that 7.2 per cent of women surveyed used family planning services. More recent figures from the World Population Reference Bureau (1997) puts this figure at only 4 per cent for Ethiopia as a whole.

Despite their unfamiliarity with Western contraception, abstinence and coitus interruptus are both recognized as having an effect on pregnancy. In the traditional understanding of conception, women have a finite number of potentials (Amharic: *fitrat*) in the body that become all the children she will have. A man's *zer* (Amharic: seed) gives life to the conceptus.[8] One woman explained, 'all the babies you will ever have are in the belly already, waiting for their time to come out. When you lie with a man, this causes you to become pregnant, but the *fitrat* is already there.' Alternatively, some women believe that the *zer* mixes with a woman's blood to become the child. Another woman explained,

> I'm *b'mergem* [menstruating: Amharic, lit: 'cursed'], right? So I'm outside for seven days.[9] Then, at night, I cleanse myself and I return to my husband. I lay with him that night and I will become pregnant. His seed mixes with my blood. His seed gives the bone, and my blood, the flesh. The heart – it depends on who the child takes after. For example, Yaacov [her three-year-old son] is like me, so that means his heart came from me. Avraham [her new infant] – he's still young, so I'm not sure – but he's more like his father. So his heart is from [his father].

Without sexual relations or if a man 'finishes outside,' pregnancy can be prevented. However, traditionally at least, people seemed to take the biblical injunction against 'spilling seed' seriously and avoided coitus interruptus. Among younger Ethiopian Jews in Israel, it seems more acceptable: several couples told me that they used 'natural methods,' by which they meant coitus interruptus.

Since immigrating to Israel, Ethiopian Jews have adopted family planning methods fairly quickly. Contraception is readily available at local health centres for low or no cost and is promoted by health care practitioners. Contraception is also freely available to unmarried women and teenagers without parental consent. In my study, 54 per cent of women surveyed had used birth control at one time or another since immigrating. Oral contraceptives are the most popular method, followed by the IUD (Table 6.3).

Table 6.3. Percentages of current contraceptive users, by method type (n=33)

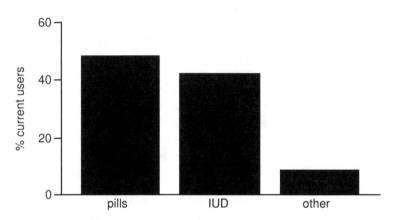

Contraceptive prevalence (current use) among Ethiopian Jews in Israel is about half that of the prevalence in the general Israeli Jewish population. Thirty per cent of the Ethiopian Jewish women in my survey were currently using contraception. The number of women who used birth control continuously between two subsequent pregnancies (that is, for birth spacing) is lower, about 15 per cent. Few contraceptive users rely on any method for more than a year or two; only four women (n=57 users, 124 total) surveyed had used contraception longer than three consecutive years. More commonly, women use one method for a period of months, then switch methods or stop altogether.

As these numbers indicate, while Ethiopian Jewish women seem ready to accept contraceptives, they don't use them consistently or for any length of time. This may be because, as I argue below, most women use contraception as a method of spacing their births to a preferred optimum of three years, particularly in the absence of long lactational amenorrhoea due to a reduction of breast feeding in Israel. In their efforts to control the pace of childbearing, they do not necessarily view contraception's goal as fertility reduction.

Ethnophysiology and the Traditional Ideal Birth Spacing

'I was lucky, God gave me my children slowly, only every three or four years. My mother had many children, one every second year, it was really difficult – several babies died. God saw my mother's problem and gave them to me slowly.' Twenty-seven-year-old Tesfe[10] speaks for many

Ethiopian Jewish women who desire many children, well spaced. The ideal birth spacing is three years – this allows a woman to nurse a child for two years before becoming pregnant again.

Pregnancies too close together are feared for a number of reasons. In the traditional conception, the body is a more or less fluid space, with a few central organs attached by a series of cords (see Young 1970). Regular blood flow is essential to *tena,* good health. In women's bodies, blood is particularly central: the shedding and renewal of menstrual blood among fertile women is important to their overall wellbeing. Two or more pregnancies close together also make women's blood weak (Amharic: *dam manes* or Hebrew: *dam chalash*). Weak blood results in a lack of energy, headaches, and dizziness (Amharic: *ras mazor,* 'spinning head').[11]

For the sake of the health of both mother and child, informants said, pregnancies should ideally be spaced three years apart. This gives women a chance to recoup energy lost from one pregnancy and nursing child that then can be channelled into the next. Women in my sample appeared to achieve nearly the ideal in Ethiopia – average inter-birth interval (closed birth interval) was 32 months. Birth intervals were clustered around a median of 36 months, with more than 40 per cent of women reporting birth intervals between 33 and 36 months.

Changing Patterns of Lactation and Birth Spacing

In the absence of a long post-partum abstinence period and without contraception, lactation is widely believed to be the primary determinant of post-partum infecundity, and thus, birth spacing and through it, lifetime fertility (Wood 1994, Bongaarts and Potter 1983). Lactation, particularly in the early months when nursing frequency and milk output are at their peak, suppresses ovulation by raising prolactin and b-endorphin levels in the bloodstream (Wood 1994, Johnson and Everitt 1988). Prolactin appears to inhibit follicular development in the ovary and also inhibits progesterone secretion, resulting in luteal phase inadequacy even when ovulatory cycles are resumed (McNeilly 1993; Wood 1994). The link between b-endorphin and ovulatory suppression is not entirely established, but may suppress the release of gonadotropin releasing hormone (GnRH) from the hypothalamus, thereby suppressing the release of luteinizing hormone (LH) and follicle stimulating hormone (FSH), and by extension, follicular development (Wood 1994).

Among the Beta Israel, post-partum abstinence was relatively short, consisting of the forty- or eighty-day confinement period in the birth

Table 6.4. Results of a multiple regression analysis of the factors that affect the interbirth interval in Ethiopia (n=275 births)

Source	DF	Sum of sq.	F Ratio	$p <$	Sig.
	Factors Affecting the Birth Interval Ethiopian Births				
mos. lactation	1	5105.92	64.19	0.00	***
year	1	287.54	3.61	0.06	n/s
cohort	2	391.72	2.46	0.09	n/s
fetal loss	1	91.49	1.15	0.28	n/s
mother's age	1	37.7	0.47	0.49	n/s

*** results are highly significant at the $p < 0.001$ level

house. Since women rarely begin resumption of menstrual periods this quickly, this separation was unlikely to have much of an effect on fertility. Thus, as Table 6.4 shows, in a multiple regression analysis of the data collected from retrospective reports, lactation emerges as the most important variable affecting the length of the birth interval.

In Israel, patterns of lactation have changed considerably. Ethiopian Jewish immigrants refer to the superiority of breast milk (*tut*: Amharic) over formula for the health of their baby and because it delays menstruation and pregnancy. Because of this, the majority of women in this study initiated breastfeeding (88.9 per cent). But in Israel, the supplementation of breastfeeding with formula and early introduction of weaning foods is considered to be normal and good for the baby and is widely promoted by advertising. For example, a recent study of over 8,000 Israeli Jewish women of mixed ethnicity found that although 79.3 per cent of all women initiated breastfeeding, only 46.5 per cent of these continued beyond three months duration (Ever-Hadani *et al.* 1994).

Moreover, despite the introduction of breastfeeding promotion programmes in hospitals (see Palti *et al.* 1988), the free distribution of formula and processed baby foods and the recommendation of the early introduction of other solids was encouraged by local health practitioners who worked with the Ethiopian Jewish immigrant women in this study. Ethiopian Jewish women believe that formula makes their baby grow faster and larger – traits that are culturally desirable. But this excessive growth is also seen to be somewhat dangerous for the child and not necessarily a sign of health. One woman compared this growth to a balloon – it gets large, but is full of air and not substance. Formula-fed babies are described as *tsafuf*, bloated (Hebrew: lit. crowded) and considered weak. As 21-year-old Hadass said of her stepmother's baby who was formula-fed from birth:

> She's, you know [gestures to indicate the puffed-up size of her one-year-old stepsister], *tsafuf*. Big, but there is nothing inside of her. That *Materna* makes her big, but not strong. Her legs are weak. Not even one day was she breastfed. That one [her stepmother] gave her *Materna* from the start. With *tut* they are small, but they are strong.

Despite their belief in the superiority of breast milk, participants often had difficulty assimilating the contradictory information they receive from health care workers. As 29-year-old Mevit, a mother of three young boys, told me,

> *Tut* [Amharic: 'breast milk'] is the best thing for the baby. Yes, I nursed all my children because it makes them strong. *Materna* is okay if you go out or something like that. They give it to us at the health centre. [She looks at her one month old son] Do you think Shlomo is too thin? *Materna* makes them fatter. Look at Baflima's baby, he is big and she gives him a bottle.

The desire for big, fat babies and the pressure to conform to the health standards put forth by health workers and others in Israeli society correlates with the growing trend among these women to rely on supplemental formula. In my sample, more than 30 per cent of Ethiopian Jewish infants born in Israel were nursed less than six months (50/153). This compared to less than 1 per cent of the infants born in Ethiopia (1/270). Half of all reported nursing their infants in Ethiopia for two years or more, while in Israel, only 2.6 per cent of Ethiopian Jewish women nursed their infants for more than two years.

The early introduction of the bottle and of weaning foods has resulted in shorter total lactation duration in Israel, the average now being only 10.7 ± 0.68 months (n=186 infants). This effect increases proportionally over time, so that the longer a woman has lived in Israel, the shorter period of time she will nurse a child, regardless of how long she has nursed previous children.

Moreover, the frequency of nursing also appears to have shifted. Women are no longer confined in a birth house with their infant for one to two months after birth as they were in Ethiopia, when the infant had constant and exclusive access to their mother. Although many women, particularly new immigrants, attempt to observe this separation from society, they are often unable to for practical reasons (see Trevisan-Semi 1985; Anteby forthcoming). Even when women do not resume working outside the home during this period, they often have to tend to household responsibilities which can take them away from the home and their infants. Since families no longer live in villages where they could rely on support from extended family members, women have to begin cooking, cleaning, and shopping much sooner than they would have in Ethiopia. Also, the availability of formula and readily prepared cereals make it easier for women to leave their babies with their husbands or neighbours if they so desire. Thus, even women who do nurse, do so less frequently than they would in Ethiopia.

Table 6.5 Results of a multiple regression analysis of the factors that affect the interbirth interval in Israel (n=111 births)

Factors Affecting the Birth Interval Israeli Births					
Source	DF	Sum of sq.	F Ratio	p <	Sig.
contraception	1	1996.4	15.79	0.00	***
year	1	938.48	7.42	0.01	**
mos. lactation	1	596.89	4.72	0.03	*
fetal loss	1	648.23	5.13	0.03	*
mother's age	1	47.77	0.38	0.54	n/s
cohort	2	1.28	0.005	0.99	n/s

*** results are highly significant at the p< 0.001 level, ** results are significant at the p< 0.01 level, * results are significant at the p< 0.05 level

In Israel, lactation still remains one of the most important variables affecting the birth interval (Table 6.5). However, other factors are more influential. Both contraception and the year of infant's birth were highly significant (p<0.001 and 0.01, respectively). These two variables are related in that women who arrived in the 1980s (those from Operation Moses cohort) were more than twice as likely to use contraception than the more recent immigrants.

In Israel, women now resume regular menstrual cycles earlier than they did in Ethiopia as a result of the decline in duration of lactation; increased nutrition probably also plays a role. As a result, among non-contraceptive users, the mean closed birth interval in Israel is now 25 months, compared to 32 months in Ethiopia (p < 0.001). This reduction in the birth interval has practical significance: the age specific fertility rate among new Ethiopian immigrants aged 25-40 has increased, rather than decreased, after time spent in Israel. For example, national level data show that the age specific fertility rate[12] of women from the Operation Soloman cohort (the newest immigrants and the least likely to be contraceptive users) has increased 18 per cent among women in this age group after five years in Israel. Overall, the total fertility rate of this cohort has increased from 6.5 to 7.0 in the five years following immigration (between 1991 and 1996).

Many Ethiopian Jewish women recognize that the changes in nursing patterns occurring in Israel are having an effect on their menstrual cycle and on their fecundity. Women who experienced pregnancy in both contexts relate that their menstrual periods resume more quickly in Israel than they did in Ethiopia. In the following conversation, Haddas, a twenty-year-old new immigrant, and her neighbour, Bracha, a thirty-year-old veteran immigrant, discuss the fate of a relative who gives her baby formula:

Hadass: She [the baby] is weak because her mother doesn't nurse her. Also she has children too close together – two babies in two years and she is pregnant again. It's no good . . . They all worry that the babies are too small. With *tut*, they are small, but they are strong. It's because of that she is pregnant so soon. It's really no good, but what can I say?

Bracha: It's no good. You know? It's the new fashion here. When they get out of the hospital, they have no milk for a few days. You know, it happened to me. I needed to drink a lot of milk. But her, she just gave a bottle, and that's it – *gamarnu* [Hebrew: lit, we're finished]. So she gets her period a few months later and she's pregnant.

Hadass: It's no good.

Many Ethiopian Jewish women feel strongly that pregnancies too close together are dangerous for both mother and child. As a result, many women seek contraception in order to prolong the time to the next pregnancy. Use of contraception is having the desired effect: those women who use birth control in Israel have a significantly longer birth spacing than women who do not contracept. The birth interval among non-users was 25 months, compared to 35 months for users (n=101 pregnancies, $p < 0.001$).[13] As noted above, ideal birth spacing was more or less achieved in Ethiopia, for most women at least, through prolonged lactation. In Israel, however, women who want to attain ideal birth spacing do so with the use of contraception. As I will argue below, this is, in fact, the main goal of their contraceptive use, since few women use birth control for the purpose of ending their reproductive careers.

Fertility Desires and Family Planning

In Israel, Ethiopian Jewish women often express a desire to have fewer children. Economic difficulties rate among the most common complaints and women are acutely aware of the rising economic cost of children in Israel.[14] Many women echoed 25-year-old Tadila who said, 'Lots of children is good, like my mother had. But in Israel, it is too difficult. In Ethiopia it was easy to bring up eight or even ten children. Here, even two or three is hard and bothers your head.' Or as 35-year-old Anat, with six school-aged children, said,

> I don't want any more children. It's hard in this place. The salary is small . . . We need to pay for school, for food, and all that. In Ethiopia, everything is at home. There's no electricity, but [that's] OK. With farming, everything is outside. But in this place it is hard. The children always complain – why can't I wear nice clothes, why don't you buy me this or that? It's much more difficult to raise children here.

Not only are the direct economic costs of the capitalist economy difficult to manage, but there are indirect costs as well. People feel the pressure of the workday and the loss of time with their children. Parents, who already feel they lack authority because they are not 'cultural experts' in the new society, also fear that they are not able to control their children because their day-to-day influence is minimized in the face of parental employment and their children's schooling. As 33-year-old Rachel expressed it,

> In Ethiopia there was a lot of free time. Now we work eight hours a day, there is a lot of housework, and everything to do. Also, I can't go to work because I need to be home with the children. Even if I can't help them with their homework, I need to be with them. If not, they leave. Also, here the children control us – in Ethiopia, the opposite . . . In Ethiopia there was education, discipline. I could hit them and set them straight – there was no police – I could raise them the way I want to. Here it is bad – they talk back and I can't even send them to their room.

Ideal family size[15] is changing such that women who immigrated as children and have spent much of their life in Israel want, on average, two fewer children than those who arrived as adults (4.7 children vs. 6.3 children, n=125, p< 0.001). Moreover, more than half of all women expressed a desire to have fewer children than their mother had given birth to in Ethiopia and 22 per cent of all women of reproductive age at the time of the survey said they desired no more children. Not surprisingly, this varied by parity, such that the desire for more children decreased by number of live births (Table 6.6). Nonetheless, after two children, all women surveyed said they wanted more children. And even after six live births, more than 40 per cent still wanted more children.

Statistical analysis shows no correlation between the desire for no more children and contraceptive use. Of the women who said they wanted no more children (n=26), only 40 per cent were using contraception at the time of the survey. Women who stated that they wanted more children made up a slightly larger proportion of birth control users than those who did not want more children (Tables 6.7 and 6.8).

Table 6.6. Number of responses to the question 'Do you want any more children?' by number of live births (n=72)

| Live births | Fertility Desires | | |
	No	Yes	% yes
1	0	11	100
2	0	16	100
3	2	9	81.8
4	5	12	70.6
5	3	2	40.0
6+	7	5	41.7

Thus, most women said they were using birth control because they did not want more children at that time, rather than never. Most women would agree with 29-year-old Mevit, who told me, 'I take the pill, one every day. Yes, I want more children, but when this one grows a little more. It's too hard with too many little children in the house. And if I got pregnant now, I would have to wean this one – he's too little!' Ethiopian Jewish women feel that the strategic use of contraception to limit births to a desired timeframe helps them to effectively manage their lives in Israel.

My data support anthropologist Caroline Bledsoe's (Bledsoe with Banja 1996: 10) contention that among people in high fertility societies 'desires to space children at safe intervals are so strong that it is fair to conclude that the intervals themselves, not numbers of children, are the focus of conscious choice calculus.' Bledsoe posits that conserving maternal energy and physical reserves for future childbearing, not the reduction in fertility, are the main goals of contraceptive use. A number

Table 6.8. Number of responses to the question, 'Do you want any more children?' by current use of contraception. Number is expressed as a per cent; the total is in parentheses (n=78). Chi Square Likelihood Ratio = 0.34, p < 0.56

		Desired Fertility	
		Yes	No
Currently Using	Yes	32.8 (19)	40.0 (8)
Birth Control?	No	67.2 (39)	60.0 (12)

Table 6.7. Number of responses to the question 'Do you want any more children?' by ever-use of contraception. Number is expressed as a per cent; the total is in parentheses (n=90). Chi Square Likelihood Ratio = 0.193, p < 0.66

		Desired Fertility	
		Yes	No
Ever used	Yes	55.2 (32)	50.0 (13)
Birth Control?	No	44.8 (26)	50.0 (13)

of other researchers have shown that birth spacing was the primary goals of contraceptive use among women in non-Western countries (Caldwell *et al.* 1992, National Research Council 1993, Bledsoe *et al.* 1994).

Like Bledsoe, I find that the use of contraception is not logically inconsistent with the desire for high fertility. However, despite the fact that women do appear to use contraception in order to manage their reproductive health, and perhaps more profoundly, to protect the health of their children, I believe this is only to the extent that they are making up for what has been lost from the reduction in nursing. That is, they are not using birth control to compensate for other losses in maternal reserves such as miscarriage, infant deaths, or other types of 'reproductive mishaps' (Bledsoe *et al.* 1998). In the context of their increased nutritional status and readily accessible health care system in Israel, Ethiopian Jewish women do not have the same pressures to manage their reproductive health that they might have had in the Ethiopian setting.

For Ethiopian Jews, however, there are overriding factors that limit the use of birth control for the purpose of maintaining health and proscribe its use among women who actually do desire to limit fertility. Foremost among these are cultural understandings of the health consequences of contraceptives that contradict their regular use. This is discussed in the following sections.

The Importance of Blood

A number of researchers have discussed the importance of blood as a symbol in Beta Israel cosmology (Trevisan Semi 1985, Salamon 1993, Seeman 1997, Anteby forthcoming). Ethiopian Jews distinguish between good blood, which circulates in the healthy body, and bad blood (or black blood, Amharic: *tukur dam*] that causes illness (see Chemtov *et al.* 1990). Traditionally blood letting or blood suction was practised by Ethiopian Jews to treat specific illnesses that are perceived to result from bad blood, such as *moygnbabegn*, a culturally specific neurologic disorder, and *wugat,* chest pains (see Hodes and Teferedegne 1996).

In Ethiopian Jewish cosmology, menstrual blood is *irkuz*, unclean, and the menstruating woman herself is *b'mergem,* cursed. Traditionally, women were separated during menstruation (and following childbirth) in order to keep the rest of the community clean (Amharic: *qidus*, lit: holy) and out of contact of the blood. Corpses and dead animals were also *irkuz*, and any one coming in contact with them would have to separate themselves from the village until sundown, at which point they could rejoin the community following ritual immersion in running water. Menstrual taboos thus were part of a wider framework of pollution beliefs that were important to the Beta Israel in Ethiopia for demarcating social boundaries (see also Anteby, forthcoming, Salamon 1993, Quirin 1992).

Although menstrual blood is unclean and linked ideologically and semantically to the black blood of illness, menstruation itself is seen as a necessary process that maintains balance. Blood is continuously renewed in fertile women and menstrual flow is necessary to maintain *tena*, or good health. Without good flow, illness follows. Retained menstrual blood following a miscarriage, for example, could lead to *attent hono kere*, another culturally specific illness that Ethiopians believe to be caused by a foetus that is retained and turned to bone (the name of the illness itself literally means 'it remains bone') (Hodes and Teferedegne 1996). Twenty-two-year-old Wanitu explained to me, 'If the *quolle* [Amharic: guardian spirit] is angry with you, then you will lose the baby or the blood will stay there and turn to bone. Also, if the black blood doesn't come out, then it will turn to bone.'

Ethiopian Jews in Israel at times complained of having 'too much blood,' a problem manifest by high blood pressure. This problem can also be relieved by blood letting, even if in the Israeli context this is through the actual drawing of blood for blood tests (see Chemtov and Rosen 1992)[16] Having too much blood or bad blood in the system causes headaches, dizziness and weakness and a general feeling of malaise.

The birth control pill has two actions that make its use undesirable for prolonged periods of time. First, since menstrual periods become lighter while taking the pill, women believe that it limits the output of menstrual blood, thereby retaining some of the *tukur dam* that should be released. Second, it is believed to make the circulating blood in the body 'weak' (Hebrew: *chalash*). *Dam manus* (Amharic, lit. 'low blood') a condition of weak blood, is responsible for fatigue and dizziness which women complain about when they are taking the pill. Thus, while 'low blood' may be caused by pregnancies too close together, it is also caused by prolonged use of the birth control pill. Twenty-two-year-old Wanitu explained to me why she was pregnant with her third child, when she really did not want to be pregnant again so soon:

> I was taking pills, you remember? I really didn't want to have another baby yet. But I stopped taking the pill for a week because it made me feel sick and bloated [Hebrew: *tsafuf*, lit: crowded]. It made my belly crowded [*tsafuf*] when I ate, or even when I hadn't eaten. I didn't like it. It also made my head spin. It makes your blood weak. Afterward, I didn't get my period, so I thought maybe I was pregnant. I waited another month and then I went to the doctor for a test. I didn't want to get pregnant, but God wanted me to, I think.

Since the pill is believed to interfere with normal menstrual flow, it is seen to be indirectly responsible for these symptoms. Women related that they believed the pill caused them to feel bloated or nauseous and to lose their appetite; their bellies were 'crowded' (Hebrew: *tsafuf*), so that they could not eat. Rather than a baby filling their belly (which is never described as *tsafuf*), the belly is filled with black blood or just 'full.'

Among Ethiopian Jews, 'full bellies' is an idiom for expressing distress and negative emotions (Ben-Ezer 1994). Sadness and despair surrounding displaced and separated families, poverty, or general problems with assimilation may be expressed as having a 'full abdomen' whose 'stomach got filled up with troubles' (ibid.: 113). When women's bellies are too full, i.e. they have too many negative emotions, they may refuse to eat, stating that there is 'no room' for anything else. For some women, this turns into a chronic malnutrition similar to anorexia nervosa (Ben-Ezer 1990). Thus, not only is the pill associated with the physical discomfort of bloating, it is blamed for lack of appetite and a feeling of weakness and poor health; it also may be an expression of their dissatisfaction with contraception in general.

The Long-Term Effects of Contraception

Besides the short-term discomfort of symptoms such as bloating, fatigue, and the general problems of 'weak blood,' there is a fear of the long-term effects of this ill health on the ability to bear children in the future. As one man told me,

> You know it's no good to be on pills for a long time before you have your first child. I don't know what it does, but it closes everything there. It's better to have your first child early and then take pills for a while. If not, everything is closed. It happens to Ethiopians, to everyone, not just *ferenjim* [Amharic: 'whites'] – just like you – they use the pills for a few years and then when they want to have a baby they can't.

> It's also no good to stay on the pill for too long between children. You know Fantanesh, the one with that retarded child? Well, look at that child, she didn't have any, you know, [gestures to skin] – she was thin, nothing when she was born. Her mother used the pills for too long, and that's what happened to the baby. If she had taken pills like that before her first child, she never would have gotten pregnant, or the child would have been worse, maybe would have died. It was only because she had that healthy boy before that this one was born alive.

'Medicines' (Hebrew: *trufot*) have powerful attributes that last longer than the period of time in which they are taken. The fact that a woman takes the birth control pill for a period of more than three years at any point in her life may have unforeseen consequences later on. Likewise, past health and in this context, past healthy births, can have far reaching effects. In the case of the woman mentioned above, both the fact she had been on the pill 'too long' and that she had given birth to a previous child who was healthy influenced the pregnancy and the birth outcome.

Newly available Depo-Provera injections[17] are considered by Ethiopian Jews to be so powerful that they should be avoided by younger women altogether. Thirty-year-old Mevit told me,

The *chisun* [Depo-Provera, Hebrew: lit. 'vaccine'] is only for women that wouldn't miss [Hebrew: *mitgagaat*, lit. 'be homesick for'] children. It does something to the body and can cause problems if you want children later. Maybe in five or six years I want to have a daughter, so I can't take the *chisun*. It's only for women who don't want any more children.

All of the contraceptive options that are categorized by Ethiopian Jews as medicines, *'trufot'* (i.e. the pill and Depo-Provera) are feared for their long-term effects and they avoid any that may endanger future reproduction (see Bledsoe *et al.* 1998). The fears of the long-term effects of *trufot* are not due to an irrational misunderstanding of the actual physiological affects of the contraceptive agent. Ethiopian Jews, like most people in high fertility societies, see reproduction as an ongoing process that takes place over a lifetime. Each birth concerns them not only for itself, but in the context of a lifetime of giving birth, for future childbearing as well. The effects of all reproductive events – and this includes births, reproductive losses, and postponements – 'reverberate throughout reproductive life' (Bledsoe with Banja 1996:14).

Sexuality, Gender and Contraceptive Practice

Despite the fact that contraception is part and parcel of sexual activity, surprisingly little attention is paid in most research to how sexual relationships and local understandings of proper sexual behaviour impact its use. An exception is Santow's (1993) work on coitus interruptus. Santow discusses a number of factors that influence the reliance on withdrawal; of particular relevance here: dominance of men in reproductive decision making, women's shame concerning sexual matters, and a minimizing of the importance of sexual encounter in the overall personal relationships between partners. Although coitus interruptus is not very popular among Ethiopian Jews (practised by only 9 per cent of all birth control users), in general, contraceptive use among this population is constrained by notions of marital fidelity, sexual shame, and female modesty.

For example, the diaphragm, I was told, 'is no good' because it requires women to be immediately pro-active and precognisant of the sex act. 'This is a *busha* [Hebrew: 'embarrassment'], we [women] are not supposed to know about that before it happens. No one would ever use that thing,' one woman told me. Men are to take the initiative in instigating the sexual encounter; if a woman has sexual desires, she must communicate them to her husband subtly, if at all.

Moreover, for effective use, the diaphragm requires a certain amount of knowledge and familiarity with the internal female body, which most Ethiopian Jews do not have. In the traditional understanding, there are few internal organs (see Young 1970; Ravid *et al.* 1995). *Hod* is the catch-all term for the abdomen; it is envisioned to be a large sack that contains both food and babies. Because of this, women worry that there is nothing to keep the diaphragm (or for that matter, IUD) from floating around the body. In addition, Israeli physicians do not encourage the use of the diaphragm, since they see it as a troublesome and less reliable method than either the birth control pill or the IUD (Shtarkshall, pers.comm.).[18]

Even though men are expected to be dominant in the sexual encounter, there is no preference for 'male' methods such as the condom. They are, as a rule, unpopular and no-one in my sample reported using them. Because of their association with sexually transmitted diseases condoms are believed to promote promiscuity, so are discouraged by Ethiopian Jewish religious leaders (Chemtov and Rosen 1992). Married couples would not use a condom since it is believed that the only purpose of a condom is to prevent STDs, which they would only be exposed to if one partner were unfaithful to the other. Thus, condoms symbolize infidelity and distrust among married partners. Moreover, they are feared to cause impotence or to become lodged in the woman's abdomen (ibid.).

According to one prominent health educator in Israel, however, condom use is on the rise among young, unmarried Ethiopian Jews (Shtarkshall, pers. comm.). Sexual norms are in flux, such that teenagers, while perhaps as sexually active as they were in Ethiopia, are no longer bound by the tradition of early, arranged marriages (see Phillips Davids 1998b). The fear of AIDS in the community, combined with aggressive AIDS education, appears to be effectively changing opinion about the condom and is responsible for its new popularity among the young.[19]

Conclusions

Among Ethiopian Jewish immigrants in Israel, birth control is used strategically for the management of the reproductive life and, in some cases, to maximize lifetime fertility. Couples do this with the serial use of a variety of methods. The ability to 'pick and choose' both the method itself and the timing of use gives couples more flexibility in their reproductive choices. Nonetheless, most couples do not choose to use contraception in order to adopt an 'Israeli' pattern of low fertility. Instead, they are managing in many cases to replicate the pattern found in

Ethiopia, or simply modify it in a way that balances their new needs of reproductive management with their traditional desires for high fertility.

These conclusions challenge the basic tenets of some international family planning programmes. First, in Israel, there should be no 'unmet' need for contraception. According to the logic of many family planning providers, all women who desire to use contraception should be using it, since it is widely available at low cost and minimal inconvenience. Contraceptive prevalence (current use) among Ethiopian Jewish women is, in fact, higher than the desire to stop reproducing (33 per cent and 22 per cent, respectively). Thus those that use contraception are not necessarily doing so because they desire no more children and, more significantly, those who want no more children are not necessarily using contraceptives to achieve this goal. According to the logic of latent demand, those who desire no more children should be the most committed contraceptive users.

Second, the assumption among some family planning providers that women use contraception for the conscious purpose of limiting lifetime fertility is also challenged by this research. I have shown how Ethiopian Jewish couples selectively target their contraceptive use to manage women's health and the health of their infants, which is made possible, they believe, by the spacing of births three years apart. The effect of such spacing may, of course, be to reduce total fertility, however unintentionally. Yet the cultural barriers to contraceptive use, which are linked to ethnophysiological beliefs about women's health, limit the use of contraceptives for both purposes.

This research contributes to the growing body of evidence that even in high fertility societies where some couples may desire to limit the total number of children they have, they often act with intentionality to try to control the timing of pregnancy so that those that are born (and their mothers) are healthy. In new social settings, such as Israel, where there are few economic or social barriers to fertility control, couples view modern contraception as one or a series of means to an end. Some of the Ethiopian Jewish couples interviewed had no desire to limit their total number of children. These results, following the work of Caroline Bledsoe (Bledsoe *et al.* 1998; Bledsoe *et al.* 1994), urge us to trace in more detail the ways that the biological framework of human fecundity is manipulated by social actors to produce observable fertility. It demands that we take seriously the idea that cultural beliefs and practices are pervasive in reproductive behaviour. Rather than relying on socially decontextualized models of these patterns, we need to develop ethnographically detailed explanations of fertility behaviour that account for the context and meaning of the actions as well as the outcome of those actions.

Notes

1. Sections of this chapter were presented at the Third International Congress for the Society for the Study of Ethiopian Jewry in Milan, October 1998. I thank conference participants for their insights and comments. In particular, Gadi Ben-Ezer was very helpful in sharing his research on 'full bellies' and anorexia nervosa. I am indebted to Rachel Waxman of the Barzilai Hospital in Ashkelon for facilitating my work in that community. Interviews were conducted in the absorption centres in Ashkelon with the gracious cooperation of The Jewish Agency. Esther Germai, Pnina Malako, and Einav Pikado were instrumental in data collection. Many thanks to them and to the Ethiopian Jewish men and women who opened their hearts and their homes to me. I am also grateful to Andrew Davids and Steve Kaplan for their encouragement and helpful insights on the issues discussed in this chapter and the research project as a whole. Thanks also to Don Seeman, Barbara Okun, and the editors of this volume for their comments on an earlier draft. This research on which this chapter is based was supported by the Fulbright Foundation, the National Science Foundation (dissertation improvement grant), the Jacob K. Javits graduate fellowship program, *Sigma Xi*, and the Memorial Foundation for Jewish Culture.
2. The relationship between fertility and socio-economic variables has a long history that is outside the scope of this chapter. For recent reviews of the issues see volumes by Greenhalgh 1996; Kertzer and Hogan 1997). For a discussion of these issues as they pertain specifically to Ethiopian Jewish immigrants, see Phillips Davids 1998a and 1999.
3. The total fertility rate of Israeli Jews was 2.6 in 1993 (Central Bureau of Statistics 1996).
4. I follow the growing convention of researchers who use the term 'Ethiopian Jew' to refer to the population in Israel, while 'Beta Israel' is used when referring to the community in Ethiopia. The term 'Falasha,' by which the group was known by their Christian neighbours (and historically in scholarly literature), is considered derogatory and is rarely used by researchers today. See Weil 1995, Salamon 1994; for a dissenting opinion on the use of the term 'Ethiopian Jews' see Seeman 1997.
5. Most modern historians disagree that the Beta Israel have a direct, phylogenetic relationship with the ancient Jewish community. The details of their origins have been the focus of a number of recent books (see Kaplan 1992, Quirin 1992, Kessler 1996, Shelemay 1977).

6. Unless otherwise noted, all population statistics come from data provided by the Central Bureau of Statistics in Jerusalem.

7. For heuristic and analytical purposes, the sample was divided into three immigration cohorts: Operation Moses (1980–85), Interim (1986–1989), and Operation Soloman (1990–1992). Historically, these rescue operations did not span such a long period of time, but in terms of immigration experience both in Ethiopia and in Israel, the women in these cohorts are similar. In other words, my 'Operation Moses' cohort includes all women who left their villages between 1980–1985 and walked through the Sudan whether or not they actually arrived in the series of airlifts dubbed 'Operation Moses'. They comprise the early wave of immigrants to Israel; for this reason, I also refer to this cohort as 'veteran' immigrants, which is the common reference in Israel (Hebrew: *vatikim*). With the exception of a few women who arrived in late 1990 and a few who joined their families in early 1992, all women from the 'Operation Soloman' cohort actually arrived in the airlift on 25 May 1991. These women are also referred to as 'new immigrants' (Hebrew: *olim chadashim*).

8. When I initially began my research, women spoke of these 'potentials' as nearly complete essences of a foetus that only need the 'seed' to spark life into them. Today women often use the Hebrew term *betziot* (eggs), although the understanding of sperm and egg uniting to form a child is very recent.

9. Traditionally, menstruating women were confined to a menstrual house (Amharic: *mergem gojo*) for the duration of their bleeding. Women were also confined for forty days following the birth of a boy and eighty days following the birth of a girl, according the their interpretation of Leviticus 12: 2-5 which states: 'When a woman conceives and bears a male child, she shall be unclean for seven days, as in the period of impurity through menstruation. . . The woman shall wait for thirty-three days because her blood requires purification; she shall touch nothing that is holy, and shall not enter the sanctuary until her days of purification are completed. If she bears a female child, she shall be unclean for fourteen days as for her menstruation and shall wait for sixty-six days because her blood requires purification.'

10. All names are pseudonyms. In some cases, personal details have been changed to protect the identity of informants.

11. Both the linguistic convention ('weak blood') and symptoms seem to roughly correspond to iron deficiency anaemia. Women complaining of 'weak blood' often receive iron supplements from their local physicians. Thus, women receive biomedical explanations of their complaints from Israeli doctors, which are then mapped onto to local understandings.

12. The age specific fertility rate (ASFR) is the number of births per women of a given age group x 1000. It is often chosen as the basis for comparison with other populations because it is unaffected by differences between the groups in age-sex composition (Shryock and Siegal 1976).

13. The open birth interval (i.e. including women who did not have a next pregnancy) was 40 months for users vs. 28 months for non-users ($p<0.007$).

14. For a more in-depth discussion see Phillips Davids 1998a.
15. The concept of 'ideal family size' or 'desired fertility' and how it relates to fertility behaviour and outcome has been discussed in of a number of articles (e.g. Pritchett 1994, van de Walle 1992, Westoff 1990). In the 'natural fertility' model (Henry 1961), low fertility regimes are distinguished from high precisely by the existence of a 'target' number of desired births in the former, while the latter are assumed to desire an unlimited number of children. In support of this, a number of researchers point to the fact that women in high fertility contexts have trouble giving a numerical answer to the question 'how many children do you want?' and instead answer 'it's up to God' or 'ask my husband' (see Bledsoe *et al.* 1994, Bledsoe *et al.* 1998, van de Walle 1992, Handwerker 1986a). This does not necessarily mean that women do not have some understanding of what appropriate and normative family size is, however. In my study, for instance, women could easily tell me how many children were 'too few.' As Penn Handwerker has put it, '"natural fertility" cannot be distinguished from "target" fertility when the target is a large number' (1986b: 9). While a number of women I interviewed did have trouble giving an exact number for the 'ideal', stating rather 'as many as God gives me', most were able to come up with a numerical response. For details see Phillips Davids 1999.
16. Several women told me that when they were ill with a fever, in particular, they liked the doctor to take blood tests because the drawing of blood itself was believed to relieve their symptoms. Chemtov, Kalka, and Fassberg (1990) discuss this ideology in its opposite context: people complained that routine blood tests for Hepatitis B among the healthy population were making them ill because it draws the good blood from the body. As one of their informants stated, 'the more you treat us the more ill we become. You take blood and we become weaker and weaker' (p. 222).
17. Depo-Provera was not available at the time of my formal survey, but came on the market at the end of the period of research.
18. Ronnie Shtarkshall is a leading authority on sex education and HIV prevention among Ethiopian Jews in Israel.
19. One could argue that ideology is only being re-appropriated. The association with STDs and promiscuity is still upheld, by teenagers and older people, alike. Outside of the framework of marriage, the loading of condom use with these associations is, on one hand, revered (male promiscuity is something to which to aspire), but also feared.

References

Anteby, L. (forthcoming), 'There's Blood in the House': Negotiating Female Rituals of Purity among the Ethiopian Jews in Israel', in R. Wasserfall (ed.), *Women and Water: Purity Rituals in Jewish Lives*, Boston: New England University and Brandeis University.

Ben-Ezer, G. (1990), 'Anorexia Nervosa or an Ethiopian Coping Style?' *Mind and Human Interaction,* 2(2): 36–9.

—— (1994), 'Ethiopian Jews Encounter Israel: Narratives of Migration and the Problem of Identity', in R. Benmayor and A. Skotnes (eds), *Migration and Identity*, Oxford: Oxford University Press, pp. 101–17.

Bledsoe, C., with F. Banja (1996), 'Reproductive Mishaps and Western Contraception: Tiny Numbers, Far-reaching Challenges to Western Theories of Fertility and Ageing', paper presented to the Demography Workshop, Population Research Centre, University of Chicago, 31 October 1996.

Bledsoe, C., F. Banja and A. Hill (1998), 'Reproductive Mishaps and Western Contraception: an African Challenge to Fertility Theory', *Population and Development Review*, 24(1): 15–57.

Bledsoe, C., A. Hill, U. D'Alessandro, and P. Langerock (1994), 'Constructing Natural Fertility: the Use of Western Contraceptive Technologies in Rural Gambia', *Population and Development Review*, 20(1): 81–113.

Bongaarts, J. (1991), 'The KAP-Gap and the Unmet Need for Contraception', *Population and Development Review*, 17(2): 293–313.

—— (1994), 'The Impact of Population Policies: Comment', *Population and Development Review* 20(3): 616–20.

Bongaarts, J. and R. Potter (1983), *Fertility, Biology, and Behavior: an Analysis of the Proximate Determinants*, New York: Academic Press.

Caldwell, J., and P. Caldwell (1994), 'Rapid Population Growth and Fragile Environments: the Sub-Saharan African and South Asian Experience', *Annals of the New York Academy of Sciences*, 709: 355-69.

Caldwell, J., I. Orubuloye and P. Caldwell (1992), 'Fertility Decline in Africa: a New Type of Transition?' *Population and Development Review*, 18(2): 211–42.

Central Bureau of Statistics (1996), *Vital Statistics* 1017, Jerusalem.

Chemtov, D., I. Kalka and Y. Fassberg (1990), 'Research Note: Blood Drawing and Hepatitis B: the Case of Ethiopian Jews in Israel,' *Sociology of Health and Illness*, 12(2): 216–26.

Chemtov, D., and C. Rosen (1992), '*Be "Gobez" for the Sake of Your Health*,' Report from the Multi-agency Committee for Education and Information on HIV Infection and Related Diseases, Jerusalem.

De Silva, I. (1991), 'Consistency Between Reproductive Preferences and Behaviour: the Sri Lankan Experience', *Studies in Family Planning*, 22(3): 188–97.

Ever-Hadani, P., D. Seidman, O. Manor and S. Harlap (1994), 'Breast Feeding in Israel: Maternal Factors Associated with Choice and Duration', *Journal of Epidemiology and Community Health*, 48: 281–5.

Goldscheider, C. (1996), *Israel's Changing Society: Population, Ethnicity and Development*, Boulder: Westview.

Greenhalgh, S. (ed.) (1996), *Situating Fertility: Anthropology and Demographic Inquiry*, Cambridge: Cambridge University Press.

Gruber, R. (1987), *Rescue: the Exodus of the Ethiopian Jews*, New York: Atheneum.

Haile, A. (1990), 'Fertility Conditions in Gondar, Northwest Ethiopia: an Appraisal of Current Status', *Studies in Family Planning* 21(2): 110–17.

Hailemariam, A., and H. Kloos (1993), 'Population', in H. Kloos (ed.), *The Ecology of Health and Disease in Ethiopia*, Boulder: Westview.

Handwerker, W. (1986a), '"Natural Fertility" as a Balance of Choice and Behavioral Effect: Policy Implications for Liberian Farm Households', in W. Handwerker (ed.) *Culture and Reproduction: an Anthropological Critique of Demographic Transition Theory*, Boulder: Westview, pp. 90–111.

—— (1986b), 'Culture and Reproduction: Exploring Micro/Macro Linkages', in W. Handwerker (ed.), *Culture and Reproduction: an Anthropological Critique of Demographic Transition Theory*, Boulder: Westview, pp. 1–28.

—— (1989), *Women's Power and Social Revolution: Fertility Transition in the West Indies*, Newbury Park: Sage.

Henry, L. (1961), 'Some Data on Natural Fertility', *Eugenics Quarterly* 8: 81–91.

Hodes, R., and Teferedegne, B. (1996), 'Traditional Beliefs and Disease Practices of Ethiopian Jews', *Israel Journal of Medical Sciences*, 34(7): 561–7.

Johnson, M., and B. Everitt (1988), *Essential Reproduction (3rd Edition)*, Oxford: Blackwell Scientific.

Kaplan, S. (1988), 'The Beta Israel and the Rabbinate: Law, Ritual, and Politics', *Social Science Information*, 27(3): 357–70.

—— (1992), *The Beta Israel (Falasha) in Ethiopia*, New York: New York University Press.

Kaplan, S. and H. Salamon (1998), 'Ethiopian Immigrants in Israel: Experience and Prospects', *Jewish Policy Research*, 1: 1–24.

Karadawi, A. (1991), 'The Smuggling of the Ethiopian Falasha to Israel through Sudan', *African Affairs*, 90: 23–49.

Kertzer, D., and D. Hogan (1997), *Anthropological Demography: Towards a New Synthesis*. Chicago: University of Chicago Press.

Kessler, D. (1996), *The Falashas: a Short History of the Ethiopian Jews (3rd Revised Edition)*, London: Frank Cass.

Lesthaeghe, R., and C. Jolly (1994), 'The Start of the Sub-Saharan Fertility Transitions: Some Answers and Many Questions', *Annals of the New York Academy of Sciences*, 709: 379–95.

Martin, T. (1995), 'Women's Education and Fertility: Results from 26 Demographic and Health Surveys', *Studies in Family Planning*, 26(4): 187–202.

Mauldin, W., and S. Segal (1988), 'Prevalence of Contraceptive Use: Trends and Issues', *Studies in Family Planning*, 19(6): 335–53.

McNeilly, A. (1993), 'Breastfeeding and Fertility', in R. Gray, H. Leridon, and A. Spira (eds), *Biomedical and Demographic Determinants of Reproduction*, Oxford: Clarendon Press, pp. 391–412.

National Research Council (1993), *Factors Affecting Contraceptive Use in Sub-Saharan Africa*, Washington, D.C.: National Research Council Press.

Noam, G., E. Benita and R. Levy (1993), *The Absorption of Ethiopian Immigrants: a Census in Kiryat Gat*, Jerusalem: Joint Jewish Distribution Committee.

Okun, B. (1997), 'Family Planning in the Jewish Population of Israel: Correlates with Withdrawal Use', *Studies in Family Planning* 28(3): 215–27.

Palti, H., C. Valderama, R. Pogrund, J. Jarkoni and C. Kurzman (1988), 'Evaluation of the Effectiveness of a Structured Breast-feeding Promotion Program Integrated into a Maternal and Child Health Service in Jerusalem', *Israel Journal of Medical Sciences*, 24: 342.

Pankhurst, R. (1992), 'The Falashas, or Judaic Ethiopians in their Christian Ethiopian Setting', *African Affairs*, 91: 567–82.

Parfitt, T. (1985), *Operation Moses: the Story of the Exodus of the Falasha Jews from Ethiopia*, London: Weidenfeld and Nicolson.

Phillips Davids, J. (1998a), 'Spoken Words, Hidden Meanings: Fertility Decisions of Ethiopian Jews in Israel', Paper Presented at the Third International Congress of the Society for the Study of Ethiopian Jewry, Milan, October 1998.

—— (1998b), 'Fertility Transition and Changes in the Life Course among Ethiopian Jewish Women in Israel', in D. Appleyard, and E. Trevisan Semi (eds), *The Beta Israel in Ethiopia and in Israel: Studies of the Jews of Ethiopia*, London: Curzon, pp. 137–59.

—— (1999), *Fertility Transition and Changes in the Life Course among Ethiopian Jewish Women in Israel*, unpublished Ph.D. dissertation, Department of Anthropology, Emory University.

Pritchett, L. (1994a), 'Desired Fertility and the Impact of Population Policies', *Population and Development Review*, 20(1): 1–55.

—— (1994b), 'The Impact of Population Policies: Reply', *Population and Development Review*, 20(3): 621–9.

Quirin, J. (1992), *The Evolution of the Ethiopian Jews: a History of the Beta Israel (Falasha) to 1920*, Philadelphia: University of Pennsylvania Press.

Ravid, C., A. Spitzer, B. Tamir, M. Granot and R. Noam (1995), 'Internal Body Perceptions of Ethiopian Jews who Emigrated to Israel', *Western Journal of Nursing Research*, 17(6): 631–46.

Ross, J., and W. Mauldin (1996), 'Family Planning Programs: Efforts and Results, 1972-1994,' *Studies in Family Planning*, 27(3): 137–47.

Salamon, H. (1993), 'Blood between the Beta Israel and their Christian Neighbors in Ethiopia: Key Symbols in an Intergroup Context', *Jerusalem Studies in Jewish Folklore*, 16: 117–34. (Hebrew)

—— (1994), 'Between Ethnicity and Religiosity: Internal Group Aspects of Conversion among the Beta Israel in Ethiopia', *Pe'amim*, 58: 104–19. (Hebrew)

Santow, G. (1993), '*Coitus interruptus* in the Twentieth Century', *Population and Development Review*, 19(4): 767–92.

Seeman, D. (1997), *One People, One Blood: Religious Conversion, Public Health, and Immigration as Social Experience for Ethiopian-Israelis*, unpublished Ph.D. dissertation, Department of Anthropology, Harvard University.

Shelemay, K. (1977), *Music, Ritual, and Falasha History*, East Lansing: University of Michigan.

Shryock, H., and Siegal, J. (1976), *The Methods and Materials of Demography*, New York Academic Press.

Trevisan-Semi, E. (1985), 'The Beta Israel: from Purity to Impurity', *Jewish Journal of Sociology*, 27:103–14.

van de Walle, E. (1992), 'Fertility Transition, Conscious Choice, and Numeracy', *Demography* 29(4): 487–502.

Wawer, M., R. McNamara, T. McGinn, and D. Laura (1991), 'Family Planning Operations Research in Africa: Reviewing a Decade of Experience', *Studies in Family Planning*, 22(5): 279–93.

Weil, S. (1991), *Ethiopian One-Parent Families in Israel*, Jerusalem: Hebrew University. (Hebrew)

—— (1995), 'Collective Designations and Collective Identity among Ethiopian Jews,' *Israel Social Science Research*, 10(2): 25–40.

Westoff, C. (1990), 'Reproductive Intentions and Fertility Rates', *International Family Planning Perspectives*, 16(3): 84–9.

Wood, J. (1994), *Dynamics of Human Reproduction: Biology, Biometry, Demography*, New York: Aldine de Gruyter.

World Bank (1993), *Effective Family Planning Programs*, Washington, D.C.: World Bank.

World Population Reference Bureau (1997), *World Population Data Sheet 1997*, Washington, D.C.: World Population Reference Bureau.

Young, A. (1970), *Medical Practices of the Bagemder Amhara*, unpublished Ph.D. thesis, Department of Anthropology, University of Pennsylvania.

7

New Reproductive Rights and Wrongs in the Galilee[1]

R h o d a   K a n a a n e h

Introduction

When I asked my old friend and classmate Fadia how some of the girls
we had gone to school with were doing, she told me that many of them
had married upon graduation and had several children. She called them
primiteevim (a Hebrew word derived from the English word primitive).
My elderly aunt who had nine children herself said that people today no
longer have large families because life has 'advanced': 'Before we didn't
know anything. But now only those who are wild (*mitwa'hsheen*) keep
on having a lot of children, living by their instincts.' Another high-school
acquaintance told me about her neighbours: 'They never plan anything.
They're like goats, like Barbarians, living by their instincts. They just
give birth and throw the children out on the streets without thinking of
how they are going to provide for them.'

'Primitive; barbarian; irrational; we must advance': these words have
entered the vocabulary of Palestinians in the Galilee in profound ways.
The modernisation/development discourse that constructs the 'Third
World' as uncontrollably and irrationally over-reproductive and thus poor
(Greenhalgh 1996), has been taken up by some people within that so-
called Third World. It has infiltrated Palestinian day-to-day constructions
of self and other. I argue that a new lens or social standard has emerged –
that of reproduction – for assigning social value, negotiating relationships
and envisioning progress. Using this measure, many Palestinians today
describe other Palestinians of being just like the Third World – wild,
animalistic, herd-like, driven by their reproductive instincts, unable to
control their reproduction, as opposed to themselves who are rational,
cultured, civilized, who carefully plan their sex and reproduction and are
advancing in the footsteps of the First World. Palestinians increasingly

distinguish themselves and define progress by looking through a modernist lens at how they have sex and make babies and 'by looking askance at other people's children' (Schneider and Schneider 1996).

It should be noted that this newly formed modernist discourse also has its flip side: the counter discourse of romanticized traditionalism and anti-modernization nationalism that reverses the terms of the argument.[2] Although less common than the modernist version above, some Palestinians also label others as selfish, rabid individualists, frivolous, materialistic, sexually loose, unthinkingly imitating the West, not wanting to have children. They consider themselves self-sacrificing, 'real' Arab mothers/fathers, bearing children and upholding traditional Arab sexual morals, families and the nation.

But in both cases (whether pro- or anti-modernization), supposed differences in number of children, spacing of births and especially contraceptive use have come to be important markers of status. To borrow Betsy Hartmann's term from a different context, 'reproductive rights and wrongs' are strategically deployed as part of the local negotiations of personal and collective identity and daily engagements of power (Hartmann 1987). The negotiation of reproductive decisions has become a central arena of struggle not only over women's bodies and lives, but also over significant social concepts such as 'the feminine', 'the masculine', 'the household', 'our culture', 'the nation' and 'progress'. Family planning has thus become an important locus of contest in the Galilee.

Contraceptives play a key role in these social negotiations. From the modernist point of view, reproductive control and family planning especially through modern medical contraceptives is widely esteemed. From the less popular anti-modernist perspective, 'natural' reproduction and fecundity are valued. Palestinians in the Galilee often subscribe to one of these views and sometimes oscillate between them. But for all the gradations of opinion, reproduction and contraception are topics of concern to almost all.

Background

The Palestinians in this study, unlike those living in the Occupied Territories or in the Diaspora, are citizens of the state of Israel.[3] They are largely descendants of the relatively few Palestinians who were not expelled outside the borders of the emerging state of Israel during the 1948 war. Nearing one million people, these Palestinians today find themselves an ethnic minority of about 20 per cent. The northern region of the Galilee where this study is based includes a large concentration of

Palestinians – estimates range from 50 to 75 per cent of the region's population, depending on how its boundaries are defined (Falah 1989: 232; Yiftachel 1995: 222). As non-Jews in a Jewish state, they are in many ways marginalized, second-class citizens (Jiryis 1976; Kretzmer 1989; Lustick 1980).

Despite (or perhaps because of) their marginalization, I argue that one of the reasons for the emergence of the reproductive measure among Palestinians in the Galilee is that this measure is central to *Israeli* definitions of self and Palestinian other. Palestinian acceptance of this measure is partly an internalization of these state discourses and policies. The Israeli state, by its very definition as a Jewish state, has long striven to maximize the number of Jews in the area relative to non-Jews (Friedlander and Goldscheider 1979; Said 1988). Thus the state characterizes Palestinians, especially those living within its borders – as the Galilee Palestinians in this study do – as an undesirable problem population whose backward fertility and reproduction are highly threatening (Kanaaneh 1997; 1998). The largely unquestioned (by Israeli Jews) need for a Jewish majority in Israel has produced the menace of an 'Arab demographic time-bomb' (e.g. Hadawi 1991: 157–8; Koenig 1976). Thus Israel's views of Palestinians inside its border are dominated by images of them as primitive breeders, irrational and uncontrollable reproducers. A powerful example comes from Professor Arnon Sofer, a prominent political geographer from Haifa University and Ministry of Interior planner, who stated on public television in 1995 that the most serious threat Israel faces is the wombs of Arab women in Israel. (Masalha 1997: 149) The rhetoric of development and modernization – that 'they' need to stop breeding – is heightened here and takes on strong ethnic overtones, as it does in many other locations around the world (see articles in Ginsburg and Rapp 1995).

It is thus ironic that Palestinians have partly come to mimic Israeli discourse – by defining themselves in terms of fertility and using sexual control as a measure of modernity or alternatively, Arab authenticity. It is not however surprising that options for empowerment and advancement in the Galilee largely follow lines of power that Palestinians simultaneously are subject to and try to resist. It is not uncommon that dominant structures define the few means through which empowerment is conceivable (Comaroff and Comaroff 1990). Thus Israeli state policies and rhetoric are part of the reason why Palestinians use reproduction as a register of difference, the same register with which they have been evaluated and marginalized.

A second reason for the salience of the reproductive measure, especially its more common modernist version, is the incorporation – as uneven and hierarchical as it is – of Palestinians into the Israeli economy, or more accurately, the bottom of the Israeli economy, and their exposure to a highly consumerist culture. This process began earlier in the century with massive land purchases and expropriation by Jewish agencies and later the Israeli state, thus effectively eliminating agriculture, the main source of livelihood for Palestinians prior to the establishment of the state. The result has been the forced proletarianization of Palestinians, who were then compelled to work for wages on lands they used to own, or in other Jewish enterprises, as the cheapest of blue-collar workers (Tamari 1981; Owen 1982; Bornstein 1998). The Israeli economy, bolstered by massive influxes of US government aid and private capital, has long benefited from cheap Palestinian labour from inside Israel as well as from the West Bank and Gaza.

But along with these forced and violent changes, a kind of 'seduction' has taken place as well. Many Palestinians have come to aspire to some version of the American dream for themselves or at least for their children. Many people indeed describe themselves as trying to 'follow in the footsteps of the First World'. By having fewer children many parents hope to provide them with recently conceived necessities: computers, Coca-Cola, Adidas footwear and Swatch watches. This reminds us that we are not dealing with some romanticized isolated location, but one that is intimately linked to a global network of markets and technologies of mass communication. These economic transformations involve new patterns of employment, but also changing patterns of need and consumption and changing conceptions of household economy and economic rationality that idealize small modern consuming families. Family planning thus becomes part of a consumerist strategy to provide more of these new-found needs to a smaller number of children. Increasingly, high fertility and large families are associated with poverty, backwardness and primitiveness. A certain 'economic rationality' has thus become a significant marker of modernity in the Galilee. Although most Palestinians are at the bottom of the consumerist system,[4] they are largely enveloped by it and express their hopes and fears from within it. Aihwa Ong writes that 'the disciplining of the labor force is an intricate, long-drawn-out process involving a mixture of repression, habituation, co-optation, and cooperation within the workplace and throughout society' (Ong 1991: 286). Thus these processes of globalization in the Galilee have been accompanied by an adoption of many tenets of modernization ideology, including ideas about the primitive reproductive practices of the 'Third World'.

A third factor contributing to the salience of the reproductive measure is medicalization. The past decades have witnessed the rapid penetration of modern medical services into the Galilee. That hospital deliveries in the Galilee went from zero to 100 per cent in the space of forty years suggests the extent of this change. The Palestinian community is relatively under-served and basic indicators such as infant mortality rates, or life expectancy lag considerably behind the better-served Jewish community (Central Bureau of Statistics 1996; Swirski *et al.* 1992, Reiss 1991). Yet Western medicine now shapes the way people view their bodies, conceive of sickness and health, and seek care. This has also given shape to new conceptualizations of reproduction and sexuality. In *The Woman in the Body*, an important text on the medicalization of reproduction in the United States, Emily Martin argues that not only does medicalization transform the physical processes of birthing, but new cultural values become embedded in these processes as well (Martin 1987). Martin tries to get at 'what else ordinary people or medical specialists are talking about when they describe hormones, the uterus or menstrual flow. What cultural assumptions are they making about the nature of women, of men, of the purpose of existence?' (ibid: 13). This chapter contains some parallel to Martin's work, in that I explore the cultural values that have emerged in the processes of medicalization in the Galilee. Medical expansion and scientific innovations not only transform the processes of body care physically, but can also transform social concepts and values as well. It is clear that basic assumptions about the superiority of science and modernity are embedded in talk about reproduction in the Galilee. Moreover, with the introduction of scientific methods of contraception, they have become entangled in the construction of identities.

Until the 1980s, contraceptives were available in Israel primarily through private physicians and required individual payment (i.e. were not covered by insurance). (Friedlander and Goldscheider 1979: 128) In the 1980s, the Ministry of Health partially initiated a family planning project that was pioneered in the Arab sector through governmental Family Health Centres. The Ministry was eager to start family planning programmes for Arabs, yet reluctant to do so among Jews (Kanaaneh 1998). Although the state's motivations for providing Palestinians with subsidized fertility control services are widely questioned, contraceptives are commonly known and used, including IUDs, hormonal pills, rhythm method, coitus interruptus and condoms (ibid.).[5] Moreover, my research suggests that reproductive control has become an important social measure of status.

Before discussing specific examples of reproductive rights and wrongs in the Galilee, I should note that the data for this study were gathered during a year of fieldwork (1995-96) and consist of open-ended interviews with a hundred Palestinians from various parts of the Galilee, eighty of whom were women and twenty men. The people I interviewed came from a wide range of economic, educational, familial and religious backgrounds, as well as from a range of urban and rural locations. However, in addition to these interviews my study draws extensively on what is inadequately termed 'participant-observation' in this community in which I was born and raised. Indeed the boundaries between formal research and the everyday were fuzzy. My fieldwork months were spent doing formal research activities which included (amongst other things) setting up interviews, visiting Maternal and Child Health clinics, being invited to lecture at a women's leadership group, discussing research methods with other researchers in the area, attending a conference on women and violence in Haifa, and e-mailing back and forth with a sociologist in Belgium. But I also went to shopping centres with my cousins, was invited to friends' engagement parties and relatives' children's birthday parties, helped my aunt with her gardening, watched music videos with my friends, and went to congratulate a neighbour on the success of her in-vitro fertilization. These wide range of activities have all informed this study.

Inexcusable mistakes

Dalal,[6] one of the women who participated in my research in the Galilee, is a 36-year-old secretary and mother of two girls, who grew up in the city of Haifa. She assured me that villagers have the most children in all of Palestinian society, much more than urban Palestinians. According to Dalal, villagers who move to cities were prone to change, but those who stayed in villages 'continue to have families that are too large'. She explained:

> I have a sister in law back in the village who knows her family's economic situation is difficult and still she keeps on having children, one after the other – they have four and live in one room. Sometimes they don't have the price of a bag of milk . . . This is shameful – it's not fair to the children. They don't go to school, they're just thrown in the streets. This is ignorance.

Indeed urban Palestinians often consider themselves superior to 'backward' village Palestinians, who in turn consider themselves superior to Bedouin Palestinians.[7] My point is that this hierarchy is increasingly constructed through the lens of sexual and reproductive control, and through the use, avoidance or 'misuse' of contraceptives.

While it is not my intention to elaborate on urban, rural and Bedouin differences in Palestinian society, I quote Dalal's emphasis on their reproductive ranking to illustrate the centrality of control and contraception in contemporary articulations of these differences. On several occasions of talking to Dalal, she characterized people in the cities as able to overcome their supposed 'reproductive instinct'[8] and become what she described as responsible, civilized reproducers. When I asked her about Bedouins, she said: 'Oh forget about them, they don't even know what contraceptives are. If they saw a condom they probably would think it's a piece of gum in a wrapper.' Her husband added 'They think that honour means having a soccer team for a family. They are oblivious to the modern world.'

Under this modernist regime of reproductive control, contraception has become widely esteemed. According to this perspective modern, advanced people have planned, small families with the assistance of medical science and contraceptives, while backward, primitive people have unplanned, irrationally large families because they do not use these contraceptives or fail to use them properly. Certain parents are thus labelled irrational and their pregnancies and births regarded as untimely and unplanned. In this light, 'mistakes' (unplanned pregnancies) become key markers of backwardness. Dalal's husband told me; 'It depends on a couple's background, on their level of culture. People who are not cultured and civilised have children by mistake.' Dalal, the wife, added: 'Certainly it is natural that a human being makes mistakes, in certain cases. For example with the day-counting [rhythm] method, it is possible to miscalculate a day or two. But I use a thermometer and keep a record so that everything is scientific and precise – you need a woman who has awareness, then you won't have mistakes.'

The planning of reproduction and the control of sex emerge as instruments of advancement. The use of contraceptives, and their proper use, becomes central. Men and especially women must manage their bodies in particular ways. Another woman, Suha, who has one son and one daughter, expressed sympathy for her 'mistake-prone' sister-in-law, but construed her repeated pregnancies as a failure to manage her body which Suha could not fathom:

There are a lot of women that can't manage themselves. They keep on getting pregnant when they don't want to because they can't manage themselves, they forget pills, or they get pregnant on top of the IUD – I don't know how that happens. My sister-in-law keeps on complaining about her children and her husband tells her it is her own fault, that she didn't manage herself. She used the day counting method and it somehow didn't work. I just don't understand why it didn't work so many times. I felt sorry for her, but some women just don't know how to take care of themselves.

Suha's sister-in-law is thus stigmatized for lack of control and planning. Her supposed mistakes or unplanned pregnancies were a source of some social devaluation, at least by Suha's standards.

'Making a mistake' for someone who is considered from an educated background is perhaps more stigmatizing than a mistake by someone who is 'the type that makes mistakes'. Rawan's sister-in-law, Salwa, got pregnant by mistake (according to Rawan) soon after she got married while still attending teachers' seminary. Rawan told me how embarrassing it was for her that Salwa did this. She said that Salwa had decided not to take pills because her mother thought that if a newly-wed woman took pills they would effect her ability to have children. Rawan said that Salwa's mother had these 'stone age' beliefs even though she was a Family Health Centre nurse. Rawan added 'what kills me is that her sister, who is getting her Masters degree at the Technion (University), supported her. "Yes, pills are harmful to newly-weds," she said. I couldn't believe what I was hearing from these educated people.' Rawan and her family were especially embarrassed since Saleem, Rawan's brother (and Salwa's husband), had not yet built a house and established himself economically. Thus the newly formed 'by mistake' family was cramped in the parent's household. Note that the entire family was delighted with the birth of the first child of a new generation. I do not wish to imply that people's embarrassment about mistakes made babies unwanted or resented. Nor do I wish to imply that stigmatization of mistakes as unmodern pregnancies is over-determining of identity or status. Rather, I suggest that a modernist discourse on contraception and reproduction is a major means through which identity, boundaries and power are negotiated.

Haniyyeh defended certain mistakes: 'Some women do get pregnant on top of the IUD. Some women even close their tubes and continue getting pregnant. You can't control that. There is a good percentage, probably 50 per cent, of women who say that they made a mistake and it is true. For people who make few mistakes you can believe them, but if they have more than five children and they are all mistakes . . .' Haniyyeh said that women could not be blamed for 'real mistakes'. Thus according to the modernist narrative there are also 'fake mistakes': certain women who claim to have made a mistake when in fact they wanted to get pregnant in the first place. According to this narrative, many women who want more children but in a modernist environment cannot admit to it, excuse their unmodern pregnancies as 'mistakes'. These women are seen as unable to justify their reproductive decisions within the modernist regime and thus resort to calling it a mistake – a pregnancy that occurred beyond their control or in spite of their modernist desires. It is very common to hear statements like Salam's that 'the real mistakes are just 3 to 5 per cent. The rest just say it.' According to Ahmed, the reason for these allegedly fake mistakes is that 'Women are ashamed to admit that they want more children so they say it is a mistake.' Thus most mistakes are inexcusable signs of the primitive in the modernist eyes of many Palestinians in the Galilee.

Nisreen, an older woman who was a social worker, told me:

> People need to match themselves to the times. If Arabs used to have so many children in the past, times are different today and they need to change. It is amazing how many women tell me they got pregnant mistakenly – 'mistake, mistake'. This is an impossible situation. I really don't think they are real mistakes, not the majority of cases. Only 5 per cent or so are real mistakes . . . There is a pathology in women's psychology. And it really takes a great effort and personal strength to separate yourself, to stop identifying with this traditional fecund model mother. It takes an incredible degree of self control.

When I asked Nisreen if she thought there might be a problem with the way the medical establishment offers contraceptive information and services she said: 'In the [government] clinic they have everything written, everything about the IUD and the pills and even coitus interruptus which people call "the method between the man and the woman" – and each one's pros and cons and the percentage of its certainty. Every woman knows that there are pills, and that it is easy to get them. But maybe inside her, she wants children.' Nisreen thus did not accept the excuse of mistakes, and saw women who continued to have 'mistaken' children as pathological.

Khadijeh, however, suggested that 'really, a lot of the blame lies on the gynaecological doctors, they don't give enough time and attention to their patients. Many of them never explain to the women how the IUD they are inserting or the pills they are prescribing work or what the woman needs to do. So it is not her fault if she remains ignorant.' An article in an Arabic daily newspaper is titled '16% of Women have Unwanted Pregnancies Because of Lack of Awareness'[9] (Sh'hadeh 1996). In spite of these qualifications, contraceptive mistakes and ignorance are still considered signs of a backward woman. Similarly, Suha said that she had developed some 'infections' and when she last asked the doctor to prescribe contraceptive pills for her 'the doctor told me "pills I won't give you" and that was it. She didn't explain to me what other options I had. If I weren't educated and aggressive I would have gotten pregnant. These doctors are just out to make money.' Despite the criticism of doctors, their women 'victims' are not free of the stigma of 'too many', unwanted or unplanned pregnancies.

Georgeina, who had four boys and used an IUD, also did not accept mistakes as justification: 'Mistake, this is just a word. This generation knows everything, they don't need to make mistakes. They learned at school and they are very smart. Some women say they got pregnant by mistake even though they weren't doing anything to prevent pregnancy. This is not a mistake.'

The counter discourse to this valuation of modernity and contraception is evident in the following quote from Ghanem, a male insurance agent and father of four: 'Some people want to try and forget their culture and origins. They just blindly imitate the West and do anything that is done in the West. But look at the results, the moral decay, the sexual corruption this has led to there. I am proud to be an authentic Arab and to have an authentic natural Arab family. Children are very important to us.' While Ghanem seems to offer the opposite view on reproduction, he continues to use it as a measure of identity and to define his relationship to modernity.

Thus alongside the pro-modernist discourse of reproductive difference, there coexists a less dominant counter discourse that does not consider large families and high fertility a stigma at all. Rather, having many children is a mark of authenticity, tradition and true Arabness. Kalthum, a 61-year-old woman from a family that is frequently stigmatized in modernist eyes, said: 'We are the ones who are right. What is the meaning of life without children? What are those educated people saving their money for? We want to enjoy life, to see our children and grandchildren filling the world. We are Arabs.' Opinions diverge, sometimes within a single family. While Taghreed said that 'I have been forced by my husband and the family to have this many children. I have not been able to adapt myself to this era,' her mother-in-law did not subscribe to this view: 'We are proud of our heritage and traditions. We are not so quick to forget them. I am Bedouin and my children will be Bedouin and my children's children will be Bedouin. There will be a lot of them, God willing, and they will be real proud Arabs.' This counter-narrative of traditionalism, like the more dominant pro-modernist discourse, is configured in reproductive terms.

Methods of Modernity

It is not only the use of contraceptives and their proper management that is significant, but different contraceptives are ranked and taken to signal various degrees of modernity. For example, coitus interruptus and the rhythm method are commonly considered less 'scientific', less 'guaranteed' and thus less modern. On the other hand, methods such as the IUD or pill are praised as more scientific and accurate and their users as more modern.

A relative of mine, Samiyyeh, didn't know what her older sister, who had six children, meant by saying she used 'the method between the man and the woman'. When I told her that this meant early withdrawal, she laughed and said: 'Yuck. I can't believe my sister would do that. I haven't even heard of people today relying on this. Why would anyone use this when modern scientific methods are available?' Samiyyeh preferred her chosen method of pills which she described as more modern than coitus interruptus.

Interestingly, another woman, Lamees, who practised coitus interruptus for five years and had only one boy, reversed the usual hierarchy of coitus interruptus as less modern than other methods such as the IUD, by emphasizing the control involved in the former. She told me: 'Only the wives of men who can't hold themselves insert an IUD. I don't need one. Unlike my husband, most men don't really care about their wives' pleasure.' By emphasizing her husband's degree of control and his care for her pleasure, Lamees stigmatized the IUD as a method for the 'out of control'.

In a conversation between Manal, a Family Health Centre nurse, and her sister-in-law Karam, contraceptive methods were also ranked in terms of their costliness, and the degree of attention they required from the user.

Karam: I just recently bought a packet of pills, and each packet costs 15 shekels. So it turns out to be the most expensive method because you need to buy more each month. The IUD is cheaper. Some women say: "Why should I pay so much for pills?" They just choose the cheaper method.

Manal: But the problem is that they have to pay the whole amount for the IUD all at once. And they complain about this too.

Karam: The IUD is guaranteed, but not a hundred percent. The pills are more guaranteed, but that is only if you remember to take them every day. I think most women think that the IUD is more comfortable because they could forget a pill, and you know how these women mess up. With the IUD, they just get it inserted and they don't have to ask about it any more.

Implied in Manal and Karam's discussion with me is a hierarchy of pills and pill users over IUDs and their users.

Anna Lowenhaupt Tsing's work on the Meratus Dayaks, a marginalized group in 'an out of the way place' in Indonesia, highlights the 'instability of meaning and practice' of contraception (Tsing 1993: 104). The meaning of contraceptive pills promoted by the Indonesian state was shifting:

> The pills I knew in the United States as artifacts of medical science had been transformed by Indonesian state discourse into an icon of bureaucratic order, and transformed again [regionally] . . . into the daily health-promoting herbal tonics of folk medicine, and again into nodes for Meratus acceptance of . . . state models of civilization (ibid: 104).

Tsing does not portray these wider political developments 'as imposed on a solid core of traditional social and cultural organization' where gender and fertility are assumed to solidly lie, unchanging and ahistorical (ibid: 105) These meanings coexist uneasily, were constantly being negotiated and were linked to regional political changes.

My project follows similar lines by highlighting the construction and negotiation of the meanings of different contraceptives in the Galilee. As I read it, it is indeed political, social and economic transformations and struggles that underpin the changing meaning and value of contraceptives. Shuruq, who has three children, told me:

> At the clinic, they didn't explain anything about contraceptives to me. Explanations are only for those who don't know anything, for women that the nurse can see are unable to take care of themselves. There are many types of contraceptives in the world. Today there are books and everything. A cultured woman can read and she can decide. For example, before they used to use injections, now they don't recommend using them anymore. They barely exist. Only older women who are used to using them still request them. My doctor said that advanced people in the world today use pills, and the IUD is now the old style.

The First World and its medical advancements, books and science, the accelerating present and future, and where 'we' lie in relation to them – all these can be read between the lines of Shuruq's, and many other people's, discussions of contraception and reproduction.

Tsing's work is a reminder that the state enters women's lives to different degrees in different places. Martin suggests that for middle-class white women in the USA, the state comes relatively close to their bodies and lives (Martin 1987) while, according to Tsing, for the marginalized Meratus women, the Indonesian state does not come so close, but does affect them indirectly (Tsing 1993). Within the Galilee, processes of medicalization and modernization have affected some women more than others, and not all women subscribe equally to the modernist hierarchy of planned pregnancies over mistakes, or new medical, doctor-provided contraceptives over 'traditional' or older contraceptives. But this has obviously become an important, if not hegemonic, measure of identity in the Galilee. Khadijeh, a nurse who is coincidentally also a devout Muslim, told me that my research absolutely should look at contraceptives:

> You should ask people about the type of contraceptive they use and how much they know about it and where from. A lot of women are afraid of the pain of the IUD because they don't understand anatomy and science. Still they don't think of the pain of not using an IUD, of being pregnant and delivering. Women also don't want to get an IUD because they say they don't want to open their legs in front of a doctor. But they forget that they will open their legs even wider when they deliver.

Thus sexual and reproductive control has today become deeply entrenched in the negotiation of power and identity in the Galilee. And it has become entrenched in ways that challenge us to examine the many categories of difference, including class and global positioning.

Conclusion

While population and modernization discourses are neither monolithic nor static, they have tended to centre on the 'evolution' from 'traditional', high and 'developmentally draining' fertility to 'modern', low and 'developmentally stimulating' fertility (Greenhalgh 1996). For Palestinians this binary opposition has entered daily life and shaped their negotiations of reproductive decisions. As discussed earlier, they now measure their own success and advancement by the same standards used by powerful groups in the state, in the economy and in the medical establishment. Although perhaps not entirely unique to Palestinians in the Galilee, the emergence of this modernist reproductive measure is certainly striking in this case.

It should be emphasized that these negotiations of difference are not just abstract debates about identity and modernity – although they are that too. Much can be at stake. The potential consequences of (successfully) labelling someone as 'reproductively primitive' can be felt in very non-abstract ways. These evaluations can be germane when applying for a job, considering an offer of marriage, opening a new business, running for local elections, or organizing a political demonstration.

However, there are many nuances to this process, individual variations, internal inconsistencies, and exceptions. Reproductive valuations – both positive and negative – are not immutable, nor are they unanimously agreed upon. One person's reproductively modern friend is another person's reproductively primitive neighbour. Even those who are widely stigmatized as members of reproductively primitive clans find ways of stigmatizing their own 'others'. For example, the Sleiman family was almost mythologized by many people (including my own family) as reproductive 'others' since they had eighteen children (or twenty, depending on whom one asked). Im Yaseen, the mother of the family, told me she realized she was considered a reproductive embarrassment by her children and that she was stigmatized for her large family. Still she had her own reproductive 'others':

> The secretary at the hospital got to know me because I came back so many times and she would feel very sorry for me. She would tell Abu Yaseen [her husband]: 'Brother, you have to let your wife rest a little, please, have pity.' But Abu Yaseen said 'No way'. And I did what Abu Yaseen wanted. My children were embarrassed that I had so many children, they wanted me to rest and they gave me pills secretly. Now they hate large families. But Abu Yaseen used to take very good care of me. Each time I would give birth he would buy meat and put aside all the nutritious parts for me. At the hospital, he used to always bring me the lungs to eat. For forty days I would eat nutritious food . . . All of [my clan] take good care of their wives, daughters-in-law and daughters – they don't let them suffer. Women from the lower families used to give birth in the fields. They used to carry their shoes in their hands and run so they wouldn't wear them out. Once there was a woman from the lower neighborhood who was in the hospital with me and when she saw the lungs that my husband brought me, she put her head under the covers and started to cry because her husband doesn't take care of her. Especially when she has a girl.

Reproductive stereotypes are flexible tools. Im Yaseen who was construed by many as a reproductive 'other' stigmatized her own set of primitive reproducers. No one class or group has a monopoly on the reproductive measure.

Although a distinct pattern of 'modern' over 'backward' emerges, it is important not to overstate the case. The reproductive measure and its binary opposition are strong but not hegemonic. A few people even told me that there are *no* significant reproductive differences in society. According to Fardos, aged seventy-one , 'There is no difference between cities and villages. Arabs are Arabs, and everyone is now cutting down on their family size. Women just want suits, every occasion they want a new suit. They don't care about children anymore.'

The definitions and requirements of 'modernity' in reproduction are shifting. The measures are flexible; there is no one-to-one correlation between, for instance, how many children a woman has and how modern she is perceived. In addition, reproductive practices are not the only measures of hierarchy used. Moreover, if Palestinians frequently rank one another according to a modern/traditional reproductive binary, this does not mean that even people who strongly subscribe to this binary are incapable of making alternative, non-dualistic representations. They often do. What is clear, however, is that these deployments of reproductive stereotypes 'are implicated in a wider set of relations of power' (Stoler 1991: 55). That people are playful, manoeuvring and creative should not be understood as contradicting this. Ginsburg and Rapp have noted 'that reproduction, in its biological and social senses, is inextricably bound up with the production of culture' (Ginsburg and Rapp 1995: 2). This is certainly clear in the Galilee. Today reproductive modernity and control is widely perceived as a significant guide to escaping marginality, negotiating identity and attaining progress.

Notes

1. I would like to thank Elaine Combs-Schilling, Hatim Kanaaneh, Moslih Kanaaneh, Areen Khalil and Fadia Khoury, Roger Lancaster, Brinkeley Messick, Rayna Rapp and Jane Schneider, among many others for helping me at various stages of writing and research. Research was made possible by a Fulbright-Hays Doctoral Dissertation Research Award and a Population Council Middle East Award.
2. Although this anti-modernist discourse harks back to an authentic past, it is largely a contemporary production shaped by and in response to the modernist version.
3. My research and findings were confined to the Galilee, but some parallels might be found among Palestinians in other parts of Israel, and even among Palestinians in the West Bank and Gaza strip or in the diaspora although they have experienced different forms and levels of political and economic oppression. These regions are certainly linked, their boundaries are to different degrees porous and they are frequently considered part of one zone of identification or imagined community (Palestine), but significant practical differences and separations exist which suggest difficulties in generalizing from my research beyond the Galilee.
4. In 1997 about 46.1 per cent of non-Jews inside Israel lived below the poverty line (National Insurance Institute of Israel 1997/98).
5. No official comprehensive data on exact rates of contraceptive use exist.
6. All names have been changed to protect anonymity.
7. Bedouins are a subgroup of Palestinians of recent nomadic origins. Although

forcibly sedentarized today in the Galilee, they generally make up a poorer social strata in society.

8. This 'reproductive instinct', frequently referred to in the Galilee, is a supposedly natural and universal human drive to reproduce, to increase one's progeny, and to achieve motherhood/fatherhood.

9. The study this article discusses actually finds that 16 per cent of women being treated at a particular clinic between the ages of sixteen and twenty-five reported having unplanned and unwanted pregnancies 'because of lack of awareness' (Sh'hadeh 1996).

References

Bornstein, A. (1998), *Give Me Your Identity: Palestinian Border Struggles in the West Bank*, Doctoral Dissertation in Anthropology, Columbia University.

Central Bureau of Statistics (1996), *Statistical Abstract of Israel*, Jerusalem: Hemed Press.

Comaroff, J. and J. Comaroff (1990), 'Christianity and Colonialism in South Africa', in F. Manning and J.-M. Philibert (eds), *Customs in Conflict: The Anthropology of a Changing World*, Peterborough: Broadview Press.

Falah, G. (1989), 'Israeli 'Judaization' Policy in Galilee and its Impact on Local Arab Urbanization', *Political Geography Quarterly*, 8(3): 229–53.

Flapan, S. (1987), 'The Palestinian Exodus of 1948' in *Journal of Palestine Studies*, 20: 3–26.

Friedlander, D. and C. Goldscheider (1979), *The Population of Israel*, New York: Columbia University Press.

Ginsburg, F.D. and R. Rapp (eds) (1995), *Conceiving the New World Order: The Global Politics of Reproduction*, Berkeley: University of California Press.

Ginsburg, F.D. and R. Rapp (1995), 'Introduction: Conceiving the New World Order' in F.D. Ginsburg and R. Rapp (eds) *Conceiving the New World Order: The Global Politics of Reproduction*, Berkeley: University of California Press, pp. 1–17.

Greenhalgh, S. (1996), 'The Social Construction of Population Science: An Intellectual, Institutional, and Political History of Twentieth-Century Demography', *Society for Comparative Study of Society and History*, 10: 26–66.

Hadawi, S. (1991), *Bitter Harvest: A Modern History of Palestine*, New York: Olive Branch.

Hartmann, B. (1987), *Reproductive Rights and Wrongs: The Global Politics of Population Control and Contraceptive Choice*, New York: Harper and Row.

Jiryis, S. (1976), *The Arabs in Israel*, New York and London: Monthly Review Press.

Kanaaneh, R. (1997), 'Conceiving Difference: Birthing the Palestinian Nation in the Galilee', *Critical Public Health*, 7(3 and 4): 64–79.

—— (1998), *Desiring Modernity: Family Planning Among Palestinians in Northern Israel*, Doctoral Dissertation in Anthropology, Columbia University.

Koenig, I. (1976), 'Top Secret: Memorandum Proposal – Handling the Arabs of Israel', *SWASIA North Africa*, 3(41), October 15: 1-7.

Kretzmer, D. (1989), *The Legal Status of Arabs in Israel*, Boulder: Westview.

Lustick, I. (1980), *Arabs in the Jewish State: Israel's Control of a National Minority*, Austin: University of Texas Press.

Martin, E. (1987), *The Woman in the Body: A Cultural Analysis of Reproduction*, Boston: Beacon Press.

Masalha, N. (1997), *A Land Without A People: Israel, Transfer and the Palestinians 1949-96*, London: Faber and Faber.

National Insurance Institute of Israel (1997/98), *Annual Survey*, Jerusalem: National Insurance Institute of Israel (Hebrew).

Ong, A. (1991), 'The Gender and Labor Politics of Post Modernity' in *Annual Review of Anthropology*, 20: 279–302.

Owen, R. (1982), *Studies in the Economic and Social History of Palestine in the Nineteenth and Twentieth Centuries*, London: Macmillan Press.

Reiss, N. (1991), *The Health Care of the Arabs in Israel*, Boulder: Westview.

Said, E. (1988), 'Profile of the Palestinian People' in E. Said and C. Hitchens (eds) *Blaming the Victims*, London: Verso.

Schneider, J. and P. Schneider (1996), *Festival of the Poor: Fertility Decline and the Ideology of Class in Sicily: 1860–1980*, Tucson: University of Arizona Press.

Sh'hadeh, A. (1996), '16% of Women have Unwanted Pregnancies Because of Lack of Awareness', *Al-Ittihad*, March 5 (Arabic).

Stoler, A.L. (1991), 'Carnal Knowledge and Imperial Power: Gender, Race, and Morality in Colonial Asia', in M. di Leonardo (ed.) *Gender at the Crossroads of Knowledge*, Berkeley: University of California Press.

Swirski, B., H. Kanaaneh, A. Avgar and M. Schonbrun (1992), 'Health Care in Israel' in *Israel Equality Monitor* No. 2, Tel-Aviv: Adva Center, pp. 17–23.

Tamari, S. (1981), 'Building Other People's Homes: The Palestinian Peasant's Household and Work in Israel', *Journal of Palestine Studies*, 1(41) Autumn: 31–66.

Tsing, A.L. (1993), *In the Realm of the Diamond Queen*, New Jersey: Princeton University Press.

Yiftachel, O. (1995), 'The Dark Side of Modernism: Planning as Control of an Ethnic Minority' in S. Watson and K. Gibson (eds), *Postmodern Cities and Spaces*, Oxford: Blackwell.

8

'My Body, My Problem': Contraceptive Decision-Making among Rural Bangladeshi Women

Nancy Stark

Introduction

Reproductive anthropology has highlighted the need to recognize the restrictive influence of society and culture on women's ability to independently control their fertility (Lock and Kaufert 1998; Harcourt 1997; Newman 1995; Sen, Germain and Chen 1994; Browner 1986; Sargent 1982). Sargent (1989) cited the interaction of both extrinsic and intrinsic factors that shape reproductive decisions and result in 'juggling' multiple agendas based on both ideological and material considerations. Ideological and cultural concerns that make up fertility decisions are entwined within the family. As Newman (1995: 16) observes 'contraceptive decision-making is a product of multiple and continuing negotiations in the family arena ... a concern not only of the couple, but of the extended family' (see also Mumtaz and Rauf 1997). Further, pressures from extended family toward certain reproductive goals often stand in contrast to the goals of international family planning programmes targeting young married women of childbearing age with strong messages promoting contraceptive use (Sen *et al.* 1994).

This is especially relevant to family planning efforts in Bangladesh, a poor, overpopulated country (Hartmann and Boyce 1989, Maloney 1986). Family planning efforts have been a successful cornerstone of a broader development strategy intended to alleviate poverty (see Cleland *et al.*1994). While early family planning research in Bangladesh focused on appropriate population control policy (Paul 1986), programming (Bhatia 1980), cost effectiveness (Caldwell and Caldwell 1992; Simmons et al. 1991) and factors affecting fertility, more recently attention has turned to cultural factors – specifically considerations of gender (Aziz and Maloney 1985, Simmons et al. 1988, Simmons *et al.* 1992) – affecting fertility and contraceptive use. Married women of childbearing age in rural Bangladesh possess little autonomy, and childbearing is central to their roles as women. Family planning messages compete with strongly held beliefs of family and community, but little research has addressed how these factors shape women's personal reproductive goals (see Schuler and Hashemi 1994), nor addressed how women negotiate competing pressures regarding fertility regulation in order to further their own reproductive goals within the household. Nevertheless, an understanding of how women who lack autonomy pursue their reproductive agendas despite family and community pressures is key to providing accessible family planning services which women will use.

In this chapter I discuss how rural women in Bangladesh negotiate the competing pressures of society, family and health care system in order to pursue personal reproductive goals. I argue that gender ideology is manifest in women's fertility regulation and decision-making. I describe the social and cultural context in which women make decisions, features of contraceptive use, including the methods used and their side-effects, and I discuss how the side-effects of contraception may undermine a woman's autonomy. Finally, I describe how women in this study who have direct access to contraceptive technology utilize these services despite cultural and familial opposition and problems with side-effects, yet avoid conflict within the family. I will show that women with few avenues for autonomy eagerly embrace the opportunity to control their fertility and suggest that women develop strategies that enable them to do so without jeopardizing their long-term social and economic security. The strategies employed by women are fragile, however and subject to complications that arise from contraceptive use.

Methodology

My findings are based on a twelve-month study conducted in two villages within block C of the Matlab Maternal Child Health and Family Planning (MCH-FP) project intervention and service area of the International Centre for Diarrhoeal Disease Research, Bangladesh (ICDDR-B). I lived in a house that I shared with a research assistant located within a homestead in the study village where the market and ICDDR-B health subcentre were located. Homesteads consist of several houses that face a central courtyard occupied by patrilineal kin. Once a man's sons marry they live with the new wife in a house within the homestead. Living in a homestead afforded the opportunity to observe day-to-day village life, as well as family interaction, since families live in close proximity to one another. I was able to become familiar with the range of concerns and issues affecting the study population. We talked with women as they carried out their daily work responsibilities and were able to attend special events such as marriage ceremonies and religious observances.

The research consisted of structured and unstructured interviews with 150 women ranging in age from 15 to 75 years of age in 103 households and included 17 Hindu and 133 Muslim families. Data collected on contraceptive decision-making and use was part of a broader research project that included obstetrical decision-making. Thus I mainly interviewed pregnant women, although I often interviewed other women within a pregnant woman's household as well. I employed as a guide, a woman who lived in my homestead that knew many of the families in the village and often provided introductions. The community health worker (CHW) also assisted in identifying participants. Information was obtained about present and past fertility regulation, including documentation of the decision-making process with regard to contraceptive use, problems or complications that occurred as a result and how women resolved those problems. The findings presented here are from data collected during formal and informal interviews with women as well as participant-observation.

Health Care in the Village Setting

Health care in the study villages, both served by ICDDR-B, may be obtained from numerous practitioners including ICDDR-B staff, market-based village doctors, homeopathic practitioners and spiritual healers who are consulted within their homes. Health care is available from a government hospital, however, though it was located in a nearby village, few women reported receiving services there. However, ICDDR-B provides regular dependable home-based family planning services free of charge to women through the Community Health Worker (CHW) who is herself a contraceptive user and village resident with at least a sixth grade education. The CHW aims to visit each married woman of reproductive age and every child under five years once every two weeks and maintains records of vitamins, contraceptives and other services dispensed. She offers a number of family planning methods including condoms, Depo-Provera injection, and oral contraceptives and refers women to the local, village-based ICDDR-B health subcentre for IUD insertions and to Matlab hospital for sterilization.

In addition to the services of ICDDR-B, several traditional practitioners provide contraception in addition to treatment for other health problems. They are the *kobiraj* (a shaman who provides spiritual cures and contraception that is herbal or in the form of an amulet), homeopathic practitioner, and 'village doctor'. The village doctor is not a trained, licensed physician; rather, he is trained usually through an apprenticeship with another village doctor, or by completing a formal government-training programme for health assistants. Despite limited training, the village doctor is called upon to diagnose and treat problems that are believed to require allopathic medicine, or have failed to respond to *kobiraj* or homeopathic therapy. Homeopathic practitioners, like village doctors, may learn their trade through apprenticeships or may be self-taught.

The location of the practitioner is important factor for women's access to services. While the *kobiraj* is consulted in his/her home in the village, and rarely has a shop in the market, the village doctor often works out of the market where men go to consult him about a problem and purchase medicine. The homeopathic practitioner may or may not have a shop in the market area, but are available to women who can either visit his house or send a child to his home to obtain medicine. Generally, women have limited access to market-based health services and must have a son, husband, or other relative who is willing to obtain the therapy they require. Village-based practitioners, i.e. practitioners who conduct their practices from home rather than from the market, are easier for women to access, as they can send a young boy to a nearby homestead, to request treatment or a visit to an ailing infant. The *kobiraj,* most accessible to women, may live within the woman's homestead or nearby, and may be an elderly woman herself. All practitioners expect payment, with the exception of certain *kobiraj* who are beggars or simply concerned with earning spiritual status.

The CHW is the only practitioner on whom women can readily rely for free, in-home service. This is central since women otherwise must obtain permission from their husband or his mother and possess enough money to obtain contraceptives. Thus, the CHW provides direct access to contraceptive services and methods *in the home* that are not otherwise available. Furthermore, because she maintains regular follow-up, the CHW can counsel women when they experience side-effects. That women have access to free contraception through the CHW enables women to control fertility decisions in contrast to other areas of their lives that are limited by physical and social restrictions.

Women's Lives: Family and Marital Relations

Life for rural women, particularly young wives, is characterized by severe limitation and strict sexual division of labour. Women do not travel unaccompanied or without permission from a husband, mother-in-law or other relative. They possess little authority or control over major events of their lives such as marriage, sexual activity, or finances. Shortly after menarche women are married to a man chosen by their families and live with the husband's family under the supervision of the mother-in-law. The new bride is completely dependent upon her husband and his family, especially the mother-in-law, for access to household resources. The mother-in-law permits the young wife to eat, take work breaks, and as one young wife reported, decided when she could resume sleeping with her husband following childbirth.

The young wife's responsibilities include both productive and reproductive labour. Indeed a woman is expected to produce offspring, particularly sons, and is subject to divorce or desertion if she fails to do so. As Rabia, an educated, urban woman reflected, 'the young wife is expected to work hard, produce sons, eat very little and never complain. In this way she brings wealth and fortune to her husband's family.'

These behavioural restrictions in turn shape the way women communicate with their spouses, particularly in communicating health-related needs. For example, rather than complain of pain in her husband's house, a woman may moan or more often become unusually quiet. One young wife related how she tried to communicate her miscarriage. Ambia reported that she cried all day with pain but no-one came to help her. Although she was alone in the house, she stated that she had cried loudly enough for her brother-in-law who was at home in the next house to hear, yet he did nothing. Why Ambia's brother-in-law did not respond to Ambia's cries is unclear; however, other women reported that they had been refused health care because of the cost involved. What is clear is that women are dependent upon a gatekeeper or intermediary within the household such as the mother-in-law to 'see' their unvoiced discomfort, acknowledge it, and obtain treatment. Cultural norms limit how women express need, when they allow the decision-maker within the household to see the problem, and whether they decide to obtain treatment which may incur unwanted or unaffordable expense. Consequently, ideal behaviour places women at a disadvantage, vis-à-vis resources within the household, and bars them from communicating their needs directly. These limitations are further compounded by the poverty that pervades most rural households. Considering the lack of decision-making power or access to otherwise limited resources, women value the direct access to free contraceptives provided by the CHW.

Contraceptive Use and Decision-Making

Fertility regulation is an integral part of reproductive decisions by women in the study villages; nevertheless, fertility control remains a disputed arena and a source of power conflicts within the family. Those who choose contraception, therefore, may do so secretly in order to avoid such conflicts. Negative attitudes toward fertility control persist, especially among older women. These attitudes are expressed in what may be termed 'contraceptive parables', related by older women. These stories are instructive and warn the listener of the pitfalls of contraceptive use in particular and, more broadly, about the result of defying gender role expectations. For instance, village women often remarked that tubectomy prevents the birth of children given by Allah. The unborn child becomes angry and complains to Allah who holds the woman accountable. Concern about Allah's wrath and access to heaven is further illustrated in the oft-quoted statement, 'A woman cannot go to heaven if she dies with an IUD inside her body.' This remark focuses on the disadvantage of using a method that may be discovered. In fact, physical evidence of contraceptive use is a real concern for a surreptitious user. A strident message to those bold enough to control their fertility was related by one elderly woman's story:

> A wife lived in a foreign village and took herbal contraception but became pregnant anyway. When labour began, the birth attendant arrived and checked up inside her only to be bitten by a snake. So the family called the snake catcher who pulled the snake out and cut it open. Inside the snake were all the pills the woman had taken.

This highly symbolic tale suggests that any attempt to control fertility is doomed, for more powerful forces ultimately control women and their fertility. Negative social and familial attitudes toward fertility regulation, however, did not deter the majority of women interviewed from using contraception at some time. Despite the social pressures, ninety-four women (62.7 per cent) interviewed admitted to past or present use of contraceptives, or in two cases, planned future use of contraception. Of those, five had undergone tubectomy and three reported that they were not current users because their husbands were working out of the area.

The most popular method was Depo-Provera (55.2 per cent), followed by the pill (32.6 per cent). Respondents preferred Depo-Provera because it was easy – one injection every three months – and left no evidence. Women worried about forgetting to take the pill, and surreptitious users feared that spouses might discover the contraceptive. The IUD was the least popular (7.6 per cent) because the device required insertion inside the body and an embarrassing internal examination. Furthermore, the woman had to take time off from domestic responsibilities and obtain permission from her husband or mother-in-law to leave home in order to have one fitted.

Few women reported using herbal contraceptives and those who did used them for brief intervals only. One reason given for the limited use of herbal methods was efficacy. One woman explained to me that she saw her sisters-in law using amulets and herbal contraceptives and they became pregnant, so she decided to take the contraception offered by the CHW instead. Despite their use of modern contraception, women maintained traditional beliefs about reproduction. In one instance this led to confusion over taking birth control pills. Rehana, a young pregnant woman, married ten months, denied ever using contraception, although she was listed in the CHW's record as an acceptor. When asked about the discrepancy, she explained that her husband, an apprentice village doctor, had told her to use contraception to delay the first child, so she obtained pills from the CHW. However, she suffered from *kalir dristi* (an ailment characterized by menstrual cramps and believed to cause infertility), so she never took birth control pills. Her mother-in-law meanwhile gave her an amulet to cure the *kalir dristi* and soon she was pregnant. Rehana blamed her mother-in-law for the unexpected pregnancy.

When asked why they had decided to use contraception, women cited the need to space their children (75 per cent) most often followed by the desire not to have more children (16.3 per cent). Mothers expressed the need for spacing so one child could mature and require less care before having another infant. The care demands of two small children, in the view of those women competed with remaining household responsibilities. Interestingly, the need for child spacing was a key message used by the CHW to encourage contraceptive use among young women. The message was successful perhaps because the emphasis is on timing rather than preventing the birth of children, yet the ultimate result is limiting the number of children. Furthermore, spacing children is an acceptable, face-saving alternative explanation to the admission that poverty is driving the decision to limit family size. Economic considerations were cited by only 5.4 per cent of respondents, but underlie much decision-making. As a result of my observations of daily life, and my informal discussions with women, I recognized how poverty shaped behaviour and decisions in all spheres of life for people living in the study villages. Just as women reported that their families ignored their cries of pain in order to indirectly avoid the unwanted expense of providing health care, the CHW message of spacing offers families a reason to limit family size without acknowledging the economic benefits of limiting their family size. While a family often wants no more children because economic resources are limited and they fear having more children than they can feed, they may not directly state economic considerations as a reason, in order to save face.

Reasons for contraceptive use were not limited to spacing and economics, however. In two instances, young wives without children reported using contraceptives as part of a strategy to escape unhappy marriages. In one case, Ambia, a young childless wife living in a strict, religious household confided that she planned to use contraception, and although I queried her for a reason, she offered none. Three months later I learned that this young woman had left her husband, causing considerable embarrassment to the household. Another woman's attempt to extricate herself from an unhappy marriage proved less successful. Following her marriage, Rinu took oral contraception without her husband's consent or knowledge. Once he found her pills, he confronted her and threw them out, but she obtained more from the CHW. She planned to leave her husband, and knew that she could not do so if she became pregnant. Rinu complained that her husband lacked education, was unemployed and behaved badly. During his brother's visit, several people, including her mother-in-law, slept in one room, with only a divider separating them; nevertheless, her husband insisted on having sex. Despite her attempts to leave, however, she lacked family support and finally abandoned her plan and discontinued her use of the pill.

Attempts by the women in this study to control their fertility, and thus their social world, by using contraception is indicative of active, goal-oriented behaviour in the face of many obstacles within the society that restrict their personal autonomy. One further complicating factor for women using contraception, which also undermined their independence, was the problem posed by side-effects.

Contraceptive Side-Effects

Side-effects were reported frequently, as was method switching. Thus, a woman may have taken three different contraceptives and reported side-effects from each one. Of the ninety-four women who reported engaging

Table 8.1. Reported side-effects of contraceptive methods (n=50)

Side effect	% Reported
Bleeding	50 n=25
Head/body aches	20 n=10
Amenorrhoea	14 n=7
Dizziness/weakness	12 n=6
Other (forgetful, infection, problem for husband)	4 n=2

in some form of fertility regulation either through contraceptive use or sterilisation, forty-two (44.7 per cent) reported experiencing side-effects. The first contraceptive caused side-effects for thirty-five (37.2 per cent) women whereas only ten (10.6 per cent) women reported side-effects with the second contraceptive they used. Of those women reporting side-effects with contraception, six reported experiencing problems with both their first and second methods. Irregular bleeding was cited most often followed by headache/body aches and amenorrhoea (Table 8.1). Bleeding was the primary problem reported for the most popular methods – injection (52 per cent), pill (46.2 per cent) and IUD (66.7 per cent). Moreover injection, the most popular method, also accounted for the majority of untoward effects (53.2 per cent of all reported side-effects) compared to the pill (27.7 per cent of reported problems) and the IUD (12.8 per cent).

Besides irregular bleeding, the most frequent side-effects reported for injectable contraception included amenorrhoea (20 per cent) and body aches (20 per cent). Some complained of a condition believed to stem from anaemia, characterized by arthritis-like symptoms and weight loss. This condition was linked to the use of Depo-Provera and was considered a sign of poor health. Similarly, other methods produced ambiguous ailments. For example, after bleeding, dizziness and weakness accounted for 23.1 per cent of untoward reactions to birth control pills, and in three tubectomy cases women reported body aches and weakness.

Concerns with irregular bleeding are rooted in notions about the importance of maintaining a balance of heat and moisture in the body, attitudes about the polluting nature of reproductive blood, and the very real fear of reprisals from husbands who discover their secret use of contraception. Menstruating women are unable to pray, cook (if Hindu), or engage in sexual relations. Blood loss is associated with loss of strength and energy. Amenorrhoea, on the other hand, is linked to a build-up of blood that also causes arthritic-like symptoms or other health problems. Thus, the proper balance of menstrual blood is essential to good health. Extended amenorrhoea, common with Depo-Provera, and breakthrough bleeding associated with both pills and injections disrupts the extended pattern of bleeding. Typically one's menstrual pattern centres on pregnancy and lactation, and the amenorrhoea arising from these states is not viewed as harmful. However, contraception alters the natural pattern and creates imbalance; thus women complain of weakness. Furthermore, contraceptive users may live under the threat of the wrath of God and family. Resulting guilt and ambivalence, combined with fears and disruption that accompany irregular bleeding, may find expression in complaints of weakness, dizziness and body aches. This may also explain the frequency of method dropping or switching. An earlier study (Bhatia 1980) reported the primary side-effects of Depo-Provera to be bleeding, weakness, burning, dizziness and body aches and the primary reason women discontinued the method.

Bleeding was the primary side-effect mentioned as responsible for giving up or switching a method (58.6 per cent). When side-effects occurred, the person consulted most often was the CHW (Table 8.2). Irregular bleeding associated with injection is often treated by the CHW with birth control pills. The CHW also provides pills for amenorrhoea secondary to injection to re-establish menses, especially before becoming pregnant. For body aches and headaches, women either consulted the CHW (11.4 per cent) or no-one (11.4 per cent). Although side-effects accounted for 30.2 per cent of discontinuations amongst women questioned, they were not the most frequently cited reason for discontinuing a method: the desire for another child was cited by 42.7 per cent.

Table 8.2.   Individuals consulted for contraceptive side-effects (n=47)

Individual	Percent
CHW	55.3 n=26
No-one	19.1 n=9
Sister-in-law	10.6 n=5
Husband	6.4 n=3
Health worker	2.1 n=1
Other	6.4 n=3

Table 8.3. Treatment for contraceptive side-effects (n=48)

Treatment	Percent
Discontinued method	45.8 n=22
CHW	22.9 n=1
Did nothing	14.6 n=7
NHSC	6.3 n=3
Village doctor	6.3 n=3
Kobiraj	2.1 n=1
Other	2.1 n=1

Table 8.4. Further treatment for contraceptive side-effects (n=9)

Treatment	Number
Kobiraj	3
Discontinued method	3
Village doctor	1
NHSC	1
Matlab	1

In addition to treatment offered by the CHW, women consulted other practitioners (*kobiraj* or village doctor) but in most instances women simply discontinued the contraceptive method (Table 8.3), often prior to consulting the CHW. When side-effects persisted, women then turned to the *kobiraj* or again, discontinued the method (Table 8.4), suggesting that women believed the condition might be related to spirit possession. For the most part, women exercised independence in decision-making even when faced with complications resulting from contraceptive use. Some instances were particularly shocking, and pose questions about health and safety, in particular reported instances of IUD self-removal. Three women reported removing the IUD because, as one woman described, 'I went to the health subcentre to have the device removed, but they would only give medicine for bleeding, so I removed it myself.' A second respondent, acting on the experience of her sister-in-law, consulted a distant relative who worked as a government health worker. Her experience illustrates the articulation of family and societal attitudes, the guilt and fear experienced by women and how this affects contraceptive decisions. Champa received an IUD three months following her first delivery, a son. She kept it for two years but her son developed diarrhoea and vomiting. Despite extensive treatment – health subcentre in-patient, the *kobiraj*, and homeopathic medicine – the child died, and relatives from her family and her husband's family blamed her IUD use for the infant's death. She consulted a relative who instructed her on self-removal of the device. During her menses she reached up inside, felt the string and pulled it out.

Those who removed the IUD themselves did so because they expected health subcentre staff to balk at removing the device or to prescribe a drug rather than discontinue the method. Yet Champa, faced with the loss of her son and blame from her family, needed to discontinue contraception in order to re-establish her fertility and perhaps her proper role. She had defied her family in using the IUD, and her perception that the subcentre staff would not support her decision to discontinue the device led her to act independently to discontinue it.

Decision-Making

The decision to begin using contraception was made alone for the majority of respondents (43.4 per cent), although 19.3 per cent cited the CHW's messages and 18.1 per cent their husband's directives as motivating factors. However, not all women were willing to inform their husbands about their desire either to space births or to obtain his permission – at least initially. Whereas 52.8 per cent did ask permission before taking contraceptives, a significant 47.2 per cent reported that they did not inform their spouses (or ask permission) at the outset (Table 8.5). Using contraceptives without permission was also inversely associated with education, since women with three years or less of primary education were more likely to act without permission. This finding has important implications, for those women with less education are perhaps more vulnerable to violence or divorce if discovered. Yet women with more education are more likely to be in middle class families, and sometimes are less willing to defy familial, societal, religious authority. Middle-class women with higher education are also more inclined to aspire to ideal gender role behaviour, thus, they engage in behaviours considered proper for women. Of those women who did not tell their spouses, 12.9 per cent did reveal their actions after they began a method (Table 8.5). Still other husbands discovered contraceptive use only after finding evidence – observing their

Table 8.5. How husband learned of contraceptive use (n=70)

Method	Percent
Asked his permission before using	52.8
Told him after began	12.9
Developed medical problems	5.7
Saw me with CHW	2.9
Still does not know	25.7

wives receiving injections from the CHW, finding pills – or learned of the secret when they developed medical problems and needed medication (8.6 per cent). Surprisingly, 25.7 per cent of spouses remained unaware of their wives' contraceptive use. Wives did not consult husbands because they knew permission could be denied (65.7 per cent) or because, as one woman put it, 'it is my body and my problem' (20 per cent). Another respondent explained, 'I never consulted anyone and no-one knows – if they did, they would be angry, but we have more children than we can feed now.'

Women went to considerable effort to maintain secrecy about contraceptive use. One respondent's daughter, who lived outside the Matlab MCH-FP service area, was present during my visit with her mother. She and her mother requested my assistance in convincing the CHW to provide a six-month injectable contraceptive so that she could take the shot during the visits to her natal home without the knowledge of her husband or his family. Another woman consulted her husband about contraception. When he denied permission, she continued to listen to the CHW's contraceptive messages and to watch other women in the homestead take methods. She decided to space her births despite her husband's directive. After her fourth delivery she surreptitiously obtained birth control pills from the CHW. She discontinued the contraceptive when fever developed.

The fear this woman experienced when she became ill while using contraception is real, since repercussions for defying one's husband can be severe. A young wife related how her mother-in-law was a user until the mother-in-law's husband discovered it and beat her. Minu, an older woman whose religious husband worked in Dhaka, described how she had taken the injection for years without his knowledge because he would divorce her if he knew. Minu realized that he suspected her, since sometimes he remarked that he thought she was using contraception. Therefore, whenever he was home we were not permitted to visit, or to acknowledge that we knew her when passing through the homestead, so great was her anxiety. Finally, one wife tricked her husband into accompanying her to the health subcentre where she had an IUD inserted. Komola convinced her husband that their young son had a fever and needed to go to the subcentre. He agreed to take her and the baby to the clinic. During the visit, Komola obtained the IUD, but did not inform her husband until later when she feared that she might develop a problem and need his help. Upon learning of his wife's deceit, he remarked, 'You are bold!' But she countered, 'We are poor, we can have children every two to three years, but if we have a child every year, we'll have no food to feed them.' To this rationale he made no reply.

Komola's decision to inform her husband after using contraception was the approach used by several wives. Often spouses responded to requests to use contraception with this response: 'If you take contraception I know nothing about it, I will not be responsible.' In other words, the husband on whom the wife is dependent for care and support refuses to pay for needed health care and reasserts his dominance by denying treatment if side-effects develop. As a result, wives who know, as Komola did, that their husbands would not permit contraceptive use, secretly take a method, and later confess in order to neutralize their husband's anger if problems arise. Using this approach, a woman could contracept yet perhaps avoid more negative fallout if her husband were to learn of her covert behaviour through some other means.

The approach was successful for most women who employed it, for several possible reasons. First, the indirect approach to interpersonal relations is valued in society. Frequently, one would remark of another individual, 'He is very clever,' meaning he does not show his hand, or is careful about revealing his agenda. For a wife to engage in deceit is especially thorny because she usurps control from her husband and defies her husband and/or household head by using a method without permission. She reasserts his status and authority by confessing, thus acknowledging his control. In other words, she re-establishes – and submits to – the social hierarchy.

Second, the success of this 'take and tell' strategy perhaps is rooted in conflicting societal and economic demands upon the household and in gender roles, particularly between husbands and wives. My observations and the data I collected suggest that men and women experience ambivalence about contraceptive use. Women consider it a necessity and risk physical abuse, divorce, side-effects, and guilt by defying household and religious authority. Men may experience conflict just as their wives do, because their concerns centre around maintaining family status in the community and their own position of power in the household. Adhering to the dictates of the community and religion must be balanced against the need to control wives and remain economically solvent. Furthermore, men are responsible for economic support of their families and fertility regulation may be viewed as their failure to provide adequately. The wife understands these demands, and as a woman (i.e. lower status household member) can defy her husband, and accept the sin and blame for taking contraception rather than have her husband lose face. The husband maintains social and religious standing because he never supported contraception and 'never knew of it'. A wife's defiance is resolved when she confesses her act, restores his authority and diffuses his anger.

Finally, women's strategies involve a particular mode of communication with their spouses. First-hand experience with indirect communication, observations and discussions with women and men during the course of research raised questions about how 'uninformed' some husbands really were about their wives' contraceptive use. On several occasions in the course of the research, I questioned whether husbands were truly ignorant of their wives' activity, since privacy is so difficult to maintain in village life. For instance, during one interview, a woman sat separated from her supposedly sleeping husband by only a bamboo screen. She reported (albeit in a low voice) that her husband had instructed her to discontinue contraception, but that she had not done so. Experience with men eavesdropping on my interviews with women led me to wonder if her husband, rather than sleeping, was probably straining to hear our conversation while appearing to sleep. If he did in fact know that she had not discontinued the contraceptive, he could maintain the charade of her obedience to his authority while addressing their economic concerns about family size, as long as she was not openly defiant, or publicly challenged his authority. Through such means, women may assume the responsibility for defiance of social and familial values and have some satisfaction in their independent action, while allowing their husbands to maintain social respectability. Thus, couples, by not communicating directly about contraception, engage in an implicit agreement to deal with competing economic realities and social demands. The extent to which these circumstances exist among couples is unknown, and may provide an area for future research on spousal communication and family planning.

Discussion

The majority of women in this study with direct access to contraception used a method to further their own personal or reproductive goals at some time during their childbearing years. However, this choice was not without consequences for many women. Some women defied family and society to take contraception and at times defied family planning personnel when they discontinued a method, as in the case of IUD self-removal. Most women preferred a contraceptive that took little time away from their domestic responsibilities and one that left no evidence. The issue of health care demands that interfere with domestic responsibilities has been addressed elsewhere (Stark *et al.* 1994).

Concerns about disruption of domestic work responsibilities is also an issue with contraceptive side-effects, which pose a significant concern for women in this study, both psychologically and physically, a consideration sometimes ignored by family planning programmes (see Russell and Sobo 1997). Most often women dealt with side-effects by discontinuing the method, thus maintaining their control. However, side-effects threaten a woman's control as problems with bleeding or weakness may impede her ability to work. Further, side-effects pose a real threat of exposure to women who secretly control their fertility. Women who defy social norms are subject to feelings of guilt when sickness or death occurs within the family, particularly with other children.

Because women have direct access to contraceptive services, many controlled decisions about fertility in that they identified the need and decided on the appropriate action; nevertheless, the CHW's messages, observations of other contraceptive acceptors, and family pressure also affected women's decisions. Although the majority of women did consult a spouse before initiating therapy, nearly half did not. A portion of those women who did not tell their husbands initially only informed their spouses later because of feared or actual side-effects from the method. The findings demonstrate that women will not only control decisions about their fertility but willingly defy family and societal standards in order to do so. They support other gender research reporting the proactive, goal-oriented behaviour of women living within circumscribed roles (see Sargent 1982; Browner 1986). However, decision-making about fertility also depends upon access to contraception, careful follow-up care, and perhaps most importantly, contraceptives that do not produce side-effects severe enough to require assistance or intervention from family members. Side-effects of this type destroy the woman's autonomy and secrecy, and demand acknowledgement by family members who may suspect, but say nothing. When one considers the secrecy and potential for negative consequences that attends contraceptive use, it is no surprise that women express concern about side-effects and require close follow-up. This may partially explain why women frequently switch methods. Finally the data suggest that couples may engage in implicit agreements not to discuss contraceptive use and avoid open conflict or challenge to authority and hierarchy structures within the household.

Conclusion

This study examined how rural women in Bangladesh devised strategies to further their reproductive and social goals amid competing pressure from society, family and family planning programmes. Their agendas are the result of weighing and internalizing competing messages from health workers, family, and other women, regarding the possibility, availability, and advisability of fertility control. Women initiate and discontinue use of contraceptives based upon self-interest derived from the need to maintain social and economic security balanced with productive and reproductive labour demands. This research supports the notion that family planning services can promote independent decision-making, but also emphasized the need to address side-effects of contraception which may undermine women's independence in this process.

References

Aziz, K.M.A. and Clarence Maloney (1985), *Life Stages, Gender and Fertility in Bangladesh*, Dhaka: ICDDR-B.

Bhatia, S. (1980), 'The Matlab Family Planning Health Services Project', *Studies in Family Planning*, 11(6): 202–12.

Browner, C. (1986), 'The Politics of Reproduction in a Mexican Village', *Signs: Journal of Women in Culture and Society*, 11(4): 710–24.

Caldwell, J. and P. Caldwell (1992), 'What does the Matlab Fertility Experience Really Show?' *Studies in Family Planning*, 23(5): 292–310.

Cleland, J., J.F. Phillips, S. Amin and G.M. Kamal (1994), *The Determinants of Reproductive Change in Bangladesh: Success in a Challenging Environment*, Washington, D.C.: World Bank.

Harcourt, W. (ed.) (1997), *Power, Reproduction and Gender: The Intergenerational Transfer of Knowledge*, London: Zed Books.

Hartmann, B. and J. Boyce (1989), *Needless Hunger: Voices from a Bangladesh Village*, San Francisco: Institute for Food and Development Policy.

Lock, M. and P.A. Kaufert (1998), *Pragmatic Women and the Body Politics*, Cambridge: Cambridge University Press.

Maloney, C. (1986), *Behaviour and Poverty in Bangladesh*, Dhaka: University Press Ltd.

Mumtaz, K. and F. Rauf (1997), 'Inter-and Intra-generational Knowledge Transfer and Zones of Silence around Reproductive Health in Sunnakhi', in W. Harcourt (ed.), *Power, Reproduction and Gender: The Intergenerational Transfer of Knowledge*, London: Zed Books, pp. 98–119.

Newman, L.F. (1995*), Women's Medicine: A Cross-Cultural Study of Indigenous Fertility Regulation*, New Brunswick: Rutgers University Press.

Paul, B.K. (1986), 'Performance of Supply Oriented Family Planning Policy in Bangladesh: an Examination', *Social Science and Medicine*, 22(6): 639–44.

Russell, A. and E.J. Sobo (1997), 'Editorial. Contraception Today: Ethnographic Lessons'. *Anthropology and Medicine*, 4(2): 125–30.

Sargent, C. (1982), *The Cultural Context of Therapeutic Choice: Obstetrical Care Decisions Among the Bariba of Benin*, Boston: D. Reidel Publishing.

—— (1989), *Maternity Medicine and Power: Reproductive Decisions in Urban Benin*, Berkeley: University of California Press.

Schuler, S., and S.M. Hashemi, (1994), 'Credit Programs, Women's Empowerment, and Contraceptive Use in Rural Bangladesh', *Studies in Family Planning*. 25(2): 65–76.

Sen, G., A. Germain and L. Chen (eds) (1994), *Population Policies Reconsidered: Health, Empowerment, and Rights*, Boston: Harvard University Press.

Simmons, G., D. Balk and K.K. Faiz (1991), 'Cost Effectiveness Analysis of Family Planning Programs in Rural Bangladesh: Evidence from Matlab', *Studies in Family Planning*, 22(2): 83–101.

Simmons, R., L. Baqee, M. Koenig, and J. Phillips (1988), 'Beyond Supply: the Importance of Female Family Planning Workers in Rural Bangladesh', *Studies in Family Planning*. 19(1): 29–38.

—— R. Mita and M. Koenig (1992), 'Employment in Family Planning and Women's Status in Bangladesh', *Studies in Family Planning*, 23(2): 97–108.

Stark, N., R. Akter and J. Chakraborty (1994), 'Therapy Management and Reproduction in Matlab', in *Matlab: Women Children and Health*, ICDDR-B: Special Publication, No. 35.

PART 4

Contraceptive Policy and Practice: Provider Perspectives

9

Uzbekistan in Transition – Changing Concepts in Family Planning and Reproductive Health

Monika Krengel and *Katarina Greifeld*

Introduction

Uzbekistan became an independent Republic of the Soviet Union in 1991. It is a society in transition, where old and new values, communist and Islamic traditions, and Western influences overlap. This chapter examines the present government policy and the related position of reproductive health. We discuss continuities and discontinuities in the institutional setting, and attitudes to contraceptives and reproduction among clients and health professionals. We will show how reproductive health is conceptualized in Uzbekistan and how changes in theories regarding contraceptive choice and practice are introduced into the lives of Uzbek women. Conflicting notions regarding tradition and change, practice and policies are a central concern of this chapter.

Setting and Methods

The material presented was collected within the framework of a bilateral Uzbek-German health project, 'Promotion of Reproductive Health in Uzbekistan'.[1] K. Greifeld was a project co-ordinator in Uzbekistan between 1995 and 1997 and M. Krengel worked as intermittent co-ordinator and carried out two studies in 1996 and 1997 (of four and three weeks respectively) as part of the project. The results of these studies are previously unpublished. The first study focussed on 'Conceptions of Reproductive Health at the Village Health Centres and Midwife Level'. It was primarily based on Focus Group Interviews (FGIs) with ninety-six midwives in fifteen focus groups. The second study was concerned with 'Life Plans of Young People, their Knowledge and Conception of

Sexuality, Gender and Contraception'. The study interviewed eighty young men and ninety-five young women aged between fourteen and twenty years in twenty-five focus groups. This was complemented by eleven FGIs with parents and nine FGIs with teachers. In both studies individual interviews were carried out with gynaecologists, other health professionals and administrators, and political and religious leaders. In addition, participant-observation research was carried out in families, hospitals and village health centres. All interviews were carried out with the help of a female Uzbek-speaking interpreter.

Research and project activities were focussed on rural areas in the Oblasts (regions) Tashkent and Namangan.[2] Rural areas are very different to big cities like Tashkent (population two million), in terms of lifestyle, culture, and health infrastructure. There are also variations between rural areas. For example, Oblast Tashkent, adjoining the capital of Tashkent, and Oblast Namangan in north-eastern Uzbekistan, are rather different. In Oblast Tashkent, the influence of the large city on people's education, employment and entertainment is quite strong, and industrial settlements are more developed than in Namangan. Oblast Namangan is in the most fertile part of the country, dominated by agriculture and populated by a more traditional rural population, strongly committed to an Islamic way of life.

Parts of the republic are agricultural, fertile and green, but the larger part (about 70 per cent) is desert. In the time of the Soviet Union Uzbekistan was famous as the supplier of 'white gold' (cotton), and cotton is still the most important export crop; Uzbekistan produces a quarter of the world's supply.

Uzbekistan has a population of 24 million. About 40 per cent live in the cities and towns. Ethnically the population is relatively homogenous and 72 per cent are Uzbek. The largest ethnic minority, the Karakalpaks, live in the area known as the Karakalpakstan Autonomous Republic, which covers more than one third of Uzbekistan. It consists mainly of deserts and is situated around the drying Aral Sea. Other minorities such as Russians, Jews and Germans have mostly left the country although, amongst others, Koreans and Tadjiks remain. Apart from some interviews with Russians our research was carried out amongst Uzbek communities and variations in the reproductive behaviour of the minority groups is not taken into account.

After Independence

Independence and the reopening of Uzbekistan to Islamic nations like Turkey and Pakistan and to the non-Islamic world has brought about high aspirations for the future including the formulation of new political and social goals. The strengthening of the nation through the improvement of maternal and child health is one of these goals. In this context, a large family planning programme was started by the government in 1991 in order to improve the health of the nation and to provide a basis for the health of future generations. High levels of population growth, an average of four to five children per woman, and high maternal and infant mortality rates, to mention just a few factors, led to the revision of previous policies which had not emphasized the need for family planning.

After independence the government was confronted with a variety of old and new problems, such as the ecological devastation caused by cotton mono-culture. The widespread incidence of anaemia is directly associated with environmental problems and the unrestrained use of chemicals. These ecological problems, in combination with high birth rates, are officially seen as major causes of the unsatisfactory state of reproductive health. According to government statements, the health of approximately 70 per cent of the female population is poor. Additionally the new Republic faces growing economic problems, related to the transition from the former Soviet-planned economy. A high rate of inflation and an explosion in the cost of living has reduced buying power and caused a great deterioration in nutrition levels. The disruption of the social support infrastructure including funding for health services, is yet another problem (cf. UNFPA 1998: ix).

As well as funding, success of family planning policy and the improvement of reproductive health also depends on people's social and cultural attitudes and on the quality of the basic health institutions which mediate between government goals and the desires and opinions of client populations. People's attitudes are influenced by different traditions and experiences. Dominant influences in this case include the secular Soviet regime, which was all-pervasive at the level of institutions and workplaces, and Islamic values and guidelines for a proper way of life, which remain prevalent at the family level. These influences, and the tensions between social, cultural and political conceptions regarding reproduction, are the main focus in the following sections.

Contextualizing Reproduction

Very little research has been carried out into the social and cultural context of reproductive behaviour in Uzbekistan. The first studies were prepared within the framework of multi- and bilateral cooperation, and no ethnographic work, to the best of our knowledge, has been conducted or published since independence. Published works refer more to demographic (e.g. Barbieri *et al*. 1996) or political analyses (Heuer 1993) or concern the time of Soviet rule (Olcott 1991).

Attitudes towards conception and contraception have to be understood in their social-cultural context. They cannot be viewed as reactions to purely biological or biomedical events. Demographic policy, institutional facilities, gender and family relations, all have to be taken into consideration. The circumstances of reproduction contain or refer to complete series of connected phenomena that are always culturally interpreted and explained: the beginning and the end of menstruation, the phases of fertility, sexual intercourse and its rules of giving and taking, desire and fertilization, pregnancy and birth, and so on. The meanings of all these events are logically linked in each culture and Uzbekistan is no exception. Sexuality and reproduction are also anchored in a tight network of values, customs and beliefs. Mary Douglas and others have shown that so-called 'natural' bodily behaviour does not exist, as the body is formed by its social world (Douglas 1982, Duden 1987, Martin 1987, Pfleiderer *et al*. 1995). For this reason we use the expression 'reproductive behaviour' in a way that goes far beyond its biomedical definition.

Socio-cultural Traditions and Changes

In Uzbekistan different social and cultural forms exist side by side. This is especially felt by women. In Soviet times basic infrastructural and educational facilities could be found everywhere. For males and females alike the illiteracy rate was very low (about 3 per cent) and education standards relatively high. Forty-five per cent of qualified employees who finished technical college or university were female, and in the time of the young republic (1991) 42 per cent of all employees were female. The situation has changed since women and men have been competing for employment, and concealed unemployment has been increasing (cf. Heuer 1997). This has lead to a redefinition of women's roles.

The destruction of the former centrality of the workplace is yet another factor that has changed the situation. In Soviet times health facilities were often bound to factories and collective farms, which had their own medical stations and personnel, and/or were closely involved in the maintenance and financing of community health centres. Women in the Oblast Namangan, talking about their pregnancies in Soviet times, told us that consultation with midwives and doctors often took place during the midday break at work. Women frequently pointed out how quickly after delivery they returned to their jobs (after fifty-six days), without being able to spend much time with their babies. Now women can take a three-year break after they have given birth, of which one year is paid. Most of the women interviewed welcomed the change, because it gave them more time with their baby. However, as many mentioned, the money they receive today is so little it would not be worth giving their job preference to childcare anyway.

The situation has changed further with the continuing process of 'Uzbekization' which, in our opinion, is a more suitable expression than 'Islamization'. Uzbekization for women means consciousness of their own Uzbek traditions, which are seen to involve supporting their menfolk and seeking fulfilment through the family and their children.

An obvious change, influenced by cultural and religious notions, is the rejection of abortion, which during the Soviet time was, apart from IUDs, the most widely used practice of birth control. A midwife from a hospital in Oblast Tashkent stated: 'Earlier, we had seven to nine abortions per day. Today, we have seventeen abortions per year.' 'Abortion is murder and therefore we approve of family planning through contraceptives,' said one of the Mullahs (religious authorities) to whom we spoke. In some interviews, mainly those conducted around Tashkent, we were told that due to social and religious disapproval, abortions are increasingly carried out secretly, that is outside the public health services.

Apart from that there was no univocal agreement about what revitalization of Uzbek traditions and Islamic values implies. In some FGIs, mainly in and around Tashkent City, female adults and teenagers stated that education of girls is becoming shorter and viewed as less important. There is an increase in early marriages for girls, accompanied by increasing discrimination against pre-marital sexual relations and a strong taboo against talk about sex and contraception-related issues. In the rural environment of Oblast Tashkent and in Oblast Namangan it seemed that, despite the secular milieu in Soviet times, these taboos have always existed. The idea of pre-marital sexual relations, especially for girls, caused disgust in adults and most teenagers. For mothers the very idea of their daughters having premarital intercourse was unseemly: 'That is unthinkable . . . That would be terrible . . . It would be like death.' The taboo on pre-marital sex for women may be strengthened by the practice, common in rural areas, of 'proving' virginity on the night following the wedding. One male youth said: 'Talking about sex comes close to doing it.' The danger that sexual education and knowledge about contraceptives may have an appetizing effect was expressed in many conversations with adults and religious leaders, often followed by criticism regarding the promotion of contraceptives on television. We were also told about the shame involved in talking about sexuality and reproductive health-related issues. When we asked one mother if she talks about bodily changes such as menstruation with her teenage daughter, she answered: 'No, we would both feel too much shame.'

A very important socio-cultural factor in the control of reproduction is the authority of the family. Teenagers often stated that individual desires and choices, e.g. concerning choice of spouse and spacing of children, should be subordinated to the interests of the family, which sometimes included brothers of the father and other close relatives. This subordination to the family goes hand in hand with the subordination of younger by older generations, and with the control of men over women. A sixteen-year-old boy said he thought that, in family planning: 'The man plans the children and the woman follows him.' According to another young man: 'You cannot plan a family. Children are a gift of god, the more he gives you, the better it is.' During a family visit, one woman stated: 'If the man refuses contraception, the woman has to follow his wish, it is like that and rightly so.' Another woman continued: 'Of course a man is proud if he has five strong sons, because then he himself is strong.'

Social acceptance and status are associated with the birth of children, especially in rural areas. The majority of young people interviewed stated that a family is more important than a job, although a family and job together were seen as best, especially for a man. Interviews with several unmarried female teachers revealed that childless women see themselves as inferior, even when they are successful professionally. A large number of those surveyed, when asked about the ideal number of children, said either four (two girls and two boys) or five (two girls and three boys). The number four was predicated on the argument that both boys and girls are necessary and that a girl or boy should not be alone but should have the company of at least one sister or brother. As in many other cultures, a son is very important because he stays in the house and cares for his parents, while a daughter moves to her in-laws. In this context it is interesting that the majority of the young people interviewed did not want to have their own household after getting married but said they would prefer to live as part of a larger family. 'If a couple has already five daughters, but no son, they will try again,' a midwife said, while another pointed out: 'If they have four sons and no daughter they will try again, because girls are necessary in order to help their mothers.'

The above-mentioned attitudes were not found in interviews with Russian teenagers and adults, who predominantly stated that marriage and decisions regarding children are individual choices. They also did not share the disapproval of pre-marital intercourse and the desire for large families and many children. A man from a health centre in Tashkent demonstrated the difference between Russian and Uzbek families by pointing out that only 6.8 per cent of the inhabitants of the old people's homes in the city are Uzbek, while 60 per cent are Russian, adding 'according to our tradition children care for their parents in old age, that's why parents prefer many children'.

Until recently women who gave birth to ten and more children received medals as 'big heroines' while those who had more than five children became 'small heroines'. This goes back to the family policy of the former Soviet Union which affected all states and not just Uzbekistan. These accolades were seen as a reward for the production of the soldiers and workers necessary to maintain the strength of the Soviet Union. The former governmental approval of a large number of children is still in people's heads, and goes well with contemporary cultural-religious desires for children as the foundation of strong families.

Along with socio-cultural factors, reproduction in Uzbekistan is closely connected with various health institutions. Women aged between fifteen and forty-nine years find themselves in the so-called 'reproductive age group', which is subject to tight supervision by medical and gynaeco-logical personnel. The emphasis on care and protection of mothers and children, which is the official image of family planning and its institutional implementation, can well be linked with the high esteem mothers and children enjoyed before the introduction of the reproductive health programme. This continuity notwithstanding, the government's current promotion of contraception and reduction of birth rates represents a discontinuity embedded in metaphors that leave out the crucial sex- and desire-related connotations of reproduction and bases family planning on health-related goals and dangers.

Statistical Information on Reproductive Health

Statistical information is not only important in formulating policies, but gives a more complete picture of reproductive health and the health of women as well as highlighting the general health status of the population. Here we review published and unpublished data that either originate from the Ministry of Health (MoH) of the Republic of Uzbekistan, or were collected under its authority. We also review statistics provided by international organizations active in Uzbekistan, including World Health Organisation (WHO), United Nations Development Fund (UNDP), United Nations Population Fund (UNFPA), United Nations Children Fund (UNICEF) and the World Bank. Overall, the quality of data collection, analysis, and reporting is problematic. As a result, data is often inconsistent and leads to conflicting policies.

The following is a summary of population determinants that show at a glance the demographic situation in Uzbekistan:

Population (total)	23.7 million
Female population between 15–49 years	5.3 million (22%)
Population under 14 years	9.7 million (41%)
Birth rate	26 per 1000 population
Mortality rate	6 per 1000 population

(Source: UNFPA 1998:5)

Compared with Western countries and its Central Asian neighbours, Uzbekistan has a relatively high birth rate and this, together with a relatively low mortality rate, means the population is growing and will be doubled, at current rates, in thirty-five years. The Republic really is young in the literal sense, although trends indicate that the rate of population growth will decrease in the future. The average number of children born per woman entering the 'reproductive age group' now is 3.2 (UNFPA 1998: 5), whereas in 1992, it was 4.4 children per woman (UNICEF/WHO 1992). Today, the five- to nine-year-old cohort is a fifth larger than that of children aged one to four years (UNFPA 1998:9). Recent changes in the political-economic framework, the break-up of the former Soviet Union and the high rates of inflation and unemployment that have followed on from this, appear to be having marked effects on reproductive decision-making and behaviour.

Infant and maternal mortality rates are relatively high: twenty-six deaths of infants under age one per one-thousand births, and 32.2 deaths to women during pregnancy and childbirth per 100,000 live births in the same year (MoH 1996: 13). Women who did not want to become mothers and died as a result of faulty and unprofessional abortions are apparently included in these figures. However, women should not only be defined through their reproductive capabilities and their potential for motherhood whether planned or not (see also Rance 1997).

As many as a third of all maternal deaths were caused by haemorrhages during birth (MoH, Population, 1996). But according to national statistics (ibid.), maternal mortality halved between 1990 and 1995, although living conditions have not improved for the majority of women. Inflation has reduced buying power significantly, leading to deterioration in levels of nutrition as well as in the overall health status of women and children

(UNFPA 1998: ix). While maternal deaths are decreasing, rates of sexually transmitted diseases are increasing rapidly. As UNFPA report (ibid: xiii) states, while 'in 1990 there were 363 new cases of syphilis reported, giving an incidence rate of 1.8 per 100,000 population, by 1997 this had increased to 11,503 cases and a rate of 47.3'. This tremendous change may be attributed to external causes such as increasing travel through the region, as well as to the readiness of the new government to acknowledge that sexually transmitted diseases exist in the country.

Information on contraceptive use varies according to study and region. The Ministry of Health, together with Macro International, drew up an 'Uzbekistan Demographic and Health Survey' (1996), that is in many ways the most reliable study. These surveys are produced throughout the world, using comparable questionnaires and data processing and analysis. In Uzbekistan, according to this survey, knowledge of modern contraceptive methods is nearly universal (at 96 per cent). Fifty-six per cent of the currently married women and 40 per cent of all women are currently using one or other contraceptive method. The next table shows the different use-rates recorded for modern and traditional methods.

Method of contraception	All women currently using, in %	Married women currently using, in %
Any modern method	36.6	51.3
IUD	32.6	45.8
Oral Contraceptive	1.2	1.7
Injection	1.0	1.4
Condom	1.2	1.7
Female sterilization	0.5	0.7
Diaphragm/foam/jelly	0	0
Any traditional method	3.0	4.3
Withdrawal	2.0	2.8
Calendar Method	0.8	1.1
Douche	0.2	0.3
Other	0.1	0.1

(Source: DHS 1996: 9)

The best-known and mostly used modern method is the Intra-uterine Device (IUD), for largely historical reasons. IUDs were used almost exclusively during the time of the former Soviet Union, when other contraceptives were virtually unknown, and certainly unavailable. Induced abortion was the other main form of reproductive control used in

Uzbekistan and throughout the former Soviet Union. With the new development of a national Islamic identity, the social acceptance of abortion is increasingly called into question.

Formerly a standard out-patient procedure, today abortions increasingly take place secretly, outside the public health services. As a consequence, they are no longer registered and therefore poorly represented in official statistics. Nobody knows how many of the maternal deaths caused by haemorrhages are, in reality, the consequence of botched abortions. Until today, women have not had the choice between pharmaceutical (e.g. mefipristone, RU 486) and surgical termination of pregnancy (UNFPA 1998: 31). As we shall see in the next section, improving the health of women and children is one of the major policy issues in Uzbekistan.

Approaches and Perceptions in Family Planning

Government rhetoric, represented by posters and signboards throughout the country, repeatedly speaks of the importance of a healthy generation for the future of Uzbekistan. Only healthy mothers, they say, are able to give birth to healthy children. National goals, rather than individual desires, legitimize the idea of family planning and contraception. The policy emphasizes the wellbeing of the family and the health of the mother. This includes the encouragement of good domestic relations, for example, through the support of needy or disadvantaged families, which is at the same time in accordance with the Koran.

Health personnel to whom we spoke, amongst others, justified positive attitudes towards family planning and contraception using arguments of the state with reference to the future of the new republic. As a young married man formulated it in an interview: 'Uzbekistan has a great future and we want to take an active part in the development of our country, so that we become a sophisticated nation.' The statement by the politician Anna Ivanova (quoted in Heuer 1997: 181) points in the same direction: 'The attention with which our children are surrounded in our Republic these days, allows us to be fully confident that a new, strong and healthy generation will replace ours and lead Uzbekistan to its place in the ranks of world states' (translation by the authors). Family planning appears as a (temporary) sacrifice for the wealth of the nation. In several interviews we were told that there have to be up to three generations of healthy children born before anaemia, which is viewed as a major threat to reproductive health, is conquered.

Although family planning principles seem to be largely accepted, it is still a sensitive subject if one tries to get beyond these kinds of statements and arguments. While government rhetoric leaves out the connection between reproductive health and sexuality, in the mind of the people it does exist, and leads to taboos about talking openly and publicly about matters related to reproductive health. Another difficulty in approaching the subject in depth is the deeply held ambivalence over state-promoted family planning and personal-familial desires and constraints. As mentioned above, a large number of children was politically welcomed in the past, and culturally it demonstrates strength, honour and male potency. In a focus group with midwives it was said that some of the tea houses, the traditional meeting places for men, are especially antithetical to the promotion of family planning, because men who use contraception are often the victim of jokes by others there, who question the virility and honour of the men concerned. This is not to deny that many of the people questioned (women, men and young people alike), wanted smaller families and welcomed the opportunity provided by a larger choice of contraceptives. Among the interviews with teenagers the opinion prevailed that, apart from improving the health of the nation, the desire for fewer children is necessitated by economic constraints. A twenty-year-old man epitomized this point: 'I want only two children, because the economic base in our family is not very secure, but if I had enough money and a big house, I would like five children and even more!' We were often asked why we in the West have such small numbers of children, even though we are economically well off. In none of the interviews were children perceived as the burden that, for reasons of time, patience and reduced choices for other forms of parental self-fulfilment, they can represent in the West.

Implementation of Family Planning Policies

The government family planning programme 'For a Healthy Generation' developed the following operational goals: First, the reduction of the high birth rate and second, the reduction of maternal and infant morbidity and mortality. In order to improve maternal and child health, these goals called for:

1. three year birth intervals,[3]
2. information on and provision of various types of contraceptives,
3. improvement of health care for women of fertile age: regular medical examinations, early registration of pregnancies and early hospital care in critical cases,
4. a shortening of the reproductive phase; women under twenty and over forty years were to be advised not to become pregnant.[4]

The Ministry of Health is responsible for implementing and supervising the programme, which is supported by a differentiated network of public health institutions. This network is strongly hierarchical. At the bottom are community health facilities, so-called FAPs (*Felsher Akuschersky Points, felsher* being a 'doctor's assistant' and *akuschersky* meaning 'midwife'). These are supervised by the *Rayon* (District) Hospitals. In between are what are sometimes called SUBs ('Country Hospitals'). There is roughly one FAP per 3,000 inhabitants. Depending on the population density of the region FAPs cover a health service circle from the immediate neighbourhoods up to 10 km and more. FAPs are staffed by *felsher*'s, midwives and nurses. There is generally no shortage of health personnel, especially at the FAP level, but the number of doctors and gynaecologists varies from *Rayon* to *Rayon*. In some areas doctors visit the FAPs weekly for a consultation day, in others they come monthly or less. Contraceptives, except condoms, are generally not available in FAPs. They are prescribed and usually given out by doctors, and women sometimes go to a lot of trouble and expense in travelling to a distant *Rayon* hospital in order to get supplies. In 1997 we observed that women who wanted to use an oral contraceptive had an average of four different contacts before getting it. Although contraceptives are distributed without payment, the cost of the time that women invest in their procurement are not generally taken into consideration by health personnel. Facilities at FAPs, e.g. the examination chair, and the workload and competence of the midwives vary. In some FAPs a midwife is responsible for up to 1,000 women in the fertile age group, in others she has to care for 100 to 150 women. In some focus groups midwives told us that they give out oral contraceptives in monthly doses and renew two- and three-month injectables after these have been prescribed by the gynaecologists and that, in rare cases, they sometimes insert or take out IUDs. In other groups this was not the case, but all midwives supervise if contraceptives are well tolerated and report problems to the *Rayon* gynaecologists.

Apart from ensuring that women go through pregnancy safely, midwives also communicate the necessities and possibilities of family planning to clients in the villages. Another of their main duties is to identify pregnant women, register and monitor them. Midwives keep notes on all women of fertile age. In accordance with the national programme, these women are classified into three groups:

1. women who should not become pregnant, because of illness or age,
2. women who should temporarily avoid pregnancy, because they have just given birth to a child,
3. women who may conceive freely.

Not explicitly included in the first group were women who already had many children. Midwives said that they tell a woman not to become pregnant anymore if she already has five or more children and it seemed to be taken for granted that such women would be in bad health.

Midwives are usually members of the local community and closely involved in decision-making processes. They know the social-cultural background of their clients and often function as mediators between generations and the sexes. They also have to find a path that satisfies both their duty to supervise as well as the desires and wishes of their clients, and balances governmental policy and cultural traditions. In our interviews with midwives, numerous tensions and conflicts were reported. On the one hand doctors and gynaecologists do not consider them to be competent enough to give substantial and final advice regarding contraceptives. On the other hand their advice is frequently requested by the people because they have the most immediate contact with them. Other tensions arise through their conflicting role of having to supervise their clients and wanting to serve them at the same time. As midwives sometimes said, 'from time to time we close our eyes,' referring, in one case, to a woman of about forty years, who still wanted a baby and somehow managed to get rid of her IUD. Usually the midwife would try to influence her not to become pregnant anymore at that age, or might even report the case to the *Rayon* gynaecologist. But in this case the midwife said, 'she is healthy, why should she not have another baby?' Nevertheless, influencing clients by soft pressure, offering repeated advice and talking with a 'sweet tongue' (an expression midwives used in this context) seem to be common methods of convincing women to use contraceptives.

Men rarely enter a FAP. If they have questions or need condoms, they ask their wives to go to the FAP. As one of the midwives said: 'I have worked many years and not a single man has come. It is a matter of shame. Sometimes the wives come to us and they say: "My husband wanted to ask you . . .".' Young women don't go to a FAP either if they have problems or questions; the mother-in-law will come instead, we were told. The mother-in-law also often serves as a communicator between daughter-in-law and her son. We were told that it is easier for her to communicate subjects like contraception or contraception-related problems to her son than it would be for his wife to do so. The most important requirements for a midwife were the development of a relationship of trust with their clients, and strict confidentiality. However, principles of confidentiality are not applied in a general sense. For example, midwives frequently give information if potential would-be in-laws inquire about the state of health of the boy or girl. Confidentiality is applied more strictly where women secretly use contraceptives, without the consent of their husband or mother-in-law. A midwife commented on this practice: 'Sometimes husbands force their wives to have more and more children. In some such cases it is a big relief for the woman if we say, "Sit down, I shall insert an IUD for you".' The husband will not know about it. For a good purpose one can also deceive.'

There was clear agreement, amongst the midwives and doctors to whom we spoke, about the necessity of family planning and the government programme, and a preference for giving advice on the use of 'modern' contraceptives rather than other, less 'reliable' methods (see next section). Recommendations for contraceptives from doctors and midwives are mainly legitimated through medical indications. As the health of the nation and next generation is an issue that concerns every level of public life, sometimes *mahalla* ('quarters') committees organize meetings and programmes in order to support the promotion of smaller families and the importance of maternal health.

Contraceptive Choices and Constraints

The following material is predominantly based on interviews with health personnel of different levels, especially midwives. Besides opinions held by health personnel regarding different methods and choices of contraception, the first part of this section contains preferences and complaints of clients as reported by the midwives, however, it is sometimes difficult to distinguish where the report about clients ends and their own opinions start. Apart from asking midwives about their professional experience, their personal feelings as women, mothers and wives and their own experiences with contraceptives came up as well. Information was supplemented by talking to clients. Some of their attitudes are recollected in the second part of this section. As contraception is a difficult subject to talk about openly, these statements cannot be seen as necessarily representative of what people really think and do. Verbally there is a strong tendency to follow the choices of medical experts, because 'they know best,' as we were told several times in these interviews.

Health professionals' (and people's) choices of contraceptives are, apart from the already mentioned social-cultural influences, affected by the following factors:

1. the familiarity with IUDs which leads to a preference for this method,
2. reconsidering contraceptive practice with the revitalization of Uzbek-Islamic culture, i.e. rejection of abortion,

3. insecurity about recently introduced contraceptives (oral contraceptives and two- or three-monthly injectables) and the diversification of
   contraceptives in general,
4. individual costs (time and travel expenses).

IUDs were introduced in the 1960s. Apart from condoms, natural
contraception and abortion, IUDs were the only means for family planning
in Soviet times. In most cases IUDs are inserted shortly after giving birth
at the maternity hospital. While some medical experts said that in most
cases the women themselves want to leave the hospital with an IUD, others
remarked that it often happens on the decision of doctors. We were told
that in rare cases IUDs are inserted without the consent and knowledge
of the woman, if she belongs to the category of women that due to medical
indications should not become pregnant anymore. It was our impression
that, until recently, the health personnel felt no need to discuss advantages
or disadvantages of IUDs with their clients as there was hardly any other
choice of contraceptives. This is now changing. Different doctors stated
that they do not prefer IUDs when prescribing a contraceptive, because
IUDs can worsen anaemia (which is widespread) by causing heavy and
irregular bleeding. These and other side effects are now being taken into
consideration as more methods become available.

However, the preference for IUDs by medical experts and clients
continues. The choice is mainly justified by habit and practicality: they
are well known, simply procured, easy to care for, have high efficacy
rates and are invisible (since, as we have seen above, some women keep
their use of contraception to themselves). As midwives in one of the focus
groups pointed out: 'We ourselves have IUDs, and we recommend IUDs.
IUDs are the best. The pill is nothing for our women. They are working
very hard and they forget to take them. One can forget an IUD for a long
time.'

Attitudes of health personnel regarding the advantages and disadvantages of IUDs and other contraceptives often varied from group to group,
obviously depending on the degree of received training and possibly on
the (influencing) opinion of the leading gynaecologists of the *Rayon*.
Those who were critical about IUDs, emphasizing that they should only
be used by healthy women, sometimes were uncritical about other contraceptives. In one focus group it was pointed out, that for anaemic women
IUDs have to be replaced by oral contraceptives, because 'pills are good
against anaemia, they are blood-forming, they are a medicine, they prevent
cancer and we tell our women that the pill makes them strong'. Midwives
who thought that IUDs were the best were still in the majority. However,

they pointed out that side-effects for their clients were reduced through the introduction of modern Western IUDs. 'Women prefer foreign IUDs, for example from Finland.'

Diverse opinions were also held by health professional focus group participants regarding the question of which method of contraception is most suitable after childbirth. In two focus groups with midwives in Oblast Namangan it was argued that insertion of IUDs directly after birth should be discontinued, because it is the time of *jhilla*, where women should not have sexual intercourse for forty days. The womb is still wounded, it was said, and because of that Islamic culture does not allow intercourse during *jhilla*: 'At that time the intrusion of an object like an IUD is not good for the women, nor is it in accordance with our culture.' Subsequently discussing this issue in two other focus groups, it was maintained that this is the ideal time for the insertion of IUDs, since women should rest in this period and the IUD adjusts itself easily to the body. They agreed that during the forty days of *jhilla* contraception is not necessary, because sexual intercourse does not happen. Some midwives were of the opinion that it is not necessary to use contraceptives after childbirth at all, arguing that breastfeeding is the best and most natural prevention of pregnancy at that time. We did not enquire systematically about breastfeeding among Uzbek women. 'Some of our women nurse their child three to five years, and we have to tell them to stop,' said a member of one focus group in Namangan. In another (near Tashkent) it was maintained that breastfeeding is common but that due to environmental causes the amount and quality of milk became less, and the period of breastfeeding shorter, in recent years. Here, as in a majority of focus groups, IUDs were given preference for the time after birth, since breastfeeding was regarded as too insecure a method on which to rely, and oral contraceptives were believed by women to spoil their milk, although midwives would try to convince them otherwise.

Oral contraceptives and two- and three-monthly injectables are considered the best alternatives to IUDs, especially for anaemic women, but have a list of side-effects and fears that women report to the midwives. Headache, stomach problems, depression, backache and asthma are, according to the midwives, the main complaints of women who take oral contraceptives. Besides the consideration of side-effects midwives do not recommend oral contraceptives because of the assumed unreliability of women in taking them. In several focus groups (mainly Oblast Tashkent) the opinion prevailed that 'injectables are best, and well perceived by our women'. This was justified with recourse to social, not biomedical arguments, since injectables can be given secretly if, for example, the husband or mother-in-law are against contraception. Compared with oral contraceptives, IUDs and injectables were perceived as contraceptives requiring less investment of time and effort: one does not have to think about them every day. In other groups injectables were disapproved of. It was said that 'they lead to infertility, that's why we recommend them only to women who should not become pregnant anymore,' or 'they are only good for older women, because they supply them with hormones when reaching their menopause.' Injectables do in fact cause delays in the return to fertility after their use has been discontinued. The suspension of menstruation which sometimes accompanies the use of injectables was pointed out as being a great disadvantage of the method. Women are afraid of becoming infertile or of being pregnant and not knowing, we were told.

Natural contraception, it was said, used to be more important in the past when no modern contraceptives apart from IUDs were available: 'We explained to our women that five days before and five days after menstruation, sexual intercourse is allowed,' said one midwife. A general attitude among midwives was that cyclic sexual abstinence, especially in combination with monitoring body temperature, needed discipline and was difficult to maintain: 'We primarily recommend condoms if a woman can neither use IUDs nor hormonal contraceptives due to her state of health and the side-effects.' People's opinions about condoms were ambivalent (see below). There was no mention of herbal contraceptive tradition in Uzbekistan. Coitus interruptus remains the most popular and widespread method of natural contraception and is in accordance with the Koran,[5] the midwives and others we spoke to told us. Midwives and doctors alike try to influence their clients not to practice coitus interruptus but to use condoms or other contraceptives instead. As one midwife formulated it: 'If a woman tells us that her husband tries to prevent pregnancy by coitus interruptus, we tell her it is harmful, makes her sick and leads to psychological disturbances and that she should try to convince her husband to use other means of contraception.'

While the practice of coitus interruptus has its roots in Islamic culture, abortion is connected with the Soviet era and now widely rejected. It was said that it is not necessary anymore because other methods of contraception are available and that it is not acceptable from a religious point of view. One of the midwives narrated:

> My father-in-law is Imam (religious leader) and he said to me, 'my dear daughter-in-law, I request one thing from you, never make an abortion, that's murder, that's a sin.' These words are repeated in our mosques. If God gives a child he cares that it has a good life. But this is not quite true, that's why contraceptives are accepted by Islam but abortion is not.

This generalizing statement is not completely congruent with the words of other religious leaders, who distinguish between the first three months, when abortion is permissible as an excuse, and the remaining period.

The use of condoms is still quite limited, although health service personnel usually recommend and provide them. Opinions of clients about the use of condoms, as reported by midwives, are along the lines of: 'Men strictly reject condoms. If one can eat honey why should one eat sugar? Most men are anyway against contraception, saying that God does not want it.' 'That is nothing, it does not make fun, condoms are only useful if no other contraception is possible.' The low acceptance of condoms is probably connected with the social ideal of manly power that manifests itself in the impregnation of women. The negative image of condoms was also connected to other experiences of products from the former USSR, which were regarded as crude and of bad quality. Like IUDs, condoms from Western countries were praised for their better quality. Furthermore, we were told that the use of condoms is associated with promiscuity and prostitution, phenomena that are said to be culturally unacceptable. In focus groups with teenagers we came across the opinion that condoms are not used for the purpose of contraception, but we could not find out what they thought they were meant for. Here, as in interviews with adults, the prophylactic use of condoms to prevent the rapidly rising incidence of sexually transmitted diseases (STDs) seemed largely unknown.

Apart from being available in almost all health facilities (FAPs and hospitals), condoms can be bought at pharmacies and small kiosks in towns. The distribution at public facilities is registered, so that people have to give their name and are given a certain quantity. The lack of anonymity is a big restraint on the popularity of condoms. As already mentioned, men feel ashamed requesting condoms and ask their wives to get them. To overcome this barrier some FAPs have started depositing condoms with the male head of the *mahalla*, who distributes them among men.

Sterilization is the most uncommon and least accepted of all contraceptive methods. Midwives often did not even know how a sterilization was carried out. Although some of the midwives were of the opinion that sterilization is not bad from a medical point of view, they maintained that it is socio-religiously inconceivable. It runs against the idea of fertility as a gift of God that should be controlled for the sake of a healthy family but not terminated artificially.

As already mentioned, our information on client's attitudes and choices regarding contraceptives is limited, and the larger part of their statements are included in the preferences, complaints and choices reported above.

We summarize some of these voices, focussing on contradictory statements regarding contraceptive choice and practice.

Verbal acceptance of family planning was, as pointed out before, widespread and there was a general praise for the new possibilities regarding contraceptive choice. But these new possibilities were not always seen as positive. In a focus group with married men it was said: 'These contraceptives are drugs, they are artificially produced and contain chemicals. How can we be sure that they don't damage our children?' This and similar statements were often accompanied by complaints that the promotion of contraceptives in the mass media, especially TV, is too superficial. In one focus group with married couples it was said: 'They appear to be harmless and good for us, but no information is given about the content, and what they do. We receive many foreign products these days, issued by different producers, and even the doctors don't know what they contain and how they differ.' Other participants of the group said that one has to trust modern trials of medical products. In several interviews with males it was stated that the use of contraceptives is nonsense if a woman is healthy. One man said, for example: 'Contraceptives are only good for the sick. My wife is very healthy, so why should we wait three years to have another child?' Religious arguments were seldom used to explain a personal choice. In conversations with women it was often pointed out that it is important to choose contraception with the consent of the husband and that peace in the family is most important. We were told several times: 'I don't use contraceptives because my husband does not want it.' Most women we spoke to used IUDs and had few complaints, or used natural contraception, such as coitus interruptus. Contrary to the above-mentioned critical voices quite a few men, but also women, were of the opinion that knowledge and choice of contraceptives should be the task of medical experts: 'What do we know? They best know what is good.' One of the men interviewed did not even know what his wife used as contraceptive: 'She once used to take the pill. What she takes now, I don't know. The doctors decide what is good for her.'

Coming back to the health personnel, they themselves are not necessarily up-to-date with the latest research on side-effects and contraindications. Some of the doctors freely admitted their insecurities and suspicions, e.g. regarding the components and expiry dates of modern contraceptives. There are further conflicting notions regarding priorities. Should practical, habitual and social arguments (as seen for IUDs and, partly, injectables) be given preference or should contraceptive advice be guided strictly by consideration of side-effects and contraindications? How can all be combined? Side-effects have medical as well as social-cultural implications. Women who suffer from side-effects sometimes face a double burden. 'Many women do not communicate with their husband about their use of contraceptives and they also hesitate to talk about pains and problems they face through side-effects,' some midwives told us. Discussions on the use of contraceptives and side-effects are linked by the same taboo. Furthermore, the ideal of healthy mothers puts ill women under the suspicion that they have done something wrong on their well-guided path to be a healthy mother.

Closing Remarks

Various, often conflicting notions influence contraceptive choice and attitudes to family planning in Uzbekistan:

1. the high cultural status accorded those with many children,
2. insufficient information regarding effects and side-effects of contraceptives,
3. the cultural taboos regarding sexual education and talking openly about contraception,
4. cultural and religious values, but perhaps even more so, the population policy of the state and its influence on the opinion and decision-making of the people who show, generally speaking, a strong identification with the new state.

Health facilities now offer a variety of contraceptives. A next step would be to encourage women and men to take a greater involvement in contraceptive decision-making and to take their desires and wishes into consideration. However, there exists a cultural and institutional barrier. Women, who according to medical personnel should not become pregnant, keep their pregnancies secret as long as possible. The relation between public influence and individual decision-making regarding family planning remains somehow problematic. The former Soviet attitude to decide from above what is good, is complemented here by Islamic traditions, in which men make decisions for women, and older people make them for the young. From the institutional side fertility and contraception are set in the context of health and illness and are, so to speak, 'sterile'. In practice they are naturally connected with sexuality and subject to cultural-religious taboos. Despite the desires of policy makers, family planning and the use of contraceptives cannot be fully integrated into initiatives regarding maternal health. Issues of sexuality and sexual education have recently come to the fore in Uzbekistan, especially in relation to the spreading of STDs/HIV and an increase in prostitution in urban centres. STDs/HIV are seen as a result of the rapid transformation of Uzbekistan from a closed society to an open one necessitating participation in the global market. They are a perceived threat to the new republic: even religious authorities are recognizing this as an important issue and understand the need for educational information. Time will tell whether this leads to preventive sex education or rather if STDs/HIV continue to be the subject of fear and dire warnings, as they have been in the past.

Notes

1. We would like to thank the two German bilateral agencies, the 'Deutsche Gesellschaft für Technische Zusammenarbeit GmbH' (GTZ) and the 'Kredit-anstalt für Wiederaufbau' (KfW), who jointly funded the ongoing cooperation project to improve the health of women and children. The project is carried out by EPOS Health Consultants, Bad Homburg, Germany. It started in 1995 under the auspices of the Ministry of Health in Uzbekistan. We would like to thank everybody who contributed to the project and helped in carrying it out.
2. Uzbekistan is divided into twelve *oblast*s ('regions'), which are subdivided into *rayon*s ('districts'), followed by village and *mahalla* (neighbourhoods). In the course of decentralization more and more authority is being assigned to *oblast* level administration.
3. The median birth interval actually is 2.5 years (UNFPA 1998: xi).
4. 82.9 per cent of pregnant women are aged between twenty and thirty years; 9.2 per cent between thirty-one and thirty-five years, and only 1 per cent are more than thirty-six years old; the proportion of pregnant women under twenty years is only 6.8 per cent (Ministry of Health 1998, unofficial statistic). These figures demonstrate that the goal of limiting the upper and lower ages of childbearing women is clearly happening.
5. 'The method mentioned in the early Scriptures is of withdrawal or coitus interruptus (*azl*). The Prophet (peace be upon him) approved it, as is clear from several authenticated sayings from the Prophet's companions' (*Islam and Family Planning* (1974) Vol. II: 557).

References

Barbieri, M., A. Blum, E. Dolkigh and A. Ergashev (1996), Nuptiality, Fertility, Use of Contraception, and Family Policies in Uzbekistan, *Population Studies*, 50: 69–88.

Douglas, M. (1982), *Natural Symbols*, New York: Pantheon Books.

Duden, B. (1987), *Geschichte unter der Haut*, Stuttgart: Greif-Bücher.

Heuer, B. (1993), '"Schwarze Schatten auf dem weißen Gold". Zur Lage der muslimischen Frauen in den mittelasiatischen Staaten der GUS', in U. Grabmüller and M. Katz (eds), *Zwischen Anpassung und Widerspruch*, Beiträge zur Frauenforschung am Osteuropa-Institut der Freien Universität Berlin, Osteuropa-Institut der Freien Universität Berlin. Multidisziplinäre Veröffentlichungen, Band 3: 77–100, Berlin: Harrasowitz Verlag Wiesbaden.

—— (1997), 'Nationaler Aufbruch in Usbekistan – Perspektiven für Frauen', *Osteuropa – Zeitschrift für Gegenwartfragen des Ostens*, 47(2): 173–90.

International Planned Parenthood Federation (IPPF) (1974), *Islam and Family Planning*, Vol. II, Beirut: IPPF.

Martin, E. (1987), *The Woman in the Body: A Cultural Analysis of Reproduction*, Boston: Beacon Press Books.

Ministry of Health (1996), *Uzbekistan: Demographic and Health Survey 1996, Preliminary Report,* Tashkent: Institute of Obstetrics and Gynaecology, and Macro International, Demographic and Health Surveys.

—— (1996), *Population Health in the Republic of Uzbekistan in 1994–1995 and some Stages of Health Protection Reform*, Tashkent: Ministry of Health.

Olcott, M.B. (1991), 'Women and Society in Central Asia', in W. Fierman (ed.), *Soviet Central Asia: The Failed Transformation*, Boulder: Westview.

Pfleiderer, B., K. Greifeld and W. Bichmann (1995), *Ritual und Heilung*, Berlin: Reimer-Verlag.

Rance, S. (1997), 'Safe motherhood, unsafe abortion: a reflection on the impact of Discourse', *Reproductive Health Matters,* No. 9: 10–19.

UNFPA (United Nations Population Fund) (1998), *Uzbekistan Country Population Assessment.*

UNICEF/WHO (1992), Report of a UNICEF/WHO Collaborative Mission with the Participation of UNDP, UNFPA, and WFP, 21.2 - 2.3. 1992, Republic of Uzbekistan.

World Bank (1996), *A Survey of Health Reform in Central Asia*, Washington: World Bank Technical Paper 344.

10

Family Planning or Reproductive Health? Interpreting Policy and Providing Family Planning Services in Highland Chiapas, Mexico[1]

Mary S. Thompson

Introduction

Since giving up its long-standing pronatalist stance on the family in the 1970s, the Mexican government has increasingly viewed population control as a facet of the economic and social development of the country (Singh 1994: 217–8; Merrick 1985: 1–3). The introduction of family planning services was intended to bring about large decreases in the national fertility rate which came to be seen as an impediment to the modernization of the country. Since the widespread introduction of family planning services a major disparity has developed in the uptake of these services between urban areas, where contraceptive prevalence rates are high, and rural, and particularly indigenous areas, where the uptake of services remains very low. After the development of an international consensus on reproductive health at the International Conference on Population and Development in Cairo in 1994, which brokered a truce between reproductive health advocates and defenders of population control under the umbrella of sustainable development (cf. Hartmann 1995: 131), Mexico introduced a new programme of reproductive health in which it legitimized both concerns (Poder Ejecutivo Federal 1996: iii). In this way, population control is retained as a legitimate policy goal with respect to the modernization of the country (cf. Dirección General de Planificación Familiar 1995: 7), whilst at the same time the concerns of reproductive health advocates are also addressed through the adoption of an informed choice agenda.[2] This agenda, based upon respect for individual and cultural beliefs for the improvement of health and social wellbeing, has long been a major concern of reproductive rights advocates concerned that population control objectives undermine choice and consent in family planning service provision.

In Chiapas, the local component of the reproductive health programme, Mission Chiapas for Reproductive Health, aggressively promotes modern contraceptive methods. It does this by numerical targeting to increase the use of 'modern' contraceptive technologies and through a policy of 'systematic offering' (*oferta sistemática*) of family planning services (see Thompson, in press). Under this scheme women and couples are offered contraceptive methods every time they attend a clinic for any reason, if not already using a method. Moreover, *oferta sistemática* is taken into people's homes by doctors, *pasantes* (trainee doctors) and auxiliary indigenous health workers carrying out domiciliary promotional work, even though, as one promoter told me, people get bored or angry with continual offers of family planning services.

These features of Mission Chiapas potentially undermine stated policy intentions to promote family planning services under an informed choice agenda. On the one hand aggressive promotion raises problems for providers who are supposed to understand that people are free to decide in an informed manner whether they want to accept family planning services and what methods to choose from if they do. Given the apparent resistance to family planning in highland Chiapas the promoters are faced with a task not only of raising awareness about reproductive health in the area but also of returning target success/failure rates to their superiors once a month, and perhaps jeopardizing their careers if numbers are too low. On the other hand the strategies of Mission Chiapas raise problems for the local population in each area where people dislike the continuing emphasis on family planning, which many only understand in terms of having fewer children. Aggressive promotion of services is quite likely to cause more resistance in this instance with a conflict between expert and local understandings of policy intentions. Contested knowledge in this sense leads to different interpretations of government goals and priorities: for health workers targeting is clearly a major priority; on the other hand, local people question the prioritization of family planning services over other needs such as water and drainage supplies or roads and electricity.

In the light of these problems policy rhetoric is rendered not as a neutral or benign entity but as an umbrella which may conceal the conflicting mandates within it to increase contraceptive prevalence (with a goal of reducing local fertility) whilst at the same time proffering *choice*. Moreover, the rhetoric conceals the existence of dubious practices, such as targeting and *oferta sistemática*, designed to address the population control objective, and masks a failure to address exactly how policy might be promoted in a culturally sensitive manner involving respect for the individual: elements which are merely stated as givens.

Setting and Methods

The seventeen municipalities of Los Altos are inhabited by a majority indigenous Maya population, mainly of the Tzeltal and Tzotzil groups, with a wider ethnic mix in the departmental capital, San Cristóbal. Chiapas has amongst the highest malnutrition and maternal and infant mortality rates in the country (Gobierno del Estado de Chiapas 1996: 99; Halperin Frisch and León Montenegro 1996: 2), and Los Altos is one of the most marginalized areas. In many of the rural areas basic infrastructure is lacking, with a paucity of electricity, drainage systems and potable water. Housing is basic, generally of wood or adobe, with dirt floors. Within households women suffer disproportionately from lack of access to health services, education and economic resources and are more likely to be monolingual Mayan speakers than men, which further disadvantages them in their dealings with health service providers who are invariably *mestizo*[3] and monolingual Spanish speakers.

Politically, Los Altos is complex. Since the indigenous uprising against the government in 1994, led by the EZLN (Zapatista Army of National Liberation), the political situation has remained tense and problems were exacerbated in 1997 with the massacre of unarmed women and children at Acteal by paramilitaries associated with local government figures (Durán and Boldrini 1998). The provision of government services, including health, has been an area of continual political contestation at the grass-roots level, and family planning promotion has often been greeted with suspicion of genocidal intentions (Personal communications: NGO worker, San Cristóbal, 1996 and Ministry of Health doctor, San Cristóbal, 1996; Day 1995).

In juxtaposing providers' attitudes ascertained through in-depth interviews against the rhetoric of official policy mandates, I hope to illustrate the conflict between policy and practice, drawing out the danger or insensitivity of attempting to transfer wholesale a policy designed at international level, and full of seemingly neutral but actually quite rhetorical statements about rights (cf. Shore and Wright 1997: 8), into a culturally distinct arena which has no such history of individual rights and where local democracy, necessary to underpin such rights, is severely challenged by high levels of corruption and a one-party State which, in

Chiapas, continues to rely on clientelism (cf. Teichman 1977: 123–4) to maintain its power base.

In order to investigate the gap between policy, procedure, and the desires of the people I draw upon data gathered during eighteen months' fieldwork in Los Altos between 1996 and 1997. As I lived in San Cristóbal I travelled throughout the region to rural clinics where I interviewed staff from thirty-four government clinics in the seventeen *municipios* of the region and from nine NGOs working throughout Los Altos. I used a semi-structured interview schedule which took, on average, two hours to complete. All interviews were conducted in Spanish, recorded and later transcribed. Long-term personal relationships were established with four doctors from the government health services and staff from two NGOs from whom life histories and experiential narratives were collected. Two of the doctors made it possible for me to attend and observe government health training courses for indigenous paramedical staff in rural munici-palities. Traditional anthropological methods of participant observation were employed in the befriending of fifteen families, mostly rural migrants of mixed ethnic (Tzotzil, Tzeltal and Chol) backgrounds from the marginalized *barrios* (neighbourhoods) on the outskirts of San Cristóbal, in an attempt to gauge local attitudes towards health and family planning services. These families continued to have strong links with their rural natal communities. Though beyond the scope of this paper, I contracted two women from this group to carry out a simple questionnaire amongst ninety-eight women in their *barrios* on attitudes to family planning services.

Policy Goals and Rhetoric: What Does it all Mean?

I arrived in Los Altos a year after the introduction of the government's new Reproductive Health Programme (1995) and began the process of trying to understand what this meant to local providers, and how it was perceived by intended recipients. It is important to make absolutely clear the ethnic distinction between the majority of the intended policy recipients who are indigenous rural people or of contested ethnic back-grounds in the city, and the providers who were all socially and culturally *mestizo*. Of the allopathically qualified or trainee doctors I met, in thirty-four government clinics, none were indigenous people.

The Reproductive Health Programme resulted from the integration of the two older programmes: Mother and Child Health, and Family Planning. Many sceptical locals suggested that the only thing that had changed was the programme name. During interviews, some government health staff were unable to define the difference or implications of the change. Those doctors and *pasantes* who could not say what reproductive health meant were in a minority, though significantly some were responsible for the family planning programmes in the clinics where they worked. However, most were confident that the reproductive health programme was, in practice, more of the same: promotion of family planning services.

These responses imply that one of two things has occurred: either there has been a change of policy which has not been perceived by providers or has not filtered down to the providers in any concrete way; or the policy change is truly, in effect, just a change of name. Setting targets for the number of contraceptive acceptors is not a new feature though *oferta sistemática* is, and it was to this that many health workers referred in trying to explain how things were different. During interviews with doctors, nurses[4] and promoters, I asked how things had changed in particular medical units[5] since the new programme came into effect. Whilst some responses were given hesitantly by those not sure of the answer, other people were convinced that no real changes had been made:

I think that up to now it's, well I don't know, the same but with another name. Well, we do the same things with nothing more than a different name. What was family planning is now reproductive health.
(Qualified nurse with responsibility for family planning, SSA, Las Rosas)

Well, it's the same, because we give the same talks.
(Female trainee doctor, IMSS, Zinacantán)

In practice, for us, it's the same – the same themes, the same programmes. (Qualified nurse, SSA, Chamula)

Really, I'm not absolutely sure.
(Male trainee doctor, SSA, San Andres Larrainzar)

Well, I'm not well up on it.
(Qualified nurse with responsibility for family planning, SSA)

Absolutely nothing. Everything is the same as before.
(Qualified nurse with responsibility for family planning, DIF)

Nothing. In essence nothing has changed much. The changes have been only in name because for as long as I can remember we have carried out the same programme. I am talking about fifteen years of family planning. It's the same programme.
(Senior male doctor, family planning clinic, SSA)

Well, here [in the clinic] there have been no changes. There have been changes at the institutional level but not here . . . here we do the same as before, we offer the same service, the same methods.
(Male trainee doctor, SSA, Mesbiljá (Oxchuc))

Nothing has changed at all. It's just the same.
(Qualified nurse, SSA)

Well, it's the same. That's to say there have not been any changes except for the name, but the service that's given – for those who receive these services – nothing has changed. It's the same.
(Promoter, IMSS, El Niz (Oxchuc))

Given the preoccupation with targeting and *oferta sistemática*, it is easy to understand why health providers may perceive reproductive health as simply family planning with a new name, even when they believe that reproductive health should cover more than this. One of the problems with measuring the success of this programme hinges on the promotion of a quantitative solution, targeting, which makes few allowances for, and may even undermine, its qualitative features (cf. Justice 1989: 132) such as the informed choice element. When providers are forced to think in terms of monthly targets, they leave themselves no room to deal with a population which is not only culturally distinct but where language barriers further complicate communication between clients and providers. These cultural and linguistic factors need much attention and deliberation if informed choice is to be considered viable. To promote any health measures amongst this population requires time, patience and care. Moreover a sensitive negotiation is required not only of health practices, but also of local power structures. In Chiapas these allow the contradiction of co-optation by the State on the one hand, and on the other semi-autonomy within indigenous communities which often operate as separate entities (cf. Luiselli 1994: 54) within state boundaries. These cultural, linguistic and political pressures are borne by health providers who, apart from their own problems of physical and cultural isolation in living and working in these communities (Freyermuth 1993: 48), are under constant pressure to achieve statistical goals as a measure of their efficacy and the public success of the programme.

Mission Chiapas for Reproductive Health

The quantitative goals outlined are contextualized within a qualitative rhetoric, also defined as a goal within the reproductive health programme:

To ensure that the population knows and understands the benefits and risks of contraceptives and can choose the one which is most suitable to allow them to live in a state of physical, mental and social well-being in accordance with their expectations.

(Gobierno del Estado de Chiapas 1996: 66, my translation)

This qualitative goal is not monitored or measured in any definable way, at least in Chiapas. Any increase in contraceptive prevalence cannot stand alone as proof positive that a given population or individual understands the benefits and risks of contraceptives and has been able to make an informed decision, particularly given difficulties with this concept.[6] For providers there are more crucial questions of how to interpret this rhetoric and how to gauge for themselves whether or not the intended users comprehend promotional information, what the problems are in communicating this information, and what to do to improve the situation, which all health workers agree is poor in Los Altos.

Communicating information to a user group is not a one-way process although the inherent assumption of policy makers is that once people understand family planning they will choose to use contraceptive methods. Planners place little importance on providers' understandings of their clients' culture yet, without this understanding, how are providers to understand the 'expectations' of intended policy recipients? In Los Altos doctors and *pasantes* are exhorted to consider the cultural differences of their intended client population but all too often this translates into a perceived problem that family planning services are rejected 'because of the culture' (*por la cultura*). This generally means that as 'backward' and 'traditional' people full of superstition, client populations simply cannot understand what is good for them, since they do not speak the same language and often lack formal education. These differences are verbalized by health providers to argue that the low use of contraceptive methods, which along with other allopathic health measures continue to be resisted, is the fault of the people and not the planners and providers (cf. Salvatierra *et al.,* cited in Sánchez *et al.*[7] 1995: 74; Thompson in press).

Such problems may be expressed by providers in terms of their own frustrations and also may be framed in terms of racism. One doctor told me of feeling thwarted as a newcomer to a Tzotzil community. Unable to speak the language, and working through local bilingual members of the community, she could not understand why people often ignored her advice and why, when lives were at stake, people refused to go to the hospital. After a number of years working in the area, during which time she learned some of the language and came to understand the importance of traditional healing which she saw used concurrently with allopathic methods, she was able to incorporate her growing knowledge of the people into her work and find a balance in her approach. She contrasted her experiences to those of her friend who after only a few months gave up working in a Tzotzil area because 'she thought that the Indians were dirty and she couldn't bear touching them.'

Given these problems in communication and lack of empathy with the local population how are providers supposed to understand local expectations? Large families fulfil local expectations, and contraceptive use is often equated with female promiscuity,[8] or is framed in terms of side-effects (which many providers openly scoff at because they do not fit the narrow, medical definitions they are taught). Reported local fears included that the IUD could become embedded in the womb or in the head of the foetus; that sterilization will leave a woman weak and undermine the masculinity of a man; and that pills form balls in the stomach and/or cause cancer. The reporting of biomedically expected side-effects, such as headaches and weight gain with hormonal contraceptives, was also scoffed at by some providers who said that women complain for nothing or for very little. Merely stating biomedical risk factors and contraindications of contraceptive methods (cf. Sobo and Russell 1997: 25), alongside the presentation of bureaucratically constructed material about health benefits, does not communicate a rationale for changed behaviour especially when there is a long history of distrust by indigenous groups of State machinery and intentions. In this region of acute poverty there are few examples proving smaller families to be more economically viable. In Chiapas children provide added income and future security within the family,[9] and confer adult status and prestige upon parents (cf. Moser 1994: 45).

Expectations for health and wellbeing, then, are culturally located. Provider expectations revolve not around the social wellbeing of the targeted population but in part upon the propounded expectations of the policy makers. Their own expectations are also coloured by their views of the local population who they often blame for lack of policy successes. Policy rhetoric is framed in a would-be acultural vacuum which pays lip-service to cultural variations and to individual wants yet ultimately expects a rationalistic adherence to its commands, based upon the logical prognosis of bureaucratic aims. This leads to the prescription of desired outcomes rather than negotiation and participation with target populations. In Chiapas there is a definite lack of self-representation by the indigenous population in plans which directly affect them, no less in health than in other areas of socio-economic planning.

Policy Prescription or Local Participation

The grass-roots solution touted to bridge these gaps between policy makers, providers and intended recipients is that of local participation in policy decision-making (see Rew 1996; and Grillo and Stirrat 1997, for recent analyses of this long-standing development approach). In Los Altos this has certainly not happened with reproductive health policy which, despite being integrated into primary health care modules, continues to be shaped by vertical policy mandates. However, within the provision of family planning services, health staff in Los Altos expressed, as fact, the increased participation of women and couples in the programme through increased decision-making as a new concept within the reproductive health programme. For providers to say that women or couples now participate more in the decision about contraceptive use is to accept that they did not make these decisions before. This reversal in perception is difficult to account for in any concrete way as, rhetoric aside, health staff were unable to say why and how people now make decisions for themselves that were foreclosed to them before, and what they as providers did to ensure that people could make these decisions. This situation is reminiscent of that described by Woost writing about Sri Lankan development, who contends that

> The insertion of an alternative vocabulary of development into mainstream discourse . . . has actually done little to redefine the boundaries of 'community' and 'people's participation' in ways that would positively undercut common people's sense of powerlessness on the terrain of development, or for that matter in their struggle for survival. In fact, it can be argued that the manner in which alternative vocabularies of development are incorporated has tended to reinforce mainstream notions about how progress can be achieved. (1997: 230)

In other words, the rhetoric is empty; but as Apthorpe points out the gap between policy and practice is not. Rather it is full of 'moral practices and biases … of pre-, con-, and mis-conceptions' (Apthorpe 1997: 21). Participation might help negotiate these factors, but as long as indigenous people are represented by others working on their behalf, the gulf in political and cultural terms will remain wide. As a tool of Mexico's development strategies (Dirección General de Planificación Familiar 1995: 7) family planning is firmly embedded within and susceptible to mainstream discourses on development and participation. However, this rhetoric of participation provides a thin veil over the continuing authoritarian nature of the Mexican state and population control goals which are seen as crucial to development.

The vertical imposition of non-participatory reproductive health and population control strategies on local health staff lead to evident pressures upon women to adopt provider preferred contraceptive methods. There is a huge emphasis on the IUD, with stated preferences for promoting this method amongst many providers, rendering the possibility of participation and informed choice on the part of the client ever more remote. Doctors' views of their clients as ignorant and superstitious compound this problem making it more likely that client participation remains low whilst providers heavily exert pressure in the client's *best interest*. As one doctor working in a Tzeltal area explained to me:

> Well, first they come and ask for an injectable [contraceptive]. A little while later they come back and say: [here she put on a high-pitched whining voice and screwed up her face in a pathetic attitude] 'I don't want this one, I want pills.' So we have to change their method [shaking her head in mock disbelief]. And we offer them the operation [sterilization] but they are scared, not of the operation, but of what will happen afterwards. They think they won't be able to carry wood, carry their children, work in the fields, even though we tell them that they will have the same life, the same usefulness (*utilidad*) as before.

When talking about the promotion of family planning services government doctors used the language of paternalism and power, rather than of inclusiveness, which would surely be necessary for participation of the client. For example one *pasante* told me:

> With this new system the only new thing is that they [the government] try to control (*controlar*) more.

I asked what this meant:

> It's because people instead of, hmm, it was a question of interpreting the idea of family planning and supporting yourself, having fewer children, that is, the risks they run in having children, more children than they should have, the obstetric risks that they run. They are told about the risks they run but sometimes they take no notice. Efforts in reproductive health are very worthwhile, how they are being carried out on behalf of the users. (*Pasante*, IMSS, Oxchuc)

This *pasante* began to talk about control before finessing the issue into one of risks. It is difficult to know exactly what he meant by saying that now they 'control' more. He may have meant that, with targeting, it is easier to monitor the success of a programme in statistical terms and therefore have a basis for further targeting, or maybe he was referring to the relentless offering of family planning services. His reference to people taking 'no notice' and having 'more children than they should' indicates the *rightness* of his position in doing something good for the benefit of these people which they themselves did not perceive in the same way. He utilizes the language of knowledge and power vis-à-vis those who 'know nothing'.[10] Participative processes cannot thrive in such a climate. As Idoyaga Molina (1997: 149) points out, in these circumstances only scientifically based views constitute 'truth' and the 'patient must learn and obey'.

These views were reinforced when I asked about how information was given to clients. The need to convince (*convencer*) people arose frequently and was often related to the amount of information which might be given to a client. For example, a senior nurse in charge of family planning told me :

> We don't say too much about the operation [female sterilization]. Everything is kept simple because these people are very difficult to convince. (SSA, Las Rosas, 1996)

Her views were echoed by a doctor in Chanal who told me that, with regard to information given out on contraceptive contraindications and functioning,

> We don't go into it too deeply. We give only the basics, for example, 'the condom is a barrier method', very simple. They can't understand very well and if I were to say 'Go and take this pill. It will make you better but it might irritate your stomach a little', well, they would think that the pill would do them great harm and they would simply throw it away.

The need for compliance is seen to outweigh a regard for information which would be ideologically required in any pursuit of participation and informed choice (cf. Thompson, 1996). This contradicts one of the expressed components of the reproductive health programme which is to:

> Ensure that couples are well informed about reproductive health and contraceptive methods so that they can decide in a free manner the number and spacing of their children. (Gobierno del Estado de Chiapas 1996: 66, my translation)

Such attitudes are compounded by the effects of *oferta sistemática* wherein it is difficult to detect an inclusive, participatory approach. The following doctor's interpretation of change between family planning and reproductive health approaches seems to suggest less a case of inclusiveness and client participation than of aggressive promotion:

Look, things have changed mostly with regard to diffusion of the programmes. Before, the diffusion of the family planning programme was in a superficial form. They didn't have to insist much that the patient make a decision. Now, they take more interest in the patient and taking a stance on how they make a specific decision. It's so that they understand the message that we give them and moreover that the auxiliaries will speak the *dialecto*, the language, so it's more understood. (IMSS, Huixtán)

When the doctor insists that the patient make a decision in conjunction with comments above, having given only basic information on contraceptive methods, it seems that the decision referred to is more a case of deciding which from a limited range of methods to choose than of deciding whether to accept or reject family planning services. Notwithstanding this distinction, choice within fertility regulating methods offered by government clinics is severely limited.[11] Within the Ministry of Social Security (IMSS), choice was further limited during 1996-1997 by the withdrawal of injectable contraceptives from these clinics in the hope of increasing the prevalence of IUDs (IMSS Coordinator, San Cristóbal, 1997).

Doctors believed increased patient decision-making was a new feature within the reproductive health programme introduced in 1995. One doctor attributed this directly to Mission Chiapas but equated it not with choice but acceptance:

The offering under Mission Chiapas began very strongly. For example, methods were more accepted. Because, in fact, beforehand the programme didn't grant them the least importance. People would come for a consultation and they would just come to ask for their method and there was no 'offering'. With Mission Chiapas they [the staff] offer the method. Now there has been a lot of acceptance, I've noticed it. I've worked when the programme wasn't in place and at the moment, yes, there's a greater number of patients coming into the programme. (SSA, Yabteclum (Chenalhó))

It is interesting that whilst many doctors claimed there was no difference between the old programme of family planning and the new programme of reproductive health, many subsequently claimed that patient decision-making was a new feature. The doctor above claims to have noticed more acceptance of contraceptive methods though this does not necessarily indicate an increase in patient decision-making. Whilst the old and new programmes have registered increases in contraceptive prevalence in Chiapas, though rates remain low (Thompson 1999: 167, 300–9), there is a problem when the notion of acceptance becomes conflated with user preferences (cf. Cottingham 1997: 2; Heise 1997: 8) and *choice,* given the enormous efforts that go into promoting IUDs in particular, as well as other modern methods, in order to reach set targets. Increased rates of use do not necessarily indicate higher 'acceptance' of contraceptive methods, nor an increase in use through 'choice', but may well be attributed to aggressive promotion which can undermine both voluntary acceptance and choice. This doctor who attested to the lack of change between the programmes of family planning and reproductive health nevertheless believed, like others, that patient participation in decision-making was emphasized more under the new reproductive health programme:

> Things have changed lot. The way in which the method is offered, counselling for example, was something which changed a lot. The patient participates more of course. (Doctor, SSA, San Cristóbal, July 1997).

Of course? What seems most clear is that providers are parroting the rhetoric of participation and informed choice without being able to describe it in practice. It seems that, whilst planners have changed reproductive health policy on paper, these changes have not been fully actualized on a practical level at the provider-client interface. The offering of methods through 'counselling', claimed above, was not confirmed in any discussion I had with women who had used or were using family planning methods. On the contrary, the women portrayed grim scenarios of condescension and being treated like children, including being shouted at for refusing methods. The treatment described by one young woman who attended a clinic when pregnant with her second child was echoed by others amongst the families I knew in San Cristóbal:

> They told me off a lot (*me regañan mucho*) . . . 'Why didn't you take care? There are pills and other things' *Uyy, me regañan mucho.* 'Your son is so young', they said [the first child was a year old]. 'Now you will abandon him and he will suffer. There are pills and condoms. Why didn't you take care?' I was embarrassed. I bowed my head (*Me da pena. Me agacho).*

Although health staff told me that it was important to treat clients with respect and to be aware of cultural differences, they claimed they were not given much direction in this. Training in the new reproductive health programme, which included references to cultural sensitivity, was provided in Los Altos but according to various doctors' accounts this was an ad hoc phenomenon of short duration. New *pasantes* are sent off to the rural areas with no practical training on policy matters at all except in targeting and *oferta sistemática.* In discussing cultural sensitivity most said this was discussed with their seniors, and indeed discussed the issue with me, in terms of how difficult the client population was to convince about adopting family planning measures.

The language of policy continues to mitigate against participatory processes, not least because meanings remain evasive and hidden. Health providers are no more social development specialists than their clients and the problem of enveloping them in the rhetoric of policy makers, which is motivated in part by the need to present a good international face, is one of how health providers are to implement these ideals in their everyday work. The perception that reproductive health is only family planning under a different name suggests a number of possibilities: that the providers really do not understand the difference; that their working practices and conditions constrain them from properly implementing the new policy; or that problems of empathy and understanding between *mestizo* providers and indigenous clients are not tackled seriously in either policy or practice.

Contextualising Components of the New Reproductive Health Programme

In this final section I want to consider a number of components of the Programme of Health and Social Assistance[12] in the context of Los Altos and the findings of my own research.

A New Concept of Reproductive Health

> Inform the population of the new concept of reproductive health (through a programme of dissemination, promotion and information), with the support of those involved in health promotion. (Gobierno del Estado de Chiapas 1996: 66 *trans.*)

It is very difficult to promote reproductive health as a 'new concept' when the emphasis appears to remain resolutely on family planning promotion, and when other reproductive health areas (e.g. smear tests for cervical cancer[13]) are, at least in Los Altos, considered apart from and separate to this programme. If there is little to distinguish the new concept from the old, and if the new concept appears to be a reinforcement of the old one, in what way is it not more of the same thing? I collected no data suggesting that anything new existed that might change client perceptions and found little evidence that providers' perceptions had changed.

Risk and Sexuality

> Ensure that individuals and couples are able to enjoy risk-free reproductive health and contraceptive methods so that they can freely decide the number and spacing of their children (ibid.).

It is very difficult for doctors to ensure that individuals or couples can enjoy a life of 'reproductive health' without risks if one considers that this would, or should, entail discussing sex and sexual practices, and the risks of STDs and HIV-AIDS. One gynaecologist explained to me why, in his view, it was difficult to ask about sexual behaviour or to carry out gynaecological examinations:

> We hardly ever ask about this. If it's about pregnancy, OK, we can ask about when the last period was, and see how the baby is, these kinds of things. But their sexual activities, well, in these we can't intrude because it's taboo. Well, it's very taboo. It's embarrassing. You can bath them and wash their head, all of the body, but the genitals, no you can't wash there... You can't touch it because it's sinful. (San Carlos Hospital, Altamirano)

Risk and sexuality, in allopathic health care, are necessarily entwined in family planning narratives because of the obvious link between sexual behaviour and risk. However, for the client, not only may this link be absent but personal risk, because it is based upon known experiences of the self or others, may be linked directly to clinic visits rather than to sex or having children. A Tzeltal friend was afraid to have a cyst removed from her womb because of fears of ill-treatment by hospital staff, directly related to the fact of her race:

> But sometimes, the thing is that the doctors don't treat us [indigenous people] well, don't operate well on us and don't attend us well. I have many doubts about this. They don't attend well. What if they operated on me and left me bad?

A Tzotzil friend echoed these fears based upon her recent experiences when having her first child at the IMSS hospital in San Cristóbal by caesarean section:

> The nurses were very aggressive. They shout a lot: 'hurry up, get up, what are you doing with a husband when you can't put up with the consequences?'

Such perceptions are pervasive amongst poor women of both indigenous and *mestizo* backgrounds, and the likelihood of maltreatment is considered a definite risk when deciding whether to seek treatment in government clinics. For many, the pressures of constantly being asked about family planning practices only add to their reluctance to attend clinics.

Fostering New Reproductive Health Habits

> Encourage a change in the reproductive behaviour of the population. (Gobierno del Estado de Chiapas 1996: 66, my translation)

From studying the policy it is obvious that the main change to be encouraged is a reduction in the number of children women or couples have, though mention is also made of promoting safer sex through condom use. In practice, condoms are not considered a contraceptive method but rather a support method[14] by many doctors whose preferences for targetable methods of higher efficacy are clear. Moreover, in discussing safer sex practices with health staff, it was clear that, because of perceived cultural problems in persuading women to have smear tests or discuss sex, little actual effort is made to that end. Staff often told me that HIV/AIDS did not exist in indigenous communities, even those with large military battalions and, consequently, many prostitutes. Moreover, men in parts of Los Altos often have more than one partner yet STDs were not perceived as a problem by many providers.

Men and the Family

> Ensure the participation of the male population in responsible parenthood. (Gobierno del Estado de Chiapas 1996: 66, my translation)

There are few specific references in government literature to responsible parenthood and what it means, to the current state of affairs regarding male attitudes to paternity, and to bringing about an improvement. Indeed, the statement above was the only reference I found to men and parental responsibility was in this specific policy component. Significantly, there is no mention of how to achieve or work towards this policy goal. Similarly, in the Programme of Reproductive Health and Family Planning, 1995–2000, the only reference to men comes under 'specific objectives of family planning', which states:

> Strengthen the family structure, promote a responsible attitude amongst men and women with regard to sexuality and reproduction. Encourage the active participation of the man in family planning and his co-responsibility in decisions concerning sexuality and reproduction (Poder Ejecutivo Federal 1996: 13–14, my translation).

From these two statements we can assume responsible parenthood for men involves male responsibility in and for the family, and responsibility for sexual acts and health; and an increase in male participation with regard to decision-making in family planning (cf. Bruce 1994: 68). In practice, male participation can often be reduced to one single factor: contraceptive use by the woman is dependent on the authority of her partner. In relating their reproductive histories, women from the fifteen families I befriended were unanimous in asserting that their husbands' permission was required, though not at the clinic, if the women were to be able to use contraceptives without encountering problems. Women who were found to be contracepting in secret put themselves at risk of male violence.

Health staff in Chiapas were almost unanimous in their beliefs that men should share responsibility for family planning. There was an equally resounding unanimity in the belief that the majority of men took little or no responsibility in this area, leaving it to the women. The practical problem seemed to be in defining how male participation could be encouraged. Some health staff said that promotional talks on family planning covered issues of male responsibility towards their partners and children but there seemed to be no monitoring or evaluation in place to gauge the relative success of this strategy and no other kinds of initiatives.

Gendered Realms

According to the SSA co-ordinator of family planning for Los Altos region, women themselves control the division in responsibility between men and women in the home, using the notion of *machismo* as a mechanism:

> I believe that men should participate more on a family level. But during training sessions [for health promoters] the women laugh at the men if they appear to be interested in this area. They question their masculinity and this puts the men off. (SSA Family Planning Co-ordinator, August 1996)

Given that men are the ones who have control over most areas of life external to the home it is not surprising to find that, for women, keeping men out of domains where they have some control is a way of ensuring that they maintain it. Women do not want men to undermine the often limited power they have in the family sphere.

Birth, fertility and menstrual regulation are firmly grounded within the female sphere of influence and knowledge. It is to the *partera* (traditional birth attendant) or the *curandera* (curer/healer) that most indigenous women look when they need something to *bajar la regla* (bring on menstruation), when they are in labour, or when they or their children are sick. It is interesting that once women turn away from indigenous knowledge to the clinic the influence of the man becomes stronger. Women do not habitually seek out men's permission in practising traditional modes of fertility regulation in Los Altos but they do need such permission to use modern contraceptives. This is a phenomenon that health staff are aware of, and they lament the apparent reluctance of men to contracept or allow their women to contracept.

Male participation in family life and the strength of the family, not to mention male involvement in decision-making with regard to sexuality and reproductive health, not only depends upon a willingness of men to be involved but also upon socio-economic circumstances that affect the stability of the family unit. Women-headed households appear to be on the increase in the marginalized *barrios* of San Cristóbal whilst in rural areas men are absent for long periods working elsewhere. Though men are seen to dictate a woman's reproductive health behaviour (especially by policy makers and providers) both men and women are influenced by local attitudes to contraceptive use. Promiscuity, sterility, genocide, side-effects and ill-treatment; all feature in the complex and fluid attitudes to contraceptive use, and in the perceived intentions behind the ardent promotion of family planning services. Economic and political instability, and fears of government intentions, compound this uncertainty.

Conclusion

The selection of components taken from the Programme of Health and Social Assistance in this paper are typical of international policy edicts on reproductive health (cf. United Nations Population Information Network 1994). They are presented as neutral, value-free concepts which aim to have a *good* outcome on the health and lives of women and men through their adoption of family planning methods. Information and responsibility for one's own actions are promoted to reassure us that choice and consent are integral to provider-client relationships in the clinic. However, policy edicts cannot ensure that provider practices involve culturally sensitive dissemination of information and respect for the client, even when these appear as desirable in policy discourse. Moreover, if we construe policy rhetoric as a political instrument of power which seeks to persuade rather than inform (Apthorpe 1997: 43), we might go one step further to argue that, in setting up a worthy framework of goals, policy makers divest the body politic of responsibility for the outcome. The outcome of the health goals designed to benefit the intended recipients rests entirely upon the behaviour of those recipients. As I have argued above, many health providers in Chiapas blame the local population for their own backwardness and inability to understand that family planning is *good* for them. The gap between policy ideals and local conditions remains wide and in Los Altos there is nothing to indicate that changes might occur.

The Mexican government wishes to increase local access to family planning services in Chiapas and other indigenous, rural areas, under the auspices of economic development and modernization as outlined in the introduction to this chapter. This ideal is presented in a vacuum far removed from the processes of social change which affect everyday life at the local level, where social and economic development issues are embroiled in contested ways of life and an indigenous struggle for self-determination. This struggle includes issues of land loss, political and military strife, and economic insecurity (cf. Nash 1995, Holloway and Paláez 1998), lack of basic amenities, abandoned women and children, difficult gender and race relations, and acute poverty. Appearing as lofty ideals stripped of social and cultural context, policy components seem valid and desirable. However, at the local level the policies, or rather the effects of their implementation, are embroiled in the processes of everyday life. In effect, the policies and the aggressive manner of promoting them may serve to ensure that people have less rather than more access to family planning services, largely because of the contested knowledge with regard to fertility regulation and family ideals, and perceptions of government intentions in an area marked by military conflict. Government policy is never neutral, and less so in such circumstances.

Notes

1. With thanks to the Emslie Horniman Anthropological Fund and the University of Durham for supporting my research, and also to the Mellon Foundation for sponsoring my attendance at the conference Changing Contraceptives: Technologies, Choices and Constraints (University College Stockton, 1996), where an earlier version of this chapter was first presented.

2. The ideal of the right to an informed choice in contraceptive decision-making has its roots in Western liberal philosophy concerning the individual's right to self-determination (see, for example, Hobbes' writing from the seventeenth century (1928). The resulting twentieth century preoccupation with individual rights and autonomy (cf. Faden and Beauchamp 1986) penetrates many

disciplines with diverse implications, not least of which has been the politicization of health care as prioritized by women's rights advocates (cf. Hartmann 1995; Sen and Snow 1994).

3. The term *mestizo/a* refers to someone of mixed Spanish/Indigenous origin whilst *ladino/a* usually refers to someone of pure Spanish decent. In Los Altos these terms are often used interchangeably to refer to any Mexican who is not indigenous, and carry a heavy cultural and political significance. Many indigenous people use the term 'hombres verdaderos' (true men) to indicate that they are pure indigenous and not *mestizo*. Other indigenous people, on the other hand, try to pass as *mestizo* and become *mestizo*-ized in order to hide their indigenous origins.

4. Though all the nurses referred to here were female, I did interview both male and female nurses.

5. The main providers of family planning services in Chiapas are two Mexican government health services: *La Secretaria de Salud* (SSA, the Ministry of Health) and the *Instituto Mexicano del Seguro Social-Solidaridad* (IMSS, the Department of Social Security non-contributory wing). These are supplemented by the work of *El Sistema Nacional para el Desarrollo Integral de la Familia* (DIF, the national system for the development of the family).

6. For those lacking basic education and speaking a different mother tongue, and belonging to a different culture to that of the providers, informed choice may remain a concept of the planner's drawing board rather than a concrete possibility. As Rakusen points out, even with good education and full information, many people would be ill-equipped to make an informed decision (1981: 97).

7. Sánchez *et al.* note the findings of Salvatierra *et al.* that only 15 per cent of people in Chiapas who think they are ill actually use health services.

8. Similar links between contraceptive use and female promiscuity are made in other parts of the world where contraceptive use is contested (cf. Sobo 1993a and 1993b; Molyneux 1988).

9. This compares with findings of Nancy and Joseph Jabbra (1992: 6) that high fertility rates often correlate with weak welfare systems. In Chiapas, there is arguably such a correlation.

10. '*Ellos no saben nada*' ('they don't know anything') was frequently heard in interviews with providers when discussing the local population's attitude towards family planning and other health issues.

11. Methods offered consisted of the monthly injectable Cyclofem (Norethisterone was supposed to be available but supplies were problematic during my fieldwork term); the Copper T IUD; 28- and 21-day combined (progestogen and oestrogen) oral contraceptives (with a provider preference for the former); and female sterilization. Vasectomy was promoted but with the attitude that men could rarely be convinced, and condoms were available but not promoted and were rarely subject to targeted increases in use.

12. The Programme of Health and Social Assistance draws up guidelines on a state-level in accordance with the objectives of national programmes.

13. Officially this was not the case but doctors and *pasantes* referred to this as separate in practice.
14. Condoms were invariably referred to as a 'support method', that is, one which should be used only temporarily in lieu of adopting more dependable methods.

References

Anon. (1995), 'Situación Demográfica Nacional', *El Mercado de Valores*, Num. 8 (Agosto): 8–16.

Apthorpe, R. (1997), 'Writing development policy and policy analysis plain or clear: On language, genre and power', in C. Shore and S. Wright (eds), *Anthropology of Policy. Critical Perspectives on Governance and Power*, London: Routledge, pp. 43-58.

Bruce, J. (1994), 'Reproductive Choice: The Responsibilities of Men and Women', *Reproductive Health Matters*, No. 4 (November), pp. 68–70.

Cottingham, J. (1997), 'Introduction', in *Beyond Acceptability: Users' Perspectives on Contraception*, London: Reproductive Health Matters for the World Health Organization, pp. 1-4.

Day, M. (1995), 'Gulf of Mexico', *Nursing Times*, 91(27): 42–4.

Dirección General de Planificación Familiar (1995), *Norma Oficial Mexicana de Los Servicios de Planificación Familiar*, Mexico D.F., Dirección General de Planificación Familiar.

Durán de Huerta Patiño, M. and M. Boldrini (1998), *Acteal. Navidad en el Infierno*, Mexico, Times Editores S.A. de C.V.

Faden, R.R., and T.L. Beauchamp, in collaboration with N.M.P. King (1986), *A History and Theory of Informed Consent*, Oxford: Oxford University Press.

Freyermuth E.G. (1993), *Médicos tradicionales y médicos alópatas. Un encuentro difícil en los Altos de Chiapas*, San Cristóbal de las Casas, Chiapas: Centro de Investigaciones y Estudios Superiores en Antropología-Sureste.

Gobierno del Estado de Chiapas (1996), *Programa de Salud y Asistencia Social, 1995–2000, Chiapas (Primera edición)*, Tuxtla Gutiérrez, Chiapas: Gobierno del Estado.

Grillo, R.D., and R.L. Stirrat (1997), *Discourses of Development. Anthropological Perspectives*, Oxford: Berg.

Halperin Frisch, D.C., and H. de León Montenegro (1996), *Salud en la Frontera*, San Cristóbal de las Casas, Chiapas: El Colegio de la Frontera Sur.

Hartmann, B. (1995), *Reproductive Rights and Wrongs: The Global Politics of Population Control*, Boston: South End Press (First published 1987).

Heise, L.L. (1997), 'Beyond Acceptability: Reorienting Research on Contraceptive Choice', in *Beyond Acceptability: Users' Perspectives on Contraception*, London: Reproductive Health Matters for the World Health Organization, pp. 6–14.

Hobbes, T. (1928), *Leviathan*, London: Everyman's Library.

Holloway, J. and E. Paláez (eds) (1998), *Zapatista! Reinventing Revolution in Mexico*. London: Pluto Press.

Idoyaga Molina, A. (1997), 'Ethnomedicine and world-view: a comparative analysis of the incorporation and rejection of contraceptive methods among Argentine women', in E.J. Sobo and A. Russell (eds), *Anthropology and Medicine*, (Special Issue), 4(2): 145–58.

Jabbra, N.W., and J.G. Jabbra (1992), *Women and Development in the Middle East and North Africa*, Leiden: E.J. Brill.

Justice, J. (1989), *Policies, Plans and People: Culture and Health Development in Nepal*, Berkeley: University of California Press.

Luiselli, C. (1994), 'Chiapas: the entangled knots of modernization', *Unisa Latin America Report* 10(2), July–December: 51–7 (Translated by Marcia Lockett).

Merrick, T.W. (1985), *Recent Fertility Declines in Brazil, Colombia and Mexico*, World Bank Staff Working Papers, No. 692, Population and Development Series No. 17, Washington D.C.: The World Bank.

Molyneux, M. (1988), 'The Politics of Abortion in Nicaragua: Revolutionary Pragmatism or Feminism in the Realm of Necessity', *Feminist Review*, No. 29: 114–32.

Moser, C.O.N. (1994), *Gender Planning and Development: Theory, Practice and Training*, London: Routledge.

Nash, J. (1995), 'The New World Dis-Order: A view from Chiapas, Mexico', *Studies in Third World Societies*, part 56: 171–96.

Poder Ejecutivo Federal (1996), *Programa de Reforma del Sector Salud: Programa de Salud Reproductiva y Planificación Familiar, 1995–2000*, Mexico D.F., Secretaría de Salud.

Rakusen, J. (1981), 'Depo Provera: The Extent of the Problem. A Case Study in the Politics of Birth Control', in H. Roberts (ed.), *Women, Health and Reproduction*, London: Routledge and Kegan Paul, pp. 75–108.

Rew, A. (1996), *The Incorporation of Social and Cultural Factors and the Planning and Evaluation of Development Projects*, Papers in International Development, No. 21, Swansea: Centre for Development Studies, University of Wales.

Sánchez Pérez, H.J., H. Ochoa Díaz López and R. Miranda Ocampo (1995), 'La Situación de Salud in Chiapas: Consideraciones para su analasis', in R. Miranda Ocampo (ed.), *Chiapas el regreso a la utopia*, Universidad Autónoma de Guerrero, Mexico.

Sen, G. and R.C. Snow (1994), *Power and Decision: The Social Control of Reproduction*, Boston: Harvard Center for Population and Development Studies.

Shore, C., and S. Wright (1997), 'Introduction. Policy: A new field of anthropology', in C. Shore and S. Wright (eds), *Anthropology of Policy. Critical Perspectives on Governance and Power*, London: Routledge, pp. 3–57.

Singh, R. (1994), *Family Planning Success Stories (Asia, Latin America, Africa)*, New Delhi: UBSPD.

Sobo, E.J. (1993a), 'Bodies, Kin, and Flow: Family Planning in Rural Jamaica', *Medical Anthropology Quarterly*, 7(1): 50–73.

—— (1993b), *One Blood: The Jamaican Body*, Albany: State University of New York Press.

——, and A. Russell (eds) (1997), 'Anthropology of Contraception'. *Anthropology and Medicine*, (Special Issue), 4(2).

Teichman, J. (1977), 'Neoliberalism and the Transformation of Mexican Authoritarianism', *Mexican Studies*, 13(1): 121–47.

Thompson, M.S. (1996), 'Contraceptive implants: long acting and provider dependent contraception raises concerns about freedom of choice', *British Medical Journal*, (312): 1393–5.

—— (1999), 'Informed Choice and Targeting of Family Planning Services in Highland Chiapas, Mexico: A Fundamental Contradiction', in B. Fearon, S. Crouch and T. Muncey (eds) *Women's Reproductive Health: Educating for our Future*, Salisbury: Mark Allen.

—— (1999), *The Social Context of Family Planning Policy in Highland Chiapas, Mexico,* Ph.D. Thesis, University of Durham, Department of Anthropology.

United Nations Population Information Network (1994), *Report of the International Conference on Population and Development*, (Cairo, 5–13 September, 1994), POPIN Gopher of the United Nationals Population Division, Electronic Document.

Woost, M.D. (1997), 'Alternative Vocabularies of Development? 'Community' and 'Participation' in Development Discourse in Sri Lanka' in R.D. Grillo and R.L. Stirrat (eds), *Discourses of Development. Anthropological Perspectives*, Oxford: Berg, 229–53.

Index

abortion, 18, 203, 207–8, 212, 215–16
abstinence, 5, 44, 72, 138, 215
    post partum, 6, 19, 140–1, 214
Africa, sub-Saharan, 130–2, *see also*
    Ethiopia
African fertility
    fear of, 15, 81, 85, 86–7, 91–6
    'pathological', 91, 94–6
    white responsibility for, 91–2
'African personality', 82, 91–6
    cultural conditioning, 93–4
    sense of time, 93
    sexuality, 84
    suggested biological differences, 93
African women, aims to domesticate,
    83–5
AIDS, see HIV/AIDS
Ali, K.A., 19
amenorrhoea, 187–8
anaemia, 13, 187, 201, 213, 214
Anderson, R.B.W., 33
Ankrah, E.M., 32
anorexia nervosa, 150
Anteby, L., 142, 148
anthropological research, appropriateness
    of, 46
Apthorpe, R., 229, 238
Aziz, K.M.A., 179

'backwardness', perceived, 161–2, 163,
    166–73, 227–8
Baer, R.D., 43
Ball, P.R., 82, 83, 85, 97
Bangladesh
    decision-making re contraception,
        190–3
    family planning strategies, 179–80
    health care, 181–2
    village life, 180–1
    women's lack of autonomy, 180, 183–4

Banja, F., 131, 151
Barbieri, M., 202
Barnard, M., 33
Beck, A.T., 42
Beck Depression Inventory, 41, 42
Ben-Ezer, G., 150
Bernard, H.R., 7, 31, 56
Bedouins, 166–7, 170
Bhatia, S., 179
Bibeau, G., 8
Binnendijk, A.L., 61
birth spacing, 129–30, 132, 139–44, 153,
    185, 209
Bledsoe, C., 131, 132, 146–7, 151, 153
bleeding, excessive & irregular, 52, 116,
    117, 187, 213
blood flow, cultural importance of, 129,
    140, 148–50, 187–8
body parts, clarifying terms for, 36
body size, preferred, 37
Boldrini, M., 223
Bolton, R., 47
Bongaarts, J., 131, 132, 140
Bornstein, A., 164
Bowen, D., 33, 43
Boyce, J., 179
Brehm, S.S., 27
breast-feeding, *see* lactation
Brislin, R.W., 40, 41, 43
Browner, C.H., 31, 179, 194
Bruce, J., 111, 112, 237
Burton, N., 110, 111
Burton, P., 44

Caldwell, , J.& P., 130, 147, 179
Canez, M., 110
Carter, A., 17
Castle, W.M., 96
Catholic Church, 20, 62
Chambers, R., 15, 52, 53, 56, 58, 59, 64

Chemtov, D., 148, 149
Chiapas Reproductive Health Programme
  authoritarian nature of, 229–34
  background, 223–4
  gap between policy & provision, 227f
  goals, 224–7
childbirth, period following, 19, 140–1,
  214
  jhilla, 19, 214
choice, limitations, 112–14
Christianity, 20, 62, 63
Civic, D., 33, 35
Cizewski, R.L., 58
Clarke, D.G., 88, 89
Cleland, , J., 179
'clinical gaze', 40
Cogan, J.C., 37
coitus interruptus, 5, 18, 138, 151, 170–1,
  215
colonialist attitudes
  in Haiti, 107
  in Rhodesia, 81–97
Comaroff, J. & J., 84, 163
community health workers' role,
  Bangladesh, 181, 182, 188, 191
community involvement, in research,
  31–2
condoms
  associated with promiscuity, 63, 72,
    152, 216
  dislike of, 35, 152, 216
  impact diagramming &, 67
  & male responsibility, 73
  methods of distribution, 68, 71–3
  packaging, 73
  as protection against HIV/AIDS, 5, 27,
    63, 152
  symbolising infidelity & distrust, 152
  unorthodox use of, 59
Conlin, S., 53
contraception
  aggressive promotion of, 222–3, 230–4
  categories of, 4–7
  changing meanings & values of,
    171–2
  as cultural construct, 17–20
  economic reasons for, 185–6, 195,
    209
  fear of long-term effects, 129, 150–1

linked with promiscuity, 63, 72, 152,
  216, 228
medicalization of, 14–15, 164–5, 172,
  205
modern/technological vs traditional/
  indigenous methods, 94–5, 161–2,
  163, 170–3
modernist hierarchy of methods, 170–3
national goals context, 205, 208–12,
  218
symbol of progress & status, 19–20,
  161–2, 165, 166–75
social construct, 11–17
systematic offering (*oferta sistematica*),
  222–3, 225–6, 231, 233
unmet need for, 131, 153
'contraceptive parables', 184
contraceptive patch, 5
Contraceptive Social Marketing (CSE)
  feasibility study, *see under* Tonga
contraceptives, cost of, 112, 120–1
contraceptives, traditional, anti-modernist
  views, 162, 170
Cooper, F., 83
Cornwall, A., 9
Cottingham, J., 233
Critchlow, D., 19
Cronje, Rowan, 96
'cultural lag', 92–5

Davin, A., 84
Davies, C.S., 95
Day, M., 223
de Munck, V.C., 7
De Silva, I., 132
Depo-Provera, 13, 150–1, 185, 187, 188
Despagne, P., 110
Deutcher, I., 41
development programmes, anthropological involvement in, 9–10
diaphragm, 5, 151–2
discontinuing or method-switching,
  reasons for, 186–8, 194
doctor-patient interaction
  cultural context, 116–18
  disregard of patient, 118–21, 169
  hidden dimensions, 114–18
  manifest dimensions, 109, 111–14
  methods of observation, 108–9

patient's power over doctor, 108
quality of care, 111–18, 121–3
socio-economic context, 114–16
Dodds, Peter, 87, 90, 96
Douglas, M., 202
Draper., William, 89
Drennan, G., 39, 40, 41, 42, 43
Duden, B., 202
Duran, M., 223
Dyaks, 171–2

Edwards, J., 3
Elias, C., 108, 112
'emic' perspective, 10–11, 18–19, 41, 45,
    68
environmental concerns, 87–8, 130
Erickson, P.L., 19
Ethiopia
    contraceptive practice in, 130–2, 137–8
    understanding of conception, 138
Ethiopian Jewish refugees in Israel
    background, 133–4
    blood, as symbol, 148–50
    breast-feeding, 140–3
    change in fertility rates, 143–4
    divorce, 135
    economic pressures on, 134
    family changes, 135
    gender conflict, 135
    family planning, 145–8
    sexuality, 151–2
'etic' perspective, 41
Etkin, N.L., 6, 19
European model of family life, 84–5
Ever-Hadani, P., 141
Everitt, B., 140

face saving, 186, 192–3
Falah, G., 163
family
    authority within, 204
    changes in, 135
    defiance of, 190–3, 194
    pressures from, 179, 184, 190
family planning, aid expenditure on,
    130–1
Family Planning Association of Rhodesia
    (FPAR), 82, 86–90
family size, ideal

Ethiopean refugees, 145–6
Guatamala, 39
Mexico, 228
Uzbekistan, 204–5
Farmer, P., 34, 108, 117
'female sphere', 19, 237–8
Fisher, S., 108
Fluehr-Lobban, C., 32
formula, use of supplementary, 141–2
Foucault, M., 40
freedom of choice, *see* informed choice
Freire, P., 53
Freyermuth, E.G., 226
Friedlander, D., 163, 165

Gage, A.J., 37
Gay, J., 112
gender differences, linguistic, 44, 45
genocidal intentions, possibility of, 14,
    223
Geraty, Alfreda, 87, 95
Gergen, K., 42
Ghana, body size preferences, 37
Gilmurray, J., 88
Ginsburgh, F.D., 107, 163, 175
Goldscheider, C., 134, 163, 165
Greenhalgh, S., 106, 107, 161, 173
Grillo, R.D., 229
Gruber, R., 133
Guatamala, 38–9, 45
Guillemin, F., 40

Haile, A., 138
Hailemariam, A., 132
Haiti, Cité Soleil Clinic, 103–23
    background & setting of, 109–10
    clientele, 110–11
    community resistance to, 122
    failure of, 121–3
    quality of care, 111–21
    see also doctor-patient interaction
Halperin Frisch, D.C., 223
Handwerker, W., 131, 136
Hanks, J., 88, 89
Hanson, K.T., 85
Harcourt, W., 179
Hardon, A., 13, 19, 21
Harrison, P., 51, 52
Hartmann, B., 162, 179, 221

Hashemi, S.M., 180
Hau'ofa, E., 63
Haviland, W.A., 56, 57
Heaver, R., 58
Heise, L.L., 233
herbal cotraceptives, 6, 185
Heuer, B., 202, 208
Hill, A., 131
Hines, A., 38, 39, 40, 41, 44
HIV/AIDS
  condoms as protection against, 5, 27,
    63, 152, 236
  & culturally specific sexual
    preferences, 35
  discussing, 43
  in Haiti, 34, 110
  in Mexico, 235–6
  stigma of, 70–1
  in Tonga, 62, 63, 66, 70–1
Hodes, R., 148
Hofstede, G., 36
Holloway, J., 239
Hooker, J.R., 89, 90, 92, 94
Hunt, N.R., 83
Huygens, P., 31, 32, 36, 37, 38, 40, 44
Huntington, D., 39

illiteracy, 40
incest taboo, 64
individualist vs collectivist values, 11, 36–7
infant mortality, 12, 95–6, 206–7, 209, 223
informed consent/choice
  concept of, 10, 13, 15
  lack of, 15, 221–2, 232–4
  to psychosocial research, 31–2
injectables, 6, 187, 210, 214–15, *see also*
  Depo-Provera
International Planned Parenthood
  Federation (IPPF), 110–11
interviewers' characteristics, effects of, 32
interviewers' competence in
  communication, 33
Israel
  contraceptive availability in, 138–9
  definition of 'other', 163
IUDs, 5, 6, 13, 19, 52, 138, 152, 171,
    184, 185, 207, 210, 212, 213–15,
    230, 232, 233
  self-removal, 189–90

James, C.L.R., *The Black Jacobins*, 105–6
Japan
  notion of marital satisfaction, 44–5
  oral contraceptives in, 19
Jeater, D., 84
Jewkes, R., 9
Jiryis, S., 163
Jolly, C., 130, 131
Johnson, M., 140
Justice, J., 13

Kaler, A., 83
KAP (Knowledge-Attitude-Practice)
  studies, 131
Kaplan, S., 133, 134
Karadawi, A., 133
Kanaaneh, R., 165
Kaufert, P.A., 179
Kleinman, A., 14
Kloos, H., 132
Koo, H.P., 17
Kretzmer, D., 163
Kronen, M., 58, 59

lactation, 140–3, 214
language problems, 33, 40–4, 227–8
Latour, B., 6
Lazarus, E., 111
Leap, W., 43
Lerebours, G., 110
Lesthaege, R., 130, 131
Levene, J.M., 61, 64, 70
linguistic competence of researchers, 33
Lock, M., 179
Luiselli, C., 226
Lustick, I., 163

MacLachlan, M., 38
Malawi, 38
Malinowski, B., 56
Maloney, C., 179
Mamdani, M., 12
marriage, escape from by avoiding
  pregnancy, 186
Marshall, J.F., 52, 53
Martin, E., 108, 165, 172, 202
Martin, T., 131
maternal mortality/morbidity, 12, 110,
    206–7, 209, 223

Maudlin, W., 131, 132
McCarthy, E., 88
McGrath, B.B., 63
McNeilly, A., 140
Mechanic, D., 39
men & contraception
    dominance, 17, 151–2, 217, 236–8
    excluded, 237–8
    feelings of conflict about, 192–3
    shame, 19, 209, 211, 216
    spousal communication, 183, 190–3,
        194, 211
    sterilisation, 5, 19, 28
    taking responsibility for, 73, 236–8
menstruation
    cultural beliefs re, 129, 140, 148–50,
        187–8
    & IUD, 52
Merrick, T.W., 221
method switching, 186–8, 194
Mexican immigrants, 43
Mexico, *see* Chiapas...
'mistakes' & failures, 167–70
Molina, I., 231
Mombour, W., 43, 44
modernity, contraception as symbol of,
    19–20, 161–2, 165, 166–75
Morgan, L., 108
morning-after pill, 5
Morris, N., 43
Mosse, D., 60
mothers-in-law, 183, 211–12
Mumtaz, K., 179

Nader, L., 12
Nash, J., 239
Nelson, N., 60
Newman, L.F., 6, 18, 179
Noam, G., 134
Norplant, 116, 118, 122

Okun, B., 132
Olcott, M.B., 202
Ong, A., 164
Operation Moses, 133, 143
Operation Soloman, 134, 144
oral contraceptives, 5, 6, 19, 67, 138, 185,
    210
    methods of distribution, 68, 71–3

packaging, 71
side effects, 42, 187, 214, 228
undesirability, 149–51, 214
'other', fear & disapproval of, 85, 161,
    163, 174, *see also* 'African personality'
Owen, R., 164

Palaez, E., 239
Palestinians
    background of, 162–6
    & consumerist system, 164
    hierarchical society, 166–7
    & medicalization, 164–5
    method of study, 165–6
    modernist view of contraception,
        167–75
Palti, H., 141
Pankhurst, R, 133
Parfitt, T., 133
Parker, R.G., 35, 44, 45
participant observation, 8–9, 56–61, 68,
    136, 224
Participatory Rural Appraisal (PRA), 9,
    59, 75
Paul, B.K., 179
Perea, J.G.F., 16
Pfleiderer, B., 202
pharmaceutical companies, 12, 14
Phillips Davids, J., 135, 152
Philpott, R.H., 92, 94
Pickering, H., 45
Polgar, S., 52, 53
political economy of fertility, 106–9,
    121–3
    & culture, 107
    & history, 107
    & power, 107–8
population control, roots of, 12
population crisis arguments
    'limits to growth', 85
    'overcrowding', 86
    'race suicide', 86
Porter, M., 15
post partum sexual taboos, 6, 19, 140–1,
    214
Potter, R., 140
power, language of, 114, 116–18, 230–1
preparatory research, need for, 52–3
Preston-Whyte, E.M., 37, 46

Pretty, J.N., 59
Prieto, A.J., 33, 43
Prince, R., 43, 44
Pritchett, L., 132
pro & anti natalist stances, national, 14
provider/user relationship, 13, 15–16
  doctor/patient, *see* doctor/patient
    interaction
  perceived realities of, 53–5
  provider/user expectations, differences
    between, 226–8
  as replica of international policies,
    107–8
  as replica of society structures, 106
profit, drive for, 12

quantitive & qualitative methods, 7–8, 45,
  226–7

racial ratios, maintaining, 89–91
Rance, S., 206
Ranchod-Nilssen, S., 85
Rapid Rural Appraisal (RRA), 57–61
  shortcomings of, 60–1
Rapp, R., 107, 108, 163, 175
Rauf, F., 179
Ravid, C., 152
Rea, Kathleen, 87
Renne, E.P., 18
reproductive phase, shortening of, 209
research methods
  community involvement in, 31–2
  constraints on responses, 39–40
  cultural relevance, 38–9
  defining study population, 33–4
  emic perspective, 34–6
  for whose benefit?, 31
  impact on community, 37
  inappropriate use of western
    instruments, 29–31
  interviewers' characteristics &
    competence, effect of, 32
  method of using research instrument,
    40
  quantitative & qualitative data, 45
  scale, differences in definition of, 43–4
  sensitivity of subject, 39
  translation difficulties, 40–3
  use of indicators, 44–5

use of pre-existing material, 34–6
researcher/subject relationship, 10
Rew, A., 229
Rhodesia, population concerns
  academic & mass media, 82–3
  'cultural lag' in, 93–5
  European model of family, 84–5
  fears of African fertility, 81–2, 85,
    86–7, 91–6
  preserving status quo, 96
  racial ratios, 89–91
  Tribal Trust Land's degradation, 87–8
  unemployment, 88–9
Rhodesia Herald, 83, 89, 90–1
Rhodesia Science News, 82–3, 86
rhythm/calendar method, 5, 6, 167
Rosen, C., 148
Ross, J., 131, 132
'rural development tourism', 58
Russell, A.J., 12, 14, 194, 228
Rwanda, condom dislike in, 35

Said, E., 163
Salamon, H., 134, 148
Samuel, S., 61, 63
Sanchez Perez, H.J., 227
Sands, R., 53–5
Sargent, C., 179, 194
Satow, G., 151
Sapire, K.E., 87, 96
Saville-Troike, M., 33
Schaeffer, N.C., 43
Schellstede, W.P., 58
Schmidt, E., 84
Schneider, J., &P., 162
Schoepf, B.G., 31, 35, 39, 45
Schuler, S., 180
Scott, C., 33, 41
Seabrook, J., 51
Seeley, J.A., 10
Seeman, D., 148
Sen, G., 179
Segal, S., 131
Semin, G.R., 42
sex, as taboo subject, 63, 64, 203–4, 209,
  218, 235
sexuality, constructs of, 34–5
  seen as perverted, 84
Seymour-Smith, C., 56

shaman (*kobiraj*), 182, 189
Sh'hadeh, A., 169
Shore, C., 223
side effects, 19, 186–90, 194, 217–18
    cause of method switching, 186, 188
    doctors' disregard of, 118–19
    indigenous fears of, 228
    social, 52, 194
Simmons, R., 108, 109, 111, 112, 179, 180
Simpson, R., 8
Singer, M., 108
Singh, R., 221
Stirrat, R.L., 229
Sobo, E.J., 7, 15, 17, 18, 19, 194, 228
Society for Applied Anthropology, 31–2
Sofer, Arnold, 163
South Pacific Alliance for Family Health, 61–2, 70, 75
Soviet Union
    abortion in, 203
    family policies, 14, 205
Spilhaus, P., 89, 93
spousal communication, 183, 190–3, 194, 211, 218
Stacy, M., 15
STDs
    condoms as protection against, 5, 27
    in Haiti, 119–21
    in Mexico, 235–6
    in Tonga, 66
    in Uzbekistan, 207, 218–19
sterotypical images, 15, 34
sterilization
    female, 5, 6, 19, 216, 228
    male, 5, 19, 228
Still, E, 93–4
Stoler, A., 83, 175
Strathern, M., 3
study population, defining, 33–4
surreptitious contraceptive usage, 17, 184–5, 190–3, 211–12, 214–15
surveys & questionnaires, inappropriate use of, 29, 30–1

taboos
    incest, 64
    menstrual, 148–9, 187–8
    post partum sex, 6, 19, 140–1, 214

pre-marital sex, 203
talking about sex, 63, 64, 203–4, 209, 218, 235
Tamari, S., 164
target setting, 12, 19, 222–3, 225, 226, 233
Taussig, M., 108
Taylor, C.C., 35
Teferedegne, B., 148
'tensions of empire', 83
Terborgh, A., 30, 38, 39, 45, 47
Thiesen, R.J., 96
Thompson, M.S., 222, 227, 231, 232
Todd, A., 108
Tonga
    HIV/AIDS, 62, 63, 66, 70–1
    respect for elders, 64
    sex as taboo subject, 63, 64
    view of hospitals, 72
Tonga CSM Feasibility Study, 61–75
    background, 61–3
    ethnographic data collection, 63–4
    gender variations, 73–4
    island variations, 73
    locations, 65
    participants' enhanced understanding of problems, 70–1
    results, 69–75
    RRA sessions, 64–9
    rural/urban attitudes compared, 65
    suggested solutions, 71–3
    training & role of moderators, 64–6
Trevisan-Semi, 142, 148
Triandis, H.C., 11, 29, 31, 36, 40, 45, 47
Tsing, A.H., 171–2
tubal ligation /tubectomy, 184, 187
Tuzin, D., 34, 46

Uganda, 38
UN International Conference on Population & Development, Cairo, 1994, 12, 221
UN World Population Conference, Bucharest, 1974, 12
US Agency for International Development (USAID), 28, 131
US National Science Foundation, 46
Uzbekistan
    background 199–201

changes since Soviet times, 202–3
community health facilities (FAPs),
   209
contraceptive methods, 207–8
environmental problems, 201
government family planning
   programme, 201, 205, 208–12
midwives, role of, 210–11
population growth, 206
social cultural context, 201–5

vaginal warming, 35
Vaessen, M., 33, 41, 42
Vaughan, M., 81
van der Grijp, P., 63, 64
van Hollen, C., 13
van Rensberg, N.J., 93, 95
Van Willigen, J., 32
visual component of RRA, 59, 60

Waitzkin, H., 106, 108, 114
Ward-Gailey, C., 62
Watkins, E.S., 5, 12, 82, 83
Wawer, M., 131
weaning, early, 141–2
Weinrich, A.H., 89
Wight, D. 33
Wilmoth, J., 82, 83, 85, 97

Wilson, D., 33, 35
women & contraception
   deferring to husbands, 17, 217
   doctors' disregard of their problems,
      118–21
   'female sphere', 19, 237–8
   'failure ' in behaviour, 15, 167–70
   not empowered, 122
   not taking initiative, 151–2
   spousal communication, 183, 190–3,
      194, 211, 218
   surreptitious contraceptive usage, 17,
      184–5, 190–3, 211–12, 214–15
   treatment at clinic, 111–22
Wood, J, 140
Woodsong, C., 17
Woost, M.D., 229
World Bank, 130, 131
Wright, S., 18, 60, 223

Xhosa language, 39, 41–2

Yiftachel, O., 163
Young, A., 140, 152

de Zaluando, B., 109, 119
Zimbabwe, condom use in, 35
Zola, K., 108